*Allegorical Spectrum
of the Parables of Jesus*

Allegorical Spectrum of the Parables of Jesus

Suk Kwan Wong

WIPF & STOCK · Eugene, Oregon

ALLEGORICAL SPECTRUM OF THE PARABLES OF JESUS

Copyright © 2017 Suk Kwan Wong. All rights reserved. Except for brief quotations in critical publications or reviews, no part of this book may be reproduced in any manner without prior written permission from the publisher. Write: Permissions, Wipf and Stock Publishers, 199 W. 8th Ave., Suite 3, Eugene, OR 97401.

Wipf & Stock
An Imprint of Wipf and Stock Publishers
199 W. 8th Ave., Suite 3
Eugene, OR 97401

www.wipfandstock.com

PAPERBACK ISBN: 978-1-5326-1223-7
HARDCOVER ISBN: 978-1-5326-1225-1
EBOOK ISBN: 978-1-5326-1224-4

Manufactured in the U.S.A.　　　　　　　　　　　　JANUARY 30, 2017

Dedicated to
My parents

Contents

List of Tables | viii
List of Illustrations | viii
Acknowledgments | ix
Abbreviations | x
Introduction | xiii

Part I: Allegorical Spectrum

1 An Inspection of Allegory | 3
2 Implicit Allegory in the Parables of Jesus | 26
3 A New Allegorical Spectrum | 49

Part II: On Example Stories

4 "Example Stories" of Jülicher | 63
5 Precursors of Jülicher's Parable Categorization | 80
6 Evaluation of the Categorization of Jülicher | 104
7 Interpreting Allegory in Parables | 129
8 Application of Allegorical Spectrum | 142

Conclusion | 160
Bibliography | 167
Scripture and Ancient Document Index | 171
Author Index | 179
Subject Index | 181

List of Tables

Table 1.	Evaluation of the Allegorical Level of the Parables of Jesus | 52–53
Table 2.	Categories under Allegorical Spectrum of the Parables of Jesus | 58
Table 3.	Parables under *Gleichnisse* (Parables) of Jülicher | 66
Table 4.	Parables under *Parabeln* of Jülicher | 70
Table 5.	Relationship between Parables and Examples in Parable Categorization | 102

List of Illustrations

Figure 1.	Quintilian's Gradient | 14
Figure 2.	Frye's Sliding Scale | 27
Figure 3.	A Modified Expression of Hough's Allegorical Circle on Image and Theme | 45
Figure 4.	A Comparison of Several Allegorical Models | 47
Figure 5.	Allegorical Spectrum of the Parables of Jesus | 54

Acknowledgments

CURRENT STUDY IS A revision of my dissertation *A Categorization of Jesus's Parables: An Examination of Example Stories*. It was a study I longed to spend time on, and I was graciously allowed to accomplish it at Dallas Theological Seminary. First and foremost, I am grateful to the faculty at my school. I want to give thanks particularly to Dr. Darrell L. Bock, Dr. W. Hall Harris, and Dr. Richard A. Taylor for their advice at different stages. I also feel indebted to the editorial help of Jan Willis and Jim Larsen. Nevertheless, the encouragement from my family and friends who were afar while I was working on my dissertation in Dallas was truly my internal energy to finish the study. Last but not least, I am completely thankful to God who guides me through the study. May the Lord be glorified.

Abbreviations

AB	Anchor Bible
ABRL	Anchor Bible Reference Library
ATLA	American Theological Library Association
ANF	*Ante-Nicene Fathers*
BBR	*Bulletin for Biblical Research*
BDAG	Danker, F. W., W. Bauer, W. F. Arndt, and F. W. Gingrich. *A Greek-English Lexicon of the New Testament and Other Early Christian Literature.* 3rd ed. Chicago: University of Chicago Press, 2000.
BDB	Brown, F., S. R. Driver, and C. A. Briggs. *A Hebrew and English Lexicon of the Old Testament with an Appendix Containing the Biblcal Aramaic.* Oxford: Clarendon Press, 1907.
BECNT	Baker Exegetical Commentary on the New Testament
BJRL	*Bulletin of the John Rylands University Library of Manchester*
CBQMS	Catholic Biblical Quarterly Monograph Series
CQ	*Church Quarterly*
ELH	*A Journal of English Literary History*
GELNT	C. L. W. Grimm, and C. G. Wilke. *A Greek-English Lexicon of the New Testament.* Trans. and rev. by Joseph Henry Thayer. NY: Harper & Brothers, 1889.
ExpTim	*Expository Times*
JBL	*Journal of Biblical Literature*

Abbreviations

JETS	*Journal of the Evangelical Theological Society*
JSNTSup	Journal for the Study of the New Testament: Supplement Series
LCL	Loeb Classical Library
NovT	*Novum Testamentum*
NovTSup	Supplements to Novum Testamentum
NT	New Testament
NTS	*New Testament Studies*
OT	Old Testament
ST	*Studia theologica*
WBC	Word Biblical Commentary
WUNT	Wissenschaftliche Untersuchungen zum Neuen Testament

Introduction

It is always a challenge to interpret the parables of Jesus. Opinions vary significantly among interpreters. Although some parables provide with explanation, debates can still occur concerning what the images represent in the parables. In the parable in Luke 8:4–8, 11–15, some suggest that the seed refers to both the word and the people who listen.[1] Others argue that the seed is the word, which is the gospel.[2] However, the seed refers to the word of God or a teaching series about the word of the kingdom in the passage (Luke 8:11; Mark 4:13–14; Matt 13:11–12, 19). If the opinions in interpreting an explained parable can be so different, it should not be surprised to see a wide range of exegetical comments regarding an unexplained parable. To complicate the situation, an unexplained parable with the rhetorical use of allegory makes interpretation of the referent even more difficult.

The hindrance in understanding rhetorical allegory in the past comes from either the confusion with allegorization, or the avoidance of studying it in the parables. The habit of allegorization indeed has a long history. Kissinger suggests that allegorical interpretation has been predominately used between church fathers and the nineteenth century.[3] For instance, Irenaeus interprets the wedding garment in the parable of Matt 22:11–14 as the Holy Spirit resting on believers.[4] No wonder the rhetorical use of allegory in the parables of Jesus is never properly addressed.

---

1. Hagner, "Matthew's Parables of the Kingdom," 106.
2. Jeremias, *Die Gleichnisse Jesu*, 65.
3. Kissinger, *The Parables of Jesus*, xiii.
4. Irenaeus *Haer.* 4.36.6. (ANF 1:517)

INTRODUCTION

Interpreters of the parables of Jesus later try to avoid the mistake of allegorical interpretation by swinging the pendulum to literal interpretation. Adolf Jülicher is one of the leading advocates for such an approach, who suggests that parables and allegory "tolerate no mixing."[5] The research of Hans-Josef Klauck in recent decades overturns the bias over allegory in parable study by distinguishing it from allegorical interpretation.[6] In order to give a better understanding on what Jesus has said in the parables, allegorical interpretation or allegorization will not be included in this study. The emphasis of current research will mainly be on the rhetorical use of allegory in the parables of Jesus.

Need for the Study

Initially, I find that the four example stories do not fit very well under Adolf Jülicher's parable categorization. However, the more I dig into the issue, the more I realize what demands attention is the rhetorical use of allegory in the parables particularly those that are implicitly expressed. Although scholars like Frye and Ryken have mentioned about the allegorical features in the parables of Jesus,[7] description about rhetorical allegory in the parables is still very limited. Thus, an in-depth exploration of the allegorical features in the parables of Jesus becomes one of the reasons for current research.

Among Jülicher's three parable categories: *Gleichnisse* (parables), *Parabeln* (parables in the narrower sense), and *Beispielerzählung* (example stories),[8] the term "example stories" is never clear. Wolfgang Harnisch suggests that no figurative or aesthetic criteria can be used to justify a group as example stories.[9] Jeffrey T. Tucker doubts whether Jülicher's example stories and parables in the narrower sense show an obvious "categorical distinction."[10] Klyne Snodgrass points out that not only other parables can be used as examples like the four example stories, but also "no features of their form or content distinguish the so-called example stories from other

---

5. Jülicher, *Die Gleichnisreden Jesu*, 1:49, 74.

6. Klauck, *Allegorie und Allegorese in synoptischen Gleichnistexten*, 354–55.

7. Frye, *Anatomy of Criticism*, 89–92. Ryken, *How to Read the Bible as Literature*, 146–47.

8. Jülicher, *Die Gleichnisreden Jesu*, 1:69, 101, 112.

9. Harnisch, *Die Gleichnis-Erzählungen Jesu*, 91.

10. Tucker, *Example Stories*, 265.

Introduction

parables."[11] Ruben Zimmerman also suggests that there is no sign for example stories to be an independent group.[12] If parables in example stories cannot form a homogenous group, what should we call these parables? Should we name a new category? Or should we set up a completely new categorization? In fact, Jülicher calls this group of parables as example stories because he cannot find any referential feature in them.[13] A categorization that addresses the allegorical features in the parables of Jesus will help to demonstrate whether or not the parables in example stories belong to one group. Therefore, the other reason for current study aims at investigating the effect of the rhetorical use of allegory against example stories as well as the whole categorization of Jülicher.

In fact, different approaches to categorize the parables of Jesus are found although the focus is not on rhetorical allegory. Snodgrass uses the form and function of parables for classification.[14] He regards parables as a kind of indirect communication to switch off hearers' defense against learning things other than hard-core knowledge, an idea based on Kierkegaard's differentiation between direct and indirect communication.[15] Craig L. Blomberg, on the other hand, groups the parables of Jesus by associating the number of points with the number of main characters.[16] In other words, we can trace the main points through the main characters in the stories. As study about rhetorical allegory in the parables is so inadequate, it seems good to use it to set up a categorization for the parables of Jesus in the current study.

Methodology

The first part of this study will explore both explicit and implicit allegory in the parables of Jesus. Four screening questions are used to arrange parables on a spectrum according to their allegorical expression. A new categorization for the parables of Jesus will be developed as a result of regrouping parables under a spectrum of rhetorical allegories.

---

11. Snodgrass, *Stories with Intent*, 14.
12. Zimmermann, "Parabeln—Sonst Nichts," 395.
13. Jülicher, *Die Gleichnisreden Jesu*, 1:112.
14. Snodgrass, *Stories with Intent*, 11.
15. Ibid., 8. Kierkegaard, *Søren Kierkegaard's Journals and Papers*, 282.
16. Blomberg, *Interpreting the Parables*, 166, 325–27.

Introduction

In the second part, I want to revisit the rise of Jülicher's parable categories, in particular, example stories. A critical evaluation of his whole categorization is necessary. What I want to investigate is the effect of rhetorical allegory against his theory of parable categorization. The result of current study hopes to put together some hermeneutical guidelines for the rhetorical use of allegory in the parables. The thesis statement of this study is,

> The existence of allegorical elements in the parables of Jesus exposes the inadequacies of the definition of example stories so that a new categorization for the parables of Jesus is named for a better expression of their allegorical features.

Part I

Allegorical Spectrum

1

An Inspection of Allegory

THE RHETORICAL USE OF allegory is a peculiar tool. What can be simply stated becomes looped around in expression in allegory. It is probably a more entertaining way to deliver a speech. Jesus used many allegories in his parables but his parables were not all equally allegorical. Before diving into the exploration of rhetorical allegory in the parables of Jesus, this chapter intends to examine what allegory meant in biblical times. Owing to the complexity of parables, an understanding of what parable is brings comprehension to the relationship between rhetorical allegory and parable. The first section will unveil the nature of parable. As the rhetorical use of allegory in the parables of Jesus is constantly confused with allegorical interpretation, clarifying some issues between these two types of allegory will attain a clearer picture of rhetorical allegory. By tracing the history of the rhetorical use of allegory, it helps to refine the meaning of allegory. At the end of this chapter, a differentiation of allegory from other rhetorical devices will finalize a definition of allegory for this study.

Nature of the Parables of Jesus

The nature of the parables of Jesus is very complicated. Although there are several ways to define parables, each method contributes to some understanding as well as carries limitation.

Part I: Allegorical Spectrum

Form

One approach uses form or structure which looks for two layers in parables for definition. However, the descriptions of two levels in parables mean different things among scholars. Amos Wilder sees that there are surface and deep structures in parables.[1] He explains that surface and deep layers of parables are not referential but are only the components in a language. Robert Funk rather uses parables as metaphors to penetrate through the ordinary things in life resulting in something surprising, unexpected, or "transference of judgment."[2] Similarly, the two structural levels in parables that Madeleine Boucher searches for are the literal or direct level and the tropical or indirect level in the narrative, which is the idea of trope applied from Quintilian.[3] Using the Prodigal Son as an example (Luke 15:11–32), she refers the literal meaning to the returning home of the prodigal son, while the metaphorical meaning to the love of God over repented sinners.[4] Likewise, John Sider considers analogy as the basic unit of parables which is indeed a formula used by Adolf Jülicher.[5] However, Jülicher applies this type of analogical formula only to a particular group of parables called *Gleichnisse*, while Sider uses this formula on all parables of Jesus.[6] Before Jülicher's analogical formula, the logic in making comparison occurs in Socrates' sayings already.[7] By treating parables as analogies, parables also appear as two levels where one set of relationship makes comparison with another set of relationship in parallel.

While Wilder explores the surface and deep structure of a parable in a language linguistically, Funk, Boucher, and Sider focus on the referential two layers in a parable either as a metaphor, a trope, or an analogy. No matter what these two referential layers of parables are called, the problem with this approach is that we can also use this definition to describe allegories or other rhetorical devices. The parables of Jesus need a broader definition than merely using the structure of two realms.

---

1. Wilder, "Semeia, an Experimental Journal for Biblical Criticism," 12–13.
2. Funk, *Language, Hermeneutic, and Word of God*, 145, 159, 161.
3. Boucher, *The Mysterious Parable*, 18, 22–23. Quintilian, *Inst.* 8.6.1.
4. Boucher, *The Mysterious Parable*, 21.
5. Sider, *Interpreting the Parables*, 18–19. Jülicher, *Die Gleichnisreden Jesu*, 1:69.
6. Sider, *Interpreting the Parables*, 19.
7. Jülicher, *Die Gleichnisreden Jesu*, 1:69. Aristotle, *Rhet.* 2.20.4.

Terms

Another approach defines parables by terminology. According to Klyne Snodgrass, explaining a parable as "illustration" based on the literal meaning in Greek "to throw alongside" is a "root fallacy," for a parable means more than this.[8] He regards the parables of Jesus as fables like Theon's definition, for he sees that parables are an "imaginary world that reflects reality."[9] Theon describes a fable as a deceptive saying which is a copy of truth (λόγος ψευδὴς εἰκονίζων ἀλήθειαν).[10] This is a useful description to some parables of Jesus. However, when parables are straightforward such as the Dinner Guests (Luke 14:7–14), fables become unhelpful for definition.

Both Joachim Jeremias and Birger Gerhardsson suggest a range of meanings for defining parables. Jeremias finds that the Hebrew word *Mashal* (מָשָׁל) or the Aramaic word *Mathla* can mean metaphor, simile, parable, similitude, allegory, and illustration, whereas the word παραβολή in NT can refer to parable, comparison (Luke 5:36), symbol (Heb 9:9), proverb (Luke 4:23), riddle (Mark 4:11), and simple rule (Luke 14:7).[11] Gerhardsson generates a much longer list for parables, "A *Mashal* could be an aphorism, a proverb, a wise saying, a by-word, a song of mockery, an example, a parable, an allegory, a fable, a riddle, a pregnant prophet statement and many other things."[12] Not only do their descriptions show how complicated the meaning of parables can be, but they also demonstrate the relationship between parable and allegory: an allegory can be a kind of parable.

Boucher also recommends that the origin of parables in NT is OT, for she observes similarities between them, whether they are proverbs (Luke 4:23; 1 Sam 24:13), wisdom sayings (Mark 7:15; Prov 26:20), similitudes (Mark 4:30–32; Ezek 31:2–6), parables (Mark 12:1–12; Isa 5:1–7), or exemplary stories (Luke 10:29–37; 2 Sam 14:4–13).[13] Although מָשָׁל or παραβολή can mean various types of speeches, Boucher prefers to consider a parable as "any unusual or striking speech" owing to the difficulty to nail down the meaning for these two terms.[14]

---

8. Snodgrass, *Stories with Intent*, 7.
9. Ibid., 8.
10. Theon, *The Progymnasmata of Theon*, 1.21.
11. Jeremias, *Die Gleichnisse Jesu*, 10, 13–14.
12. Gerhardsson, "The Narrative Meshalim in the Synoptic Gospels," 340.
13. Boucher, *The Mysterious Parable*, 12–13.
14. Ibid., 13.

Part I: Allegorical Spectrum

While מָשָׁל and παραβολή cover a broad range of meaning for parables, there are parables in OT and NT that are not encompassed by these two terms. Several illustrations Boucher uses such as Ezek 31:2–6, Isa 5:1–7, Luke 10:29–37, and 2 Sam 14:4–13, indeed have neither the word מָשָׁל nor παραβολή. In other words, there is a limitation in defining the nature of the parables of Jesus by terminology alone. Perhaps we can follow ancient people which leave מָשָׁל or παραβολή non-specific and simply call these two terms special speeches. Yet it would be too general a description for defining the parables of Jesus.

Function and Purpose

Another approach uses function and purpose to define the parables of Jesus. Paul Fiebig points out that by using daily objects so fresh and vivid, the parables of Jesus become distinctive from Jewish figure of speech in that "nobody has been able to create as Jesus alone."[15] Wolfgang Harnisch suggests that the feature of the parables of Jesus is having a "purpose" so that the speech and the subject join together nicely.[16] Thus, not only the parables of Jesus are unique, but also they are spoken for a purpose.

Jeremias rather sees that Jesus uses parables as "weapons" in handling conflict situations such that each parable demands "a response at the spot."[17] Boucher finds that biblical writings are usually rhetorical, in particular the parable speeches of Jesus.[18] She explains that by decorating a speech, rhetoric aims at persuasion and "moving the addressee to decision or action."[19] Snodgrass suggests that parables are "stories with an intent" to help recipients to see truth in a completely different way.[20] The kind of "intent" in the parables is by nature prophetic message.[21] By delivering a parable in an interesting way, he points out that a parable "diverts attention and disarms" the listeners immediately while its ultimate aim desires "to awaken insight, stimulate the conscience, and move to action."[22] In other words,

15. Fiebig, *Altjüdische Gleichnisse und die Gleichnisse Jesu*, 163.
16. Harnisch, "Language of the Possible," 52.
17. Jeremias, *Die Gleichnisse Jesu*, 15.
18. Boucher, *The Mysterious Parable*, 14–16.
19. Ibid., 14.
20. Snodgrass, *Stories with Intent*, 8.
21. Ibid., 8–9.
22. Ibid., 8.

the parables of Jesus are rhetorical speeches for the purpose of persuasion, which compels the recipients to respond with a decision or an action.

However, parables are not the only rhetorical device having a purpose or an intention. According to Harnisch, similes, examples, fables, or others can also be "intentional speech" for clarifying thought and bringing awareness to the audience.[23] Therefore, using purpose or function may not be sufficient in distinguishing parables from other rhetorical devices.

Perhaps, there is no perfect way to define parables. Using the structural form of two layers, terminology, function, and purpose are only several approaches for definition. We need to admit the extensive meaning of "parables": proverbs, wisdom sayings, similes, similitudes, parables, comparisons, aphorisms, symbols, riddles, mockery songs, examples, allegories, fables, prophetic statements, simple rules, metaphors, illustrations . . . etc. In fact, parables can have allegories. Apart from that, as the parables of Jesus are special rhetorical speeches, they are by nature dynamic. On the one hand, his parables are delivered with specific purposes for handling conflict situations and persuasion. On the other hand, his parables motivate recipients to make decision and to take appropriate action in response. With the complexity of the nature of parables in view, the following looks further into the relationship between parable and allegory.

Mystery about Allegory

Can the parables of Jesus be allegorical? Jülicher's answer is no. He explains that a parable is an extended simile and it is literal, while an allegory is an extended metaphor and it is figurative.[24] He believes that allegories and parables cannot coexist.[25] He suggests that the parables of Jesus are originally literal, but the Evangelists insert allegories into the parables of Jesus.[26] However, his position concerning the relationship of allegory and parable leaves behind some problems.

First, Jülicher looks for a more concise version of the parables of Jesus. By regarding some parables as being embellished by the allegorization of the Evangelists, Jülicher cannot explain why they are similarly allegorical among witnesses. For instance, the story of the Wicked Tenants appears

---

23. Harnisch, "Language of the Possible," 42.
24. Jülicher, *Die Gleichnisreden Jesu*, 1:52, 58.
25. Ibid., 1:74.
26. Ibid., 1:49.

Part I: Allegorical Spectrum

not only in Matthew, Mark, and Luke (Matt 21:33–46; Mark 12:1–12; Luke 20:9–19), but also in the Gospel of Thomas 65–66. While these four have differences in details, the main line of the parabolic story is very similar: the vine growers murdered the son of the owner. At the end of the story, the chief priests, the scribes, and the Pharisees knew that the parable was about them even though Jesus did not make it explicit (Matt 21:45; Mark 12:12; Luke 20:19). Thus, the whole story and the owner's son involve allegories within the parable.[27] The various strands of tradition prove the authenticity of this parabolic story by multiple attestation. In light of the use of allegory in this parable, Jülicher's assumptions that allegories do not exist in parables and those found in the parables of Jesus are later addition from editors' hands do not stand very well.

The second problem with Jülicher's position is that by treating parables and allegories as two distinctive groups, he has neglected that allegory can be a kind of parable. Hans-Josef Klauck nails down the heart of the issue more clearly. Klauck finds that because of seeing simile as literal that operates through likeness, while metaphor as figurative that works from substitution for decoding, Jülicher considers simile and metaphor to be mutually exclusive.[28] Klauck observes that Jülicher extends the feature of simile to parable, and metaphor to allegory.[29] Applying the point-to-point comparison in a simile to a parable, Jülicher disapproves anything that falls outside the one-point comparison in a parable, which includes allegorical interpretation.[30] The problem in Jülicher's assumption is that parables contain more than simile style of explicit comparison. What is true of a simile does not necessarily apply to a parable. If he looks for the use of likeness as the only indication of a parable, obviously other rhetorical devices in a parable that do not use likeness as expression, such as allegory, become unacceptable. Even though simile and metaphor are two things, using the concept of simile to refute the existence of allegory in the parables is a problematic logic. In fact, Fiebig suggests that pure form of parables and allegories are hard to find.[31] A better way to handle allegory in the parables of Jesus, as

27. Blomberg, *Interpreting the Parables*, 248. Blomberg suggests that three types of characters are allegorical in the Wicked Tenants: the vineyard owner, first group of tenants, and the replaced group of tenants.

28. Klauck, *Allegorie und Allegorese in synoptischen Gleichnistexten*, 6–7.

29. Ibid.

30. Ibid., 7.

31. Fiebig, *Altjüdische Gleichnisse und die Gleichnisse Jesu*, 162–63. Brown, "Parable and Allegory Reconsidered," 37.

recommended by Northrop Frye, John Crossan, and Leland Ryken, is the use of gradation.[32]

The third problem is that Jülicher confuses allegory with allegorical interpretation. Anneus Brouwer is the first to mention the problem that Jülicher extends his rejection of allegorical interpretation to allegory in the parables of Jesus.[33] B. T. D. Smith also points out, "the creation of allegories is one thing, the allegorical interpretation of something already in existence is another."[34] Klauck further elaborates the difference in that allegory is a rhetorical and poetic form in a text, while allegorical interpretation is a kind of anachronism in interpretation violating the author's intention by reading philosophical or theological concept into a text.[35] However, Klauck suggests that interpreting an allegorical text is acceptable if the interpretation is doing according to the language structure, the intention of author, and the expected horizon of the hearers.[36] That is, whether or not a text is rhetorically allegorical, interpreters can only understand it according to the author's intention instead of adding allegorical things into the text from the perspective of interpreters.

In general, Jülicher's position of rejecting the existence of allegories in the parables of Jesus does not make his case. That is, the parables of Jesus can have allegory, as Boucher, Ryken, and Blomberg all affirm it.[37] Yet we can use the discussion here to set the limit for studying allegory: rhetorical allegory is not allegorizing or allegorical interpretation of the parables. However, we still need a clearer definition of rhetorical allegory that is close to the time of Jesus. Thus, the following section will trace the meaning of rhetorical allegory along history.

---

32. Frye, *Anatomy of Criticism*, 89–92. Crossan, *In Parables*, 7. Ryken, *How to Read the Bible as Literature*, 146–47.

33. Brouwer, *De Gelijkenissen*, 27. Klauck, *Allegorie und Allegorese in synoptischen Gleichnistexten*, 20.

34. Smith, *The Parables of the Synoptic Gospels*, 27.

35. Klauck, *Allegorie und Allegorese in synoptischen Gleichnistexten*, 354–55.

36. Ibid.

37. Boucher, *The Mysterious Parable*, 20–21. Ryken, *How to Read the Bible as Literature*, 202–3. Ryken, *Words of Life*, 65. Blomberg, *Interpreting the Parables*, 42–43.

Part I: Allegorical Spectrum

History of Defining Allegory

Early Centuries

What is allegory? Several words refer to the rhetorical use of allegory in ancient literature. Cicero defines *permutation* (allegory) as "a manner of speech denoting one thing by the letter of the words, but another by their meaning."[38] There are three types: 1) *similitudinem* (comparison); 2) *argumentum* (argument); 3) *contrarium* (contrast). The first type of allegory uses comparison by putting several similar metaphors together. The second type of allegory occurs in argument by drawing similitude "from a person or place or object in order to magnify or minify."[39] The third type applies contrast to make allegory.[40]

Quintilian utilizes two other words for allegory. One of them is *allegoria* translated as *inversio*, while the other is *ironia* called *illusio*.[41] Allegory means representing "one thing by its words" and a different thing or a contrary thing by its meaning.[42] Concerning the first type of allegory (*allegoria*), it contains series of coherent metaphors that form a closed allegory.[43] It has several subtypes. The first subtype under *allegoria* does not involve the use of metaphor in the allegory.[44] Quintilian suggests that everything in *Eclogues* 9.7–10 is explicit except the shepherd Menalcas, which is referred to Virgil.[45] Lausberg observes that the relation between the elements in this type of allegory does not need transference of an image.[46] Thus, no metaphor allegory is explicit in wordings of the images without shifting their meanings.

---

38. Cicero *Rhet. Her.* 4.34.46.
39. Cicero *Rhet. Her.* 4.34.46.
40. Cicero *Rhet. Her.* 4.34.46.
41. Quintilian *Inst.* 8.6.44, 54.
42. Quintilian *Inst.* 8.6.44, 54–55.
43. Quintilian *Inst.* 8.6.44, 50. Quintilian found a succession of metaphors in the passage of Horace. He had identified the state as a ship, the civil war as waves and storms, peace and concord as harbor. Lausberg, *Handbook of Literary Rhetoric*, 400.
44. Quintilian *Inst.* 8.6.46.
45. Quintilian *Inst.* 8.6.46–47. Virgil *Ecl.* 9.7–10. This is a personal eclogue possibly about an appeal for assistance.
46. Lausberg, *Handbook of Literary Rhetoric*, 400.

An Inspection of Allegory

The second subtype under *allegoria* is pure allegory.[47] Lausberg explains that in this type of allegory, "no lexical trace of the serious idea is to be found" and it is common in poetry.[48] Quintilian suggests that *Pro Milone* 5 is a pure allegory if the phrase "of our public assemblies" is not in the sentence.[49] Thus, pure allegory contains images but their descriptions concerning what they refer to are absent. By arranging allegories from explicitly to implicitly expressed, it helps to set up a gradient. I name this gradient as Quintilian's Gradient. The gradient starts from no metaphor allegory on the very left. Toward the right, it is pure allegory.

The third subtype under *allegoria* is a mixture of the first two subtypes (mixed allegory).[50] Quintilian points out that in *Pro Milone* 5, the explanation of the "waves" as "our public assemblies" brings the implicit idea to explicit.[51] As mixed allegory contains both implicit and explicit elements, it should be placed between no metaphor allegory and pure allegory on Quintilian's Gradient.

The fourth subtype under *allegoria* is a combination of simile, allegory, and metaphor (combined allegory).[52] Using *Pro Murena* 35 as illustration, several conditions at a strait like eddies and waves refer to just one thing: the system of elections.[53] It also comes along with explanation at the end. Although mixed allegory and combined allegory should both be placed in the middle between no metaphor allegory and pure allegory, combined allegory should be closer to pure allegory on Quintilian's Gradient owing to its more complicated involvement of metaphors than mixed allegory.

The fifth subtype under *allegoria* occurs in an example where explanation is absent.[54] Quintilian illustrates with an old phrase "Dionysius is at Corinth."[55] The story behind this phrase was about a tyrant named Dionysius. After dethroning, he fled to Corinth to be a schoolmaster.[56] In a letter

---

47. Quintilian *Inst.* 8.6.47–48.
48. Lausberg, *Handbook of Literary Rhetoric*, 399.
49. Quintilian *Inst.* 8.6.48. Cicero *Mil.* 5. The context of this quotation is about the challenge of a political career.
50. Quintilian *Inst.* 8.6.48.
51. Quintilian *Inst.* 8.6.48.
52. Quintilian *Inst.* 8.6.49.
53. Quintilian *Inst.* 8.6.49. Cicero *Mur.* 35. The context was about election for praetorship.
54. Quintilian *Inst.* 8.6.52.
55. Quintilian *Inst.* 8.6.52.
56. Quintilian *Inst.* 8.6.52n73.

PART I: ALLEGORICAL SPECTRUM

to Atticus, Cicero applied this allegorical phrase to describe his political life from having been badly defeated to later on preferring to stay out of it.[57] Demetrius uses this phrase to explain the power of using short phrase type of allegory for confrontation.[58] He suggests that if the Spartans expanded this phrase to "Although Dionysius was ever a mighty tyrant like you, he now lives in Corinth as an ordinary citizen," its powerful effect to threaten would decrease to a narrative for instruction.[59] He points out that brief saying is the feature of proverbs and maxims, while expansion of a maxim results in instruction or rhetoric.[60] He suggests that allegory is better to be less opened in order to bring the effect of fear.[61] In addition, one should avoid succession of allegories or it will be like a riddle.[62] In general, there are several things to note about this subtype of brief maxim or proverb style of allegory. Maxim-in-example allegory appears implicit to bring upon the effect of fear. It normally has an event behind it. However, instead of giving explanation of the event, the speaker uses short phrase to refer to the event and to infer implicitly to his own situation as an example. Owing to the implicit and unexplained nature, maxim-in-example allegory is better located beyond pure allegory to the right on Quintilian's Gradient.

The final subtype under *allegoria* is an enigma.[63] Using *Eclogues* 3.104–5 as an illustration, Quintilian considers this kind of *allegoria* as obscure unless with explanation.[64] As enigma allegory does imply something but completely ambiguous, it should go beyond maxim-in-example allegory to the right on Quintilian's Gradient.

Quintilian regards *ironia* as another type of allegory, which involves presenting meaning and the words in contrast.[65] The most important is "what anything said is about" because it may be something true in the other context."[66] There are several subtypes. One of them uses blame "with a pre-

57. Cicero *Att.* 9.9.1n1.
58. Demetrius *Eloc.* 8–9, 241; intro., 312–13.
59. Demetrius *Eloc.* 8–9, Innes.
60. Demetrius *Eloc.* 9.
61. Demetrius *Eloc.* 99–101.
62. Demetrius *Eloc.* 102.
63. Quintilian *Inst.* 8.6.52. Lausberg, *Handbook of Literary Rhetoric*, 400–401.
64. Quintilian *Inst.* 8.6.52–53. Virgil *Ecl.*, 3.104–5n1. There are two explanations. One uses it to refer to a prodigal called Caeli who hasn't got sufficient ground for burial. Another describes someone at the bottom of a well looking up to the sky.
65. Quintilian *Inst.* 8.6.54–56.
66. Quintilian *Inst.* 8.6.55.

tense of praise" while the other applies praise "with a pretense of blame."[67] Quintilian illustrates with *Pro Cluentio* 91 for both subtypes.[68] In the first *ironia*, it starts from commending the urban praetor Gaius Verres, but it follows with describing his misdeed of inability to put the president G. Junius on juror duty. On the contrary, the second *ironia* begins with orators, a lesser role in the court than a praetor. However, at the end, it uplifts orators for being able to influence people powerfully, probably doing a much better job than a praetor. Thus, the two subtypes of *ironia* are praising-for-blaming *ironia* and blaming-for-praising *ironia*.

Another subtype of *ironia* expresses in a sarcastic way that the real intention is the opposite.[69] Quintilian uses the illustration from Cicero in which everything is positive about Clodius but it indeed means the negative.[70] Thus, the third subtype is sarcastic *ironia*. The fourth subtype of *ironia* presents "unpleasant facts in better words" either for courtesy or for providing clues by stating the opposite."[71] In Quintilian's illustration, obviously no one likes the distinct taste of entrails nor eats them. Although irritating, this statement successfully makes an emphasis in testing a dish.[72] Thus, the fourth subtype is irritating *ironia*. Although there are some other subtypes of *ironia*, unlike *allegoria*, their differences seem to be a matter of style instead of form in expression.[73]

The discussions of Cicero and Quintilian give a definition of allegory around biblical times. Although they are slightly different in wording about allegory, their meanings are similar. While Cicero uses *permutation* to refer to allegory, Quintilian had *allegoria*. In fact, Cicero's first type of allegory *similitudinem* (comparison) is similar to Quintilian's first type of allegory *allegoria* except that *allegoria* carries a broader coverage of meaning than similitude. Cicero's third type of allegory *contrarium* (contrast) is compatible with Quintilian's second type of allegory *ironia* but Quintilian has more elaboration on *ironia*. Cicero's second type of allegory *argumentum* (argument) is the only category for which no similar term can be found

---

67. Quintilian *Inst.* 8.6.56.

68. Quintilian *Inst.* 8.6.56. Cicero *Clu.* 91nb. Vacancy of jurors in the court was usually filling up by the president under the authority of the praetor.

69. Quintilian *Inst.* 8.6.56.

70. Quintilian *Inst.* 8.6.56.

71. Quintilian *Inst.* 8.6.57.

72. Quintilian *Inst.* 8.6.57.

73. Quintilian *Inst.* 8.6.57–59.

under Quintilian's allegory, as Quintilian put his discussion on argument in a different section. Other than that, Cicero and Quintilian have very similar definition for allegory: allegory refers one thing through words to the meaning of another thing, or the meaning of a contrary thing.

Apart from that, Quintilian's description of allegory can be expressed with a gradient, which I referenced as Quintilian's Gradient, from explicitness to implicitness. With implicitness increasing toward the right, the six subtypes of *allegoria* are no metaphor allegory, mixed allegory, combined allegory, pure allegory, maxim-in-example allegory, and enigma allegory. Another type of allegory is *ironia*, which should be located further to the right beyond enigma on Quintilian's Gradient owing to its implicit nature. As the several subtypes of *ironia* are very similar in use except stylish difference, it is no need to spread them along Quintilian's Gradient.

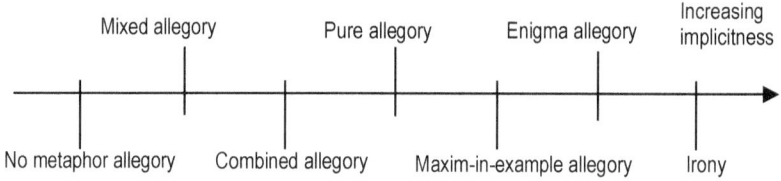

Figure 1. Quintilian's Gradient

Unfortunately, discussion about the rhetorical use of allegory is not the main trend after the early centuries. From church fathers to the nineteenth century, the "allegory" that has been used is allegorical interpretation instead of rhetorical allegory.[74]

From the Nineteenth Century to the Present

Conceptual Ideas of Allegory

In recent centuries, the rhetorical use of allegory finally has more attention. Contributors for conceptual level of rhetorical allegory include E. W. Bullinger, C. S. Lewis, and Edward Bloom. Bullinger identifies two types of

---

74. Kissinger, *The Parables of Jesus*, xiii. Bloom, "The Allegorical Principle," 165–66. The four levels of interpreting the Scriptures during Medieval period are literal, allegorical, tropological, and anagogical, but they are reduced to two levels during Renaissance period: literal and figurative.

An Inspection of Allegory

allegory, continued metaphor and continued hypocatastasis.[75] In the first type of allegory, continued metaphor, the referent and the thing used for making referent can both be seen with the expression of "one thing IS the other."[76] Bullinger illustrates with Psalm 23.[77] After using "Shepherd" to represent "the Lord" in verse 1, the metaphor continues into an allegory through verses 2 to 4 by describing how the Shepherd cares. The second type of allegory is a continuous form of hypocatastasis, which means "implied resemblance or representation."[78] In continued hypocatastasis, only the thing used to refer is seen while the referent is absent.[79] Bullinger illustrates with Psalm 80:8–15.[80] In the passage, there is no description about the referent of the "vine" but it has to imply to "Israel." Thus, the difference between the two types of allegory is that the representational relationship in continuous metaphor is explicit while in continuous hypocatastasis, it is implicit. However, there is a problem with the grouping of Bullinger. He considers a continued simile as a parable, while a continued metaphor or a continued hypocatastasis as an allegory.[81] That is, parable and allegory to Bullinger are two different things. As discussed earlier, the meaning of parable is so broad that it actually includes allegory. In addition, simile can be found in Quintilian's combined allegory.[82] Thus, Bullinger's definition of allegory is too narrow for use.

Lewis considers allegory as "the very nature of thought and language to represent what is immaterial in picturable terms."[83] Using the visible material to make allegory, it "talk[s] of that which is confessedly less real" whether it is a thought or feeling.[84] Bloom suggests that the idea of allegory "must be a subtle, intangible union of both structure and meaning" so that the "explicit statement" and "implicit meaning" are well connected.[85] In other words, the connection between the statement and its meaning in

---

75. Bullinger, *Figures of Speech Used in the Bible*, 748.
76. Ibid., 735, 748.
77. Ibid., 748.
78. Ibid., 744.
79. Ibid., 748.
80. Ibid.
81. Ibid.
82. Quintilian *Inst.* 8.6.49.
83. Lewis, *The Allegory of Love*, 44.
84. Ibid., 45.
85. Bloom, "The Allegorical Principle," 190.

allegory is undetectable. Thus, the whole concept of allegory is basically an implicit relationship between something unexplained and something visible.

Models of Allegory

Rhetorical studies on allegory later focus on arranging literature on a spectrum of allegories. Some of the advocates are Frye, Graham Hough, and E. J. Tinsley. Frye arranges allegories in literature on a sliding scale.[86] One end of the scale is naive allegory, which is "the most explicitly allegorical" literature such as discursive writing and teaching points.[87] At the other end of the scale, literature becomes "anti-explicit and anti-allegorical" with "increasingly ironic and paradoxical."[88] The midpoint of the scale is literature with allegory that has implicit relationship between image and idea.[89] Continuous allegory, free-style allegory, and allegory with poetic structure carrying doctrinal interest lie between naive allegory and the midpoint.[90] I name Frye's model of allegory as Frye's Sliding Scale.

Hough's Allegorical Circle further elaborates Frye's Sliding Scale.[91] His allegorical circle builds around two components, theme and image. While theme is about the moral and abstract elements in an allegory, image refers to the characters, actions, and objects."[92] Hough puts Frye's naive allegory at the twelve o'clock where theme dominates over image.[93] He locates Frye's midpoint at the three o'clock position and calls it "incarnation" but the term has nothing to do with the theological term incarnation.[94] He describes the relation between theme and image in incarnational allegory as fusion, which is a completely implicit spot.[95] Allegory proper or Frye's continuous allegory is at the one o'clock where image begins to have more development

---

86. Frye, *Anatomy of Criticism*, 91.
87. Ibid., 90–91.
88. Ibid.
89. Frye, *Anatomy of Criticism*, 91.
90. Ibid.
91. Hough, "The Allegorical Circle," 203–7.
92. Ibid., 203.
93. Ibid., 203–4.
94. Ibid., 204–5.
95. Ibid.

although theme still dominates.[96] At half past one, it is "humour literature" particularly the romantic one.[97] At two, it is Frye's free-style allegory, which is a kind of poetic fiction.[98] Frye's allegory that is poetic in style with "doctrinal interest" is found at half past two where fictional story is used as example.[99] Realism such as reporting and "quasi-documentary fiction" is located at six where image dominates over theme.[100] At nine, it is symbolism where theme and image "have equal weight" but are separable.[101] From the twelve to the six o'clock, the circle progresses from simple allegory to realism, and the circle returns to simple allegory from six to twelve.[102]

Tinsley explains further based on Frye's and Hough's allegorical models. He sees that the two poles from naive allegory to realism are more explicit.[103] Themes completely dominate over images in naive allegory while the reverse is the case in realism.[104] The midway between these two poles is incarnational allegory where not only theme and image appear fused, but also their relationship is "only implicit."[105] Tinsley regards incarnational allegory as more successful allegory than naive allegory or realism.[106] He explains that naive allegory makes allegorical points too obviously, while the implicit relationship between image and theme allows incarnational allegory to form a more coherent story.[107] The following chapter will provide detailed discussion with visualization regarding the complexity of allegorical models described by Frye, Hough, and Tinsley.

Inner Relationship in an Allegory

As rhetorical allegory is preferably implicit, how does the inner relationship in an allegory work? Harald Weinrich, Gerhard Sellin, Hartmut Kubczak,

96. Ibid., 205.
97. Ibid.
98. Ibid.
99. Ibid.
100. Ibid.
101. Ibid., 206, 203.
102. Ibid., 203.
103. Tinsley, "Parable, Allegory and Mysticism," 175.
104. Ibid.
105. Ibid.
106. Ibid.
107. Ibid., 175–178.

Gerhard Kurz, and Renate Banschbach Eggen give some insight to the studies of allegory in recent decades. Weinrich describes the relationship in a metaphor through the terms "image giver" and "image receiver" where the former refers to the image giving field while the latter is about the image receiving field.[108] Sellin considers the subject in a sentence as image receiver while the predicate is image giver.[109] For example, in John 1:4, "In him (the Word) was life, and the life was the light of humans." The image giver (predicate) in the verse is "the light of humans," which elaborates the image receiver (subject) namely "the life." Basically, image giver (predicate) and image receiver (subject) describe the paired relationship of a metaphorical expression.

Kubczak suggests that there are two types of metaphor, explicit metaphor and implicit metaphor.[110] He illustrates with a simple formula: x is like y to z.[111] Both x and y are present in explicit metaphor, while in implicit metaphor, x is absent.[112] Kurz goes back to Quintilian for the idea of explicit and implicit allegories. He calls Quintilian's combined allegory as explicative allegory, which indicates explicitly the allegorical meaning.[113] He regards Quintilian's pure allegory as implicative allegory, which expresses allegorical meaning implicitly.[114] That is, whether it is metaphor or allegory, the relationship of subject and predicate is clear in explicit expression, whereas the subject matter (image receiver) in implicit expression can be absent.

Eggen suggests that two distinctive features of implicit metaphors tell the differences with explicit metaphors.[115] One of them is double reference, which contains a lexical referent of the image giver and a metaphorical referent of the image receiver.[116] He explains with Weder's example by using the

---

108. Weinrich, *Sprache in Texten*, 284. Weinrich borrows the terms "image giver" and "image receiver" from Jost Trier.

109. Sellin, "Allegorie und ‚Gleichnis‚" 387 and n73. Sellin uses terms from note 65 of Wilhelm Köller's Aufnahme der Terminologie.

110. Kubczak, *Die Metapher*, 69.

111. Ibid.

112. Ibid.

113. Kurz, *Metapher, Allegorie, Symbol*, 43 and n22. Kurz gets the idea of the terms implicative allegory and explicative allegory from Renate Böschenstein. Quintilian *Inst.* 8.6.49.

114. Kurz, *Metapher, Allegorie, Symbol*, 43. Quintilian *Inst.* 8.6.47.

115. Eggen, *Gleichnis, Allegorie, Metapher*, 257.

116. Ibid., 257–58.

word "king," which can lexically refer to the head of the nation while metaphorically implying God.[117] Another feature of implicit metaphor makes use of the context either its literary or the given situation to determine the untold image receiver.[118] He suggests that like the word "herdsman" (image giver), the image receiver can refer to "God" in a Sunday sermon.[119] However, in a different context such as news, "herdsman" can mean a certain rescuer who finds a lost kid on a trip.[120] It shows that the same word can imply different things but the context determines specifically the unspoken image receiver in implicit metaphor.[121] However, the role of context is important to both implicit metaphor and explicit metaphor. While context helps to retrieve the image receiver in implicit metaphor, the clear relationship between image giver and image receiver in explicit metaphor also depends on the context for interpretation.[122]

To summarize, the inner relationship of an allegory is described by how the allegory is told. In explicit allegory, image giver (predicate) shows clearly what image receiver (subject) or allegorical meaning is. On the other hand, in implicit allegory, only image giver (predicate) is present while the explanation of its allegorical meaning (subject) needs implication.

Differentiating Allegory from Other Figures

As several terms appear similar to allegory, a differentiation among them can further help to define what allegory is. Like allegory, some of them are tropes such as metaphor, synecdoche, and metonymy. Others such as simile, similitude, and symbol are also closely related to allegory but express in a speech differently. Both Cicero and Quintilian include very similar items under tropes. However, Cicero placed tropes under figures of diction, while he put simile, comparison, and exemplification under figures of thought.[123] Cicero defines figures of diction as "the adornment is comprised in the fine polish of the language itself," while figures of thought as

---

117. Ibid., 257.
118. Ibid., 258–59, 300.
119. Ibid., 258.
120. Ibid.
121. Ibid.
122. Ibid., 299–300.
123. Cicero *Rhet. Her.* lvi-lviii.

"a certain distinction from the idea, not from the words."[124] In other words, tropes as figures of diction are decorative tools for the language, but figures of thought deal with ideas. Quintilian had a broader concept on trope. He defines trope as "a shift of a word or phrase from its proper meaning to another" for embellishment.[125] Or, it is "an expression transferred from a context in which it is proper to one in which it is not."[126] He points out the error of limiting a trope as substitution of one word with another.[127] That is, transference of meanings in tropes can occur at word levels and context levels. Another term used closely with trope is figure, which can mean "any shape in which a thought is expressed" or "a purposeful deviation in sense or language from the ordinary simple form."[128] That is, figures can occur in thoughts or stylish expressions. In fact, Quintilian put irony and synecdoche under both trope and figure.[129] Lausberg identifies two kinds of tropes, conceptual and single-word. He considers emphasis, synecdoche, hyperbole, and irony under both tropes.[130] He puts allegory under conceptual trope, while metaphor under single-word trope.[131] However, Quintilian suggests that what matters is "their effectiveness, not their name" as trope or figure.[132] In general, transference of meanings in an allegory can occur at word levels, contextual levels, and conceptual levels.

Simile, Similitude, and Allegory

Simile is good for dealing with fact either for making proofs in arguments or describing "picture of things."[133] In the latter type, comparison occurs between one thing and another thing that is "clearer than the thing it illustrates." [134]The explicit expression in simile can be indicated by the use of ὡς (as), καθώς or ὥσπερ (just as), ὅμοιος (like), or ὁμοιόω (is compared

124. Cicero *Rhet. Her.* 4.12.18.
125. Quintilian *Inst.* 8.6.1–3.
126. Quintilian, *Inst.* 9.1.4.
127. Quintilian *Inst.* 8.6.3.
128. Quintilian *Inst.* 9.1.9–11.
129. Quintilian *Inst.* 9.1.7, 8.6.22.
130. Lausberg, *Handbook of Literary Rhetoric*, 398.
131. Ibid., x, xiii.
132. Quintilian *Inst.* 9.1.8.
133. Quintilian *Inst.* 8.3.72.
134. Quintilian *Inst.* 8.6.9, 8.3.73.

to). Snodgrass suggests that the extension of a simile becomes a similitude but it does not have story development.[135] The relationship of simile and allegory is that allegory can have simile such as combined allegory of Quintilian.[136] As the nature of simile or similitude is unambiguous, allegory that carries such element appears explicit in some way. For instance, the story of the Wedding Feast almost does not provide an explanation but the use of ὁμοιώθη (is compared to) in verse 2 makes the story slightly explicit about the kingdom of heaven (Matt 22:1–14).

Metaphor and Allegory

Quintilian defines metaphor as "one thing is substituted for the other."[137] In case of explicit metaphor, the relationship between image giver and image receiver can be clearly seen just as the formula "one thing IS the other."[138] On the contrary, in implicit metaphor, the unspecified image receiver of the image giver needs to be implied from the context.[139] However, the relationship of metaphor and allegory is complicated. Quintilian comments that when a metaphor is used continuously, it "ends up as Allegory and Enigma."[140] Lewis says that "every metaphor is an allegory in little."[141] Particularly in the expression of "inner conflict," the further expansion of metaphors can ultimately turn into a "fully-fledged allegorical poem."[142] Kubczak indeed puts all metaphorical cases under the coverage of implicit metaphors.[143] In other words, the more developed metaphors can become allegories and they are all somewhat implicit. Perhaps this is why a better expression of the relationship between metaphors and allegories would be a gradient. Under Quintilian's Gradient, "no metaphor" allegory goes to the

---

135. Snodgrass, *Stories with Intent*, 12.
136. Quintilian *Inst.* 8.6.49.
137. Quintilian *Inst.* 8.6.9.
138. Kubczak, *Die Metapher*, 69. Bullinger, *Figures of Speech Used in the Bible*, 735, 744. Bullinger used hypocatastasis to refer to implicit type of metaphor.
139. Kubczak, *Die Metapher*, 69. Eggen, *Gleichnis, Allegorie, Metapher*, 257.
140. Quintilian *Inst.* 8.6.14.
141. Lewis, *The Allegory of Love*, 60.
142. Ibid., 60–61.
143. Kubczak, *Die Metapher*, 69.

end of explicit expression while the involvement of metaphors in allegories varies along the implicit direction.[144]

In Gal 4:22–24, the allegory initially develops from two explicit metaphors, the slave woman Hagar, and the free woman (image givers), which represent two covenants (image receivers). The former gave birth to children according to the flesh and the latter through the promise. The elaboration of the two women continue into explicit allegory explaining the difference between children of slavery under the Law and children of freedom through the promise of Christ (Gal 4:21–31).

Matt 9:15 uses implicit metaphors to develop into a brief allegory. The identity of the bridegroom and his attendants (image givers) lack explanation. However, in the preceding context, the disciples of John asked Jesus why his disciples did not fast (Matt 9:14). Jesus explained in the following context. The attendants of the bridegroom cannot do it now but they will fast when the bridegroom is taken away (Matt 9:15). It implies that Jesus (image receiver) refers the bridegroom (image giver) to himself and the wedding attendants (image givers) to his disciples (image receivers). The metaphors briefly develop into a short implicit allegory.[145]

Synecdoche, Metonymy, and Allegory

Cicero defines metonymy as "the figure which draws from an object closely akin or associated an expression suggesting the object meant, but not called by its own name."[146] Quintilian considers metonymy as having no big difference with synecdoche, which is "the substitution of one name for another."[147] It shows "inventions by the name of the inventor, or possessions by the name of the possessor."[148] In John 3:16, "the world" represents the people of the whole world that God loved.[149] Although synecdoche and metonymy are similar, synecdoche has a broader definition. It helps "to vary the discourse, enabling the hearer to understand many things from one, and the whole from the part, the genus from the species, the consequences from the

---

144. Quintilian *Inst.* 8.6.46–59.
145. Bullinger, *Figures of Speech Used in the Bible*, 750.
146. Cicero *Rhet. Her.* 4.32.43.
147. Quintilian *Inst.* 8.6.23.
148. Quintilian *Inst.* 8.6.23.
149. Bullinger, *Figures of Speech Used in the Bible*, 576.

antecedents, and vice versa."[150] In Rom 12:1, "your bodies" refer to the presentation of the whole persons as living sacrifice to God.[151] Both metonymy and synecdoche can be found in allegorical stories on occasion. However, they contribute to only small portions in the parables. In the Prodigal Son, "heaven" is a metonymy to refer to "God" (Luke 15:18).[152]

Symbol and Allegory

Lewis explains symbolism as "the attempt to read that something else through its sensible imitations, to see the archetype in the copy."[153] He goes on, "The symbolist leaves the given to find that which is more real."[154] Frye explains that symbols can be signs or motifs.[155] As signs, symbols can "stand for and point to things outside the place where they occur," while as motifs, they are the components in understanding "a verbal structure."[156] Tinsley says that "symbolism is metaphorical transferring" with one thing pointing powerfully at another thing such that it influences the audience in "understanding and interpretation of that" another thing.[157] Thus, symbol like allegory is representational.

However, symbolism and allegory operate very differently. Lewis explains their antagonistic relationship in that while feeling "being immaterial, can be copied by material inventions" in allegory, in symbolism, "material world in its turn is the copy of an invisible world."[158] He suggests, "Symbolism is a mode of thought, but allegory is a mode of expression."[159] Hough distinguishes the two in this way, "If the concept comes first and is then translated into a visible equivalent, this is allegory. If the visible object comes first and an immaterial reality is seen behind it or through it, this is symbolism."[160] In other words, symbol emphasizes on the copy (mate-

---

150. Quintilian *Inst.* 8.6.19–20.
151. Bullinger, *Figures of Speech Used in the Bible*, 641.
152. Ibid., 581.
153. Lewis, *The Allegory of Love*, 45.
154. Ibid.
155. Frye, *Anatomy of Criticism*, 73.
156. Ibid., 73–74.
157. Tinsley, "Parable and Allegory," 36.
158. Lewis, *The Allegory of Love*, 45.
159. Ibid., 48.
160. Hough, "The Allegorical Circle," 200.

rial or image giver) for the thought (immaterial or image receiver), while allegory points toward the expression of immaterial, namely what is being copied (image receiver) through the material (image giver). The bread and cup in the Lord's Supper are symbols (Luke 22:19–20). They are copies of the immaterial, the sacrificial death of Jesus, for the remembrance and strengthening of the thought about the inauguration of the new covenant.[161] Although allegory and symbolism are contrasting with one another, they can both be metaphorical when they bring transference from one thing to another.[162]

Although the rhetorical devices above and symbolism carry the characteristic of transference of meaning, they can be generally divided into two groups: explicit and implicit. Simile, similitude, explicit metaphor, and explicit allegory make explanation clear, whereas implicit metaphor and implicit allegory need implication. However, their relationships are very complicated. As Edwyn Hoskyns and Noel Davey suggest, "In practice most allegories contain similes, and most similitudes are tinged with metaphor."[163] Thus, it is one thing to know how these rhetorical devices differ from one another, while it is another thing to understand their enmeshed relationship in the study of rhetorical allegory for parables.

To summarize, structure or terms are not helpful to define parables. The reason is that the words מָשָׁל and παραβολή carry extensive meanings. In addition, some parables in the Bible do not use the terms מָשָׁל and παραβολή at all. The parables of Jesus are better considered as special rhetorical speeches for responding to conflict situation, making persuasion, giving insight, and moving the audience into decision and action. Although Jülicher considers allegory and parable are mutually exclusive, some of the parables of Jesus are indeed allegorical. Instead of limiting parable as simile and allegory as metaphor like Jülicher, it is better to see parables as containing a variety of meanings which include allegory. Indeed, Jülicher's avoidance of rhetorical allegory is a result of mixing it up with allegorical interpretation. Therefore, rhetorical allegory needs to be properly defined.

The rhetorical use of allegory refers one thing in word (image giver) to the meaning of another thing or contrary thing (image receiver). An allegory is comprised of image giver and image receiver. Image giver is the predicate, the visible image, or the material, while image receiver refers

---

161. Bock, *Luke: 9:51—24:53*, 1724–25, 1727.
162. Lewis, *The Allegory of Love*, 45. Tinsley, "Parable and Allegory," 36.
163. Hoskyns and Davey, *The Riddle of the New Testament*, 128.

to the subject matter, the theme, or the immaterial. The basic concept of allegory is that the immaterial or subject matter (image receiver) is represented by the visible thing of the world (image giver). The process of making rhetorical allegory involves the transference of meanings, which can occur between contexts or between words. If the transference of contexts is clear between image giver and image receiver, the allegory is explicit. On the contrary, if the transference of contexts is implicit such that only image giver is provided while image receiver is absent, the allegory is implicit. However, instead of clear distinctions between explicit and implicit allegories in parables, in reality, we find a combination of the two with gradation of allegories. Thus, an allegorical spectrum will give a better illustration. Based on several allegorical models in the past, I will develop a new categorization for illustrating the spectrum of allegories in the parables of Jesus.

2

Implicit Allegory in the Parables of Jesus

EARLY IN THE DISCUSSION of Quintilian, he has already described different kinds of allegories in literature.[1] However, the full form of expression about the allegorical spectrum in literature begins with Northrop Frye's Sliding Scale and it is further modified by Graham Hough's Allegorical Circle.[2] Both spectrums suggest that either the middle point on Frye's Sliding Scale or the three o'clock position on Hough's Allegorical Circle (incarnation) is very implicit between image (image giver) and theme (image receiver).[3] However, when their allegorical models are applied to the parables of Jesus, opinions appear conflicting.[4] I want to expand the discussion on implicit allegory in these two chapters to help in understanding the allegorical features in the parables of Jesus. In current chapter, I will elaborate the relationship between image (image giver) and theme (image receiver) based on the four sections on Hough's Allegorical Circle: naive allegory, incarnation, realism, and symbolism. In chapter 3, I will use four screening questions to indicate the rhetorical allegory in the parables of Jesus. By arranging his parables on a new allegorical spectrum, I will use it to name a new categorization.

---

1. Quintilian *Inst.* 8.6.44–59.
2. Frye, *Anatomy of Criticism*, 91. Hough, "The Allegorical Circle," 203–7.
3. Frye, *Anatomy of Criticism*, 91. Hough, "The Allegorical Circle," 204–5.
4. Tinsley, "Parable and Allegory," 39. Ryken, *Words of Life*, 66.

Allegorical Spectrum

The idea of allegorical spectrum is found embedded in the discussion of Quintilian. By setting his categories of allegories on a gradient from explicit to implicit in expression, I name it as Quintilian's Gradient in previous chapter (figure 1). The first category is "no metaphor" allegory. Progressing along the direction of implicitness, his categories of allegory include mixed allegory, combined allegory, pure allegory, maxim-in-example allegory, enigma allegory, and finally irony.[5]

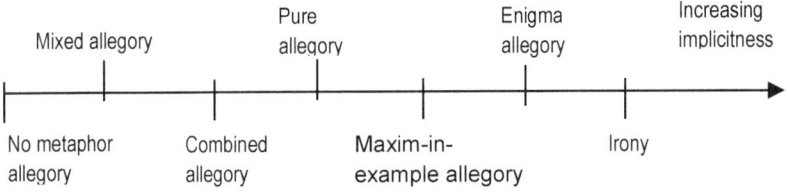

Quintilian's Gradient

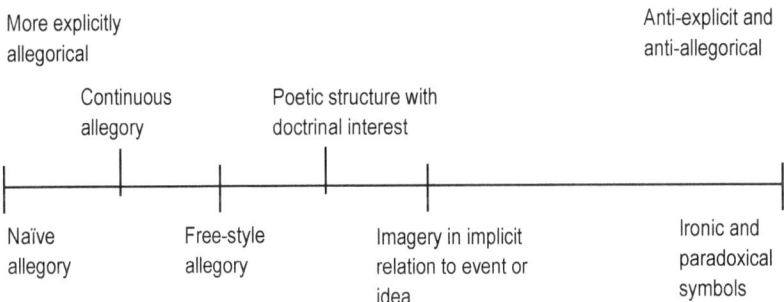

Figure 2. Frye's Sliding Scale

Frye indeed is the first to explain allegories with a sliding scale (figure 2). He says,

> Within the boundaries of literature we find a kind of sliding scale, ranging from the most explicitly allegorical, consistent with being literature at all, at one extreme, to the most elusive, anti-explicit and anti-allegorical at the other.[6]

---

5. Quintilian *Inst.* 8.6.44–59.
6. Frye, *Anatomy of Criticism*, 91.

PART I: ALLEGORICAL SPECTRUM

In other words, literature is explicit at one end of the scale. Implicitness in literature grows continuously toward the opposite end of Frye's Sliding Scale. However, while allegory begins at the explicit extremity, it ceases to be allegorical at the implicit extremity on Frye's scale. Hough further elaborates upon Frye's Sliding Scale with an allegorical circle.[7] John Dominic Crossan and Hans-Josef Klauck also suggest representing allegories either with a scale or a circle.[8] Leland Ryken shortens Frye's Sliding Scale to an allegorical continuum.[9] The following discussion on allegorical spectrum in literature is based upon Frye's Sliding Scale and Hough's Allegorical Circle.

Naive Allegory

Naive allegory appears on the explicit allegorical extremity of Frye's sliding scale, which is equivalent to the twelve o'clock position on Hough's Allegorical Circle.[10] As this type of allegory is all about using allegory to make points, it does not focus on telling a story and is found in "discursive writing with an illustrative image or two."[11] That is, the emphasis of naive allegory focuses on presenting points explicitly.

Hough further elaborates that in naive allegory, theme (image receiver) completely dominates over image (image giver).[12] He describes the image (image giver) in naive allegory as lifeless, "incoherent, insipid, or characterless."[13] In other words, while the main concern of naive allegory is presentation of theme or idea (image receiver), its images (image givers) do not need to be alive and connected. E. J. Tinsley concurs that the problem of naive allegory is poor integration between theme and image.[14] He says that naive allegory "is only just within the category of allegory at all."[15] He explains that allegory needs to show "an artistic and convincing

---

7. Hough, "The Allegorical Circle," 203–206. Blomberg, *Interpreting the Parables*, 38–39.

8. Crossan, *In Parables*, 7. Klauck, *Allegorie und Allegorese in synoptischen Gleichnistexten*, 354.

9. Ryken, *How to Read the Bible as Literature*, 146–47.

10. Frye, *Anatomy of Criticism*, 91. Hough, "The Allegorical Circle," 203–4.

11. Frye, *Anatomy of Criticism*, 91.

12. Hough, "The Allegorical Circle," 204.

13. Frye, *Anatomy of Criticism*, 90. Hough, "The Allegorical Circle," 204.

14. Tinsley, "Parable, Allegory and Mysticism," 176.

15. Ibid., 176.

blend of theme and image" to make detachment of allegorical content from the story difficult.[16] As naive allegory shows the correspondence between theme and image explicitly, it almost falls off the gradient of being considered as allegory. The reason is that naive allegory is all about making points instead of developing the images into a story.

Tinsley continues, "each detail or figure has separable significance" in naive allegory resulting in "the detachment of allegorical content from the plot."[17] This is why he regards naive allegory as bad allegory and considers it as "an allegory that has broken down."[18] He explains that "dramatic coherence" between plot and details is important in making allegory.[19] As the referential details can be easily found in naive allegory, they bring fragmentation to a story instead of forming a fluent one. In other words, what causes naive allegory to be bad allegory is the lack of coherence between the plot (theme) and the referential details (images) for storytelling.

Naive allegory is similar to "no metaphor" allegory of Quintilian in that everything in it is explicit.[20] However, they are different in that metaphor may be used in naive allegory.[21] Frye and Hough both suggest that naive allegories occur in educational materials such as moral lessons, devotional illustrations, pageant themes, and political propagandas.[22] Hough observes that naive allegory occurs "in the form of small patches in long and complex works."[23] That is, naive allegory is not extensive in length. If it occurs in a long story, it will take up just a small portion of it. Tinsley suggests that naive allegory is "the 'lifeless,' 'artificial,' 'contrived' allegory that one reads so much about in books on New Testament parables."[24] He illustrates with Rom 11:16–24 using the example that "grafting wild olives on to the stock of cultivated olive breaks down."[25] In the passage, Paul referred the wild olive branches (image giver) to Gentile believers (image receiver) and the natural olive branches (image giver) to Israel (image receiver) (Rom

16. Ibid.
17. Ibid., 177.
18. Ibid.
19. Ibid., 177–78.
20. Frye, *Anatomy of Criticism*, 91. Quintilian *Inst.* 8.6.46.
21. Frye, *Anatomy of Criticism*, 91.
22. Ibid., 90–91. Hough, "The Allegorical Circle," 204.
23. Hough, "The Allegorical Circle," 204.
24. Tinsley, "Parable, Allegory and Mysticism," 175.
25. Ibid., 178.

11:17). However, Paul just used these images to illustrate some points about the attitude of Gentile believers to Israel and the status of faith of Israel (Rom 11:18, 23–24). The allegory becomes fragmented instead of making a good story. Tinsley, on the other hand, puts the parables of Jesus under incarnational allegory instead of naive allegory.[26]

In general, the main concern of naive allegory is the presentation of points of idea or theme (image receiver). Images (image givers) merely help to illustrate the teaching points explicitly but they are poorly integrated with the theme. As a result, plot and details are so independent in naive allegory that "dramatic coherence" is absent. Thus, naive allegory is considered as bad allegory because it does not tell a fluent story.

Between Naive Allegory and Incarnation

Frye's continuous allegory or Hough's allegory proper is found at the one o'clock position.[27] Although theme still takes over, image is more alive in continuous allegory than naive allegory.[28] Frye elaborates that the stack of lively images in continuous allegory helps "to see what precepts and examples are suggested by the imagery as a whole."[29] In other words, the images have to be considered together for understanding the points of the theme. Ryken indeed begins his allegorical continuum at continuous allegory.[30] He suggests spreading the parables of Jesus between continuous allegory and incarnational allegory on his own model.[31] Ryken places the Sower (or the Seed) and the Talents under continuous allegory.[32] He explains that there is a correspondence for almost every detail in this group of allegory.[33] However, while the Sower (Seed) shows the correspondences clearly concerning the four sowing conditions (Matt 13:19–23), the Talents is only explained with a summary statement at the end (Matt 25:29) with no further explanation for the representation of the three situations of handling the talents. Thus, the Sower and the Talents are not equally allegorical

26. Ibid., 175.
27. Frye, *Anatomy of Criticism*, 91. Hough, "The Allegorical Circle," 205.
28. Ibid.
29. Frye, *Anatomy of Criticism*, 90.
30. Ryken, *How to Read the Bible as Literature*, 147.
31. Ibid.
32. Ibid.
33. Ryken, *Words of Life*, 66.

Implicit Allegory in the Parables of Jesus

under continuous allegory. Or the Talents is better put in another group on the allegorical spectrum. In general, theme still dominates over images in an explicit relationship in continuous allegory. However, the images in continuous allegory have a bit more development into short stories in comparison with naive allegory.

Hough places humor and romantic literatures such as Jonson's comedy and *The Faerie Queene* at the one thirty position.[34] Hough suggests that this type of literature carries "moral and typical significance" but he does not provide further explanation concerning how this type of allegory is different from continuous allegory.[35] In fact, Frye and C. S. Lewis consider *The Faerie Queene* as continuous allegory.[36] According to Shackford, Edmund Spenser wants to use allegory "in the form of romance of chivalry" to represent "moral virtues" with "knights" in his poems.[37] In other words, *The Faerie Queene* fits well into this group of allegory (moral allegory) and continuous allegory.

Freestyle allegory occurs at the two o'clock position where "allegory may be picked up and dropped again at pleasure" in poetic fiction.[38] Ryken calls it as "stories with obvious thematic design" on his allegorical continuum.[39] He illustrates with the Prodigal Son, "the father is God and the elder brother represents the Pharisees and scribes."[40] However, Ryken does not recommend allegorizing the details of the parable.[41] In comparison with continuous allegory, freestyle allegory concerns less with showing the obvious correspondence and more with making thematic story, which is indeed closer to the pure allegory of Quintilian.

Literature at the two thirty position such as the epics of John Milton is structurally poetic with "insistent doctrinal interest in which the internal fictions" are examples.[42]

---

34. Hough, "The Allegorical Circle," 205.
35. Ibid.
36. Frye, *Anatomy of Criticism*, 90. Lewis, *The Allegory of Love*, 297.
37. Spenser, *The Faerie Queene*, xiii-xiv.
38. Frye, *Anatomy of Criticism*, 90. Frye suggests that writings from Ariosto, Goethe, Ibsen, and Hawthorne belong here. Hough, "The Allegorical Circle," 205.
39. Ryken, *How to Read the Bible as Literature*, 147.
40. Ibid. Ryken, *Words of Life*, 66.
41. Ryken, *How to Read the Bible as Literature*, 147.
42. Frye, *Anatomy of Criticism*, 91. Hough, "The Allegorical Circle," 205.

> Of Man's first disobedience, and the fruit of that forbidden tree, whose mortal taste brought death into the world, and all our woe, with loss of Eden, till one greater Man restore us.[43]

Milton uses the account of the fall as the backdrop for his epics. The historical event is developed into fictional poem embedded with some theological themes. In comparison with maxim-in-example allegory of Quintilian, this type of poetic-doctrinal-fictional-example allegory embellishes the historical event into much longer fiction or poem. Hough suggests that this type of allegory is "the closest" to incarnational allegory at the three o'clock position.[44]

Incarnation

The midpoint of Frye's Sliding Scale, which is the three o'clock position of Hough's Allegorical Circle, is incarnation.[45] Although Hough so names it, it has nothing to do with the theological idea of incarnation.[46] Frye suggests that it is a spot where image in the literature "has an implicit relation only to events and ideas."[47] In other words, the corresponding relation between the idea (image receiver) and the image (image giver) in incarnational allegory is not obvious.

Hough further elaborates upon this kind of implicit relationship. He says that "theme and image are completely fused and the relation between them is only implicit, never open or enforced."[48] By fusion, he means, "any 'abstract' content is completely absorbed in character and action and completely expressed by them."[49] That is, the image (image giver) that is expressed through the character or the action represents entirely the "abstract content" whether it is an idea or a theme (image receiver). As a result, there is no need to obviously say what the idea or theme is. It appears as if the theme or idea were absorbed into the image. That is why, when theme (image receiver) is completely fused into image (image giver), we cannot find

---

43. Milton, *Paradise Lost*, 1.1–5.
44. Hough, "The Allegorical Circle," 205.
45. Frye, *Anatomy of Criticism*, 91. Hough, "The Allegorical Circle," 205.
46. Ibid., 204–5.
47. Frye, *Anatomy of Criticism*, 91.
48. Hough, "The Allegorical Circle," 204–5.
49. Ibid., 205.

any explanation (image receiver) in the story but only image (image giver) is shown through the character, the action, or the event.

Tinsley considers incarnational allegory as good allegory.[50] He sees that the obscurity in allegory has "at least two facets."[51] He points out that a successful allegory presents these layers "naturally and inevitably" in the narrative.[52] He explains that what shapes up the allegorical quality is "integration: whether content and form, theme and image" are tightly united.[53] In other words, how good an allegory is depends on how good the integration is between theme and image. The twofold response of Edward Bloom suggests that allegory contains a primary level of "literal and figurative surface meaning" and a secondary level of "meaning of abstract significance," which "must communicate both content and form, both idea and image."[54] That is, literal, figurative, form, and image are considered as the primary level, while abstract significant, content, and idea are the secondary level of meaning. Bloom suggests that allegory cannot be satisfied with "mere equivalences between the primary and the secondary levels."[55] Tinsley concurs that good allegory does not make endless pattern of what is represented.[56] In other words, showing the corresponding relationship between the two layers is not the main concern in a good allegory, just as in incarnational allegory. Bloom further points out that the intention of allegorical work should rather bring forth the "twofold response from the pictorial imagination and the rational intellect."[57] However, he suggests that allegory does not place the emphasis on presenting "the esthetic or the didactic" or "the primary or the secondary."[58] Rather, allegory must bring "a subtle, intangible union of both structure and meaning" in such a way that "explicit statement" is not detached from the "implicit meaning."[59] Tinsley describes the enmeshed relationship between theme and image in incarnational allegory as a powerful expression, which leads to the formation of "a

50. Tinsley, "Parable, Allegory and Mysticism," 178.
51. Ibid., 174.
52. Ibid., 178.
53. Ibid.
54. Bloom, "The Allegorical Principle," 164.
55. Ibid., 164.
56. Tinsley, "Parable, Allegory and Mysticism," 174.
57. Bloom, "The Allegorical Principle," 165.
58. Ibid., 190.
59. Ibid.

life of its own under its own impetus."⁶⁰ No matter what these two layers are called, whether they are primary and secondary, or structure and meaning, or image (image giver) and theme (image receiver), the point of making good allegory is really about the perfect union of these two layers such that the referential relationship cannot be easily discovered.

Apart from that, good allegory shows coherence between plot and details.⁶¹ Unlike naive allegory in which allegorical details or characters demonstrate "separable significance" with the plot, incarnational allegory carries the feature of "dramatic coherence."⁶² Tinsley explains that in a good allegory, the "extended and dramatized metaphor" instead of appearing unrelated to the plot, is connected with the story so well that it becomes the driven force of it.⁶³ He considers incarnational allegory as good allegory because its aliveness "reaches into the details of the plot naturally, and it can never be completely and finally 'decoded.'"⁶⁴ In other words, good allegory like incarnational allegory is a good drama. Not only the metaphor in incarnational allegory is developed at some length, but also it is the vital part of the story to which all of the details are related. The metaphor in incarnational allegory shows a good coherence between plot and details. As a result, it becomes very difficult to detach the allegorical content from the drama of incarnational allegory. That is, instead of seeing "this stands for that" decoding mechanism of naive allegory, it is expected to encounter difficulty when we attempt to fully understand the referents of the whole drama in incarnational allegory.

Hough's incarnational allegory matches well with Quintilian's pure allegory, maxim-in-example allegory, enigma allegory, and irony in the implicitness of expressing the theme. However, incarnational allegory is longer in length and more alive in drama, while Quintilian's maxim-in-example allegory and irony are short sayings. In fact, Hough's freestyle allegory is also similar to Quintilian's pure allegory when considering implicit expression. When developing something factual into allegory for illustration, Hough's poetic-doctrinal-fictional-example allegory and Quintilian's maxim-in-example allegory share some commonality. In other words, from Hough's freestyle allegory to incarnation, Hough's model is

60. Tinsley, "Parable, Allegory and Mysticism," 176.
61. Ibid., 177–78.
62. Ibid.
63. Ibid., 178.
64. Ibid.

Implicit Allegory in the Parables of Jesus

similarly implicit like that of Quintilian's Gradient from pure allegory to irony. As Hough considers incarnational allegory as "only implicit, never open or enforced," incarnational allegory becomes the apex of implicitness on his Allegorical Circle.[65] However, it is also at incarnation that several allegorical items of Quintilian are found. It seems difficult to use Quintilian's Gradient to understand Hough's model. Conversely, Hough's incarnation is probably a location that needs expansion in order to fully understand the diversity of allegory under it.

Tinsley observes that the parables of Jesus are located in the middle between naive allegory and realism, which is incarnational allegory.[66] He suggests that the Sower (Seed), the Wicked Husbandmen (Tenants), the Two Sons, the Prodigal Son, the Good Samaritan, the Rich Man and Lazarus, and the Lost Sheep should be placed under incarnational allegory.[67] In fact, the Sower (Seed) is full of explicit allegories (Matt 13:19–23). For example, the seed being sown beside the road in the parable refers explicitly to one who hears the word of the kingdom and does not understand it. As a result, the evil one comes and snatches it away from the person's heart (Matt 13:19). However, in the Good Samaritan, no referent about the characters is made except an exchange of question and answer about who the neighbor of the miserable man is (Luke 10:36–37). This is an implicit allegory. It is uncertain why Tinsley puts parables with explicit allegory and parables with implicit allegory together under incarnational allegory. In fact, Ryken only puts the Good Samaritan under incarnational allegory.[68] The disagreement between Tinsley and Ryken will be discussed in the following section.

Idea of Implicitness

What is implicitness in allegory? The kind of implicitness that occurs between image and theme at the midpoint of Frye's Sliding Scale is considered as fusion by Hough.[69] He says that the relation between theme and image becomes completely implicit in such a way that its "abstract" idea is "absorbed" into the character and action.[70] Tinsley calls this relation as

---

65. Hough, "The Allegorical Circle," 204–5.
66. Tinsley, "Parable, Allegory and Mysticism," 175.
67. Tinsley, "Parable and Allegory," 39.
68. Ryken, *How to Read the Bible as Literature*, 147.
69. Frye, *Anatomy of Criticism*, 91. Hough, "The Allegorical Circle," 204.
70. Ibid., 204–5.

Part I: Allegorical Spectrum

integration in which theme and image "may be communicated without destroying the unity."[71] Bloom considers this relation as imprecise union between the statement and the implied meaning.[72] Renate Banschbach Eggen describes the implicitness in a metaphor as "double reference," in which "[t]he lexical referent represents the image giver, the metaphorical referent the image receiver."[73] No matter the implicitness in allegory is described as fusion, integration, or theme absorbed into the image, the relationship between image (image giver) and theme (image receiver) is not obvious. That is, the image (image giver) is given in the allegory, while the theme (image receiver) is either undiscoverable or completely unexplained in the drama.

On the contrary, explicit allegory provides an obvious explanation about the relationship between image (image giver) and theme (image receiver). However, how explicit an allegory is does not equate to how allegorical an allegory is. Explicit allegory only suggests how clearly the allegorical content is told. People normally consider allegory to be like naive allegory, which shows a clear corresponding relationship between image and theme. However, Tinsley points out that the fusion of image and theme makes good allegory.[74] As in incarnational allegory, instead of making "clever juxtaposing of story and moralistic or other coding," he finds image and theme fused.[75] In other words, people normally accept allegories as those having obvious referents. However, the opposite of this assumption is the case for a good allegory. That is, image is obvious but the referential theme or idea is not explained. Although Klyne Snodgrass does not discuss extensively about the allegory in parables, he describes example stories, namely the Good Samaritan, the Rich Fool, the Rich Man and Lazarus, the Pharisee and Toll Collector, and the Unjust Steward, in this way,

> [These] stories have developed plots, but they are not metaphorical in the way that other parables are . . . These five stories do not juxtapose different realms; they are about the subjects they narrate. . . . They address the reader indirectly by telling of another person but directly by treating the subject at hand.[76]

---

71. Tinsley, "Parable, Allegory and Mysticism," 174.
72. Bloom, "The Allegorical Principle," 190.
73. Eggen, *Gleichnis, Allegorie, Metapher*, 258.
74. Tinsley, "Parable, Allegory and Mysticism," 176.
75. Ibid.
76. Ibid., 14–15.

Although Snodgrass calls these parables "single indirect narrative parables" and he considers them as having nothing to do with metaphors, he sees them as indirect.[77] The description of Snodgrass in some way supports the idea of Tinsley on good allegories in that these five parables are dramas with plots although the referential themes are implicit or indirect. Ryken also puts the Good Samaritan under incarnational allegory.[78] He says that "the story as a whole embodies the moral meaning."[79] That is, the whole parabolic story instead of the components in the story can carry referential meaning. Since incarnational allegory demonstrates fusion of image and theme, a question is raised: why does Tinsley put so many parables of Jesus in this location, including explicit allegory such as the Sower (Seed) and implicit allegory such as the Good Samaritan?[80] The only explanation is that he considers all parables of Jesus as belonging to incarnational allegory.[81] That is, regardless of explicitness or implicitness in expression, he places all parables of Jesus under the category of incarnational allegory. Unfortunately, Tinsley does not elaborate further. In the Sower (Seed), the lack of explanation of the character suggests a bit of implicitness although the parable is predominately an explicit allegory.

Apparently, opinions differ concerning how to allocate the parables of Jesus along an allegorical spectrum. Apart from implicitness in allegory, what are the other considerations for making good allegory that need to be taken into account? Criteria for evaluating the allegorical quality in parables need to be set up for distributing them along an allegorical spectrum.

Indicators of Allegory

Several features contribute to the formation of a good allegory. The first one which Tinsley mentioned for making good allegory is the fusion between image and theme.[82] As discussed above, under this kind of implicitness in allegory, the image (image giver) is clearly shown, while it leaves the theme or idea (image receiver) unexplained. Thus, one of the considerations for

---

77. Ibid., 15.

78. Ryken, *How to Read the Bible as Literature*, 147.

79. Ibid.

80. Tinsley, "Parable, Allegory and Mysticism," 176. Tinsley, "Parable and Allegory," 39.

81. Tinsley, "Parable, Allegory and Mysticism," 175.

82. Ibid., 176, 178.

Part I: Allegorical Spectrum

identifying the allegorical quality in the parables of Jesus is to look for fusion or implicitness between theme and image. That is, it evaluates whether or not explanation of the theme (image receiver) regarding its image (image giver) is provided. The image giver can be expressed through the character, the action, the event, and even the whole drama. In the case of complete fusion, there is no explanation about the theme (image receiver). If it is an incomplete fusion, we may be able to find some hints or partial explanation about the theme (image receiver) in the context. For instance, in the Good Samaritan, there is no explanation about the characters and the details. However, Jesus provided trace of hints in his reply concerning the question: who is my neighbor (Luke 10:29, 36–37)? On the contrary, in the Dragnet, not only does the statement "the kingdom of heaven is like" describe what the story is about, but also the action of separating the bad from the good is explained (Matt 13:47–50). In comparison with the Good Samaritan, the clear explanation of the Dragnet makes it less allegorical on the spectrum. Thus, the better the occurrence of fusion between image (image giver) and theme (image receiver) is, the more allegorical the drama is in the parable.

Another consideration regarding the quality of a good allegory is the "undetachability" of the allegorical content from the narrative. According to Tinsley, the plot and details of a good allegory demonstrate "a convincing coherence" in the drama.[83] Instead of being a separated unit that breaks up a story, the metaphor in a good allegory connects the whole drama tightly.[84] In other words, another indicator for a good allegory assesses how difficult it is to detach the metaphor from the story. It looks for a fluent drama instead of a story interrupted by the metaphorical details. If the flow of a story is significantly fragmented by the metaphor, whether it is "the details or characters," it will not be considered as good allegory.[85] For example, in the Wheat and Weeds, the details have clear correspondence such as the one who sows good seed is the Son of Man, the field is the world, the good seeds are the sons of the kingdom, and the weeds are the sons of the evil one (Matt 13:36–43). Instead of making a good drama, the metaphorical details limit the development of the story (Matt 13:24–30). On the contrary, the Prodigal Son does not indicate to what the characters or the story refer although the characters in the story are metaphorical (Luke 15:11–32). The Prodigal Son makes a good drama about the life change of the younger son

83. Tinsley, "Parable, Allegory and Mysticism," 177–78.
84. Ibid.
85. Ibid., 177.

and the response of the father and the older son. Thus, good allegory makes good drama without being broken up by the details of the story.

The third criterion in assessing the quality of allegory looks for the dominant image (image giver) in the drama. When a parable contains several metaphors and allegories, it is necessary to decide which metaphor or allegory is the dominant image (image giver) holding the whole story together. As Tinsley suggests, the metaphor in a good allegory connects so well that it becomes the driven force of the whole drama.[86] In other words, the dominant metaphor in allegory relates to every part of the story as if the backbone of the whole drama. The difference in emphasis between Ryken and Tinsley in placing the Sower (Seed) on the allegorical spectrum provides an illustration. Ryken puts the Sower (Seed) closer to the explicit side of his allegorical continuum under continuous allegory, while Tinsley places it under the completely implicit incarnational allegory.[87] Who is correct? As mentioned earlier, the Sower (Seed) contains both explicit and implicit elements. The sower in the story is implicit with no explanation given (Luke 8:5). However, the seed that refers to the word of God is one of the explicit metaphors in the parable (Luke 8:11). Other image givers in the parable such as the four types of soil condition after the seed is sown are explicit with explanation provided (Luke 8:5–8, 12–15). If the emphasis of the story is on the sower, the parable will probably be considered closer to the implicit side on the allegorical spectrum as Tinsley places it. If the emphasis is on the four types of soil condition after the seed is sown, the parable will probably be considered closer to the explicit side on the allegorical spectrum as Ryken locates it. Because the Sower (Seed) mainly discusses the conditions of the seed after it is sown instead of the identity of the sower, it does not make good allegory owing to the fragmentation by the explicit metaphors. Therefore, as the growing conditions of the seed are the dominant images and they are explained, the Sower (Seed) should be placed closer to the explicit than the implicit extremity on the allegorical spectrum. Ryken is correct concerning this parable.

However, in the process of determining which image (image giver) takes the dominant role, two aspects need to be taken into consideration. One of them is that an explicit image (image giver) in a drama is not necessarily the dominant one although it is easier to distinguish an explicit

---

86. Tinsley, "Parable, Allegory and Mysticism," 178.

87. Ryken, *How to Read the Bible as Literature*, 146–47. Tinsley, "Parable and Allegory," 39.

metaphor than an implicit metaphor owing to the explanation. Another concern looks into the prevention of over-interpretation of implicit metaphors in the allegorical drama. As Craig Blomberg suggests, only some components instead of all details in a longer allegory carry referential meanings.[88] In other words, not every detail in a parable needs to be considered as implicit. Therefore, a careful assessment of what the implicit metaphors or allegories are is necessary for a parable drama.

The last consideration about the quality of allegory is its length and ability to make drama. As Tinsley suggests, the metaphor in a good allegory appears "extended and dramatized."[89] In other words, apart from making good drama, the metaphor in a good allegory appears longer. It is hard to find good allegory in a brief metaphor such as a maxim and a proverb. For example, in Luke 4:23, Jesus referred to a proverb (παραβολή) that the people of his hometown said about him, "Physician, heal yourself." The people showed disbelief though they asked Jesus to do the miraculous work in Nazareth similar to what he has done in Capernaum. However, Jesus refused (Luke 4:24–30). Although "physician" (image giver) is an implicit image referring to Jesus, the statement is too brief to make a good story. However, a longer metaphor does not necessarily make a good allegory. The Sower (Seed) is long (Luke 8:4–8, 11–15). However, the dominant image (image giver) is the whole set of explicit metaphors concerning the soil conditions of the seed after it is sown. The image giver indeed heavily fragments the story by its explanation of each of the soil conditions. As a result, a long metaphor may not make a good story though its length can give room for the development of a drama. Therefore, the length of a metaphor cannot be the only consideration for the quality of a good allegory but it needs to be evaluated along with other criteria.

To summarize, four indicators help in making good allegory. The first indicator looks for fusion between image (image giver) and theme (image receiver). When fusion occurs, the image receiver (the theme or the idea) of the image giver (the character, the action, the event, or the whole drama) appears implicit with no or partial explanation provided in the drama. Second, the allegorical content is difficult to detach from a story. The plot and the details such as the character, the action, or the event, link up with the whole drama so well that instead of breaking up the story, they make it fluent. Third, there needs to be one dominant image giver among other image

---

88. Blomberg, *Interpreting the Parables*, 52.

89. Tinsley, "Parable, Allegory and Mysticism," 178.

givers in the drama. To be a more allegorical drama, the dominant image is preferably an implicit image rather than an explicit metaphor. Adding to these three, the fourth criterion is that it is better to have a longer image giver than a shorter one in order to develop into an allegorical drama.

With criteria established, subjective decisions concerning the allegorical nature of the parables of Jesus can be avoided. Although explicit allegory is often confused as being more allegorical than implicit allegory owing to the provision of explanation, it is implicit allegory that shows a good fusion of image and theme that makes good allegory. The criteria of making a good allegory will be used for expanding incarnation, the most implicit spot, on Hough's Allegorical Circle. This will be fully discussed in chapter 3.

After Incarnation

Frye's Sliding Scale and Hough's Allegorical Circle appear different after incarnation. Toward the opposite end of naive allegory, literature appears "anti-explicit and anti-allegorical" after leaving the center on Frye's Sliding Scale.[90] On the contrary, from incarnation to realism on Hough's Allegorical Circle, literature goes back to explicit with image dominated over theme.[91] Although both allegorical models start at the explicitness of naive allegory, Frye's Sliding Scale ends with implicit literature, while Hough's Allegorical Circle goes to explicit realism at the six o'clock position. How should their differences be understood? Hough confesses that after incarnation, he does not follow Frye's Sliding Scale.[92] In other words, these two allegorical models differ after incarnation.

The second half of Frye's Sliding Scale is symbolism. After passing the midpoint on Frye's Sliding Scale, imagery becomes less about "example and precept" but more about "ironic and paradoxical."[93] This kind of ironic imagery mixes with non-allegorical imagery in poetry. They are found in literature with images such as paradoxical metaphysical image, symbolic image of thing, symbolic image of emotion, heraldic symbol of emblematic image, and symbolism that does not open up for understanding.[94] In com-

90. Frye, *Anatomy of Criticism*, 91.
91. Hough, "The Allegorical Circle," 205. Tinsley, "Parable, Allegory and Mysticism," 175.
92. Hough, "The Allegorical Circle," 205.
93. Frye, *Anatomy of Criticism*, 91.
94. Ibid., 91–92.

parison with Quintilian's Gradient which has enigma allegory and irony respectively after maxim-in-example allegory, the second half of Frye's model is slightly similar in the sense of style such as with the use of paradox and irony. However, they are also very different. The second half of Frye's Sliding Scale is not allegory while Quintilian's enigma and irony are allegories. In addition, instead of irony as allegory, Frye refers to the ironic use in symbolism. Therefore, it is hard to compare Quintilian's Gradient with the second half of Frye's Sliding Scale.

Although the second half of Frye's Sliding Scale is different from Hough's realism at the six o'clock position, it matches with Hough's Allegorical Circle at other parts. For example, by using images to substitute something, Frye's *symbolisme* is similar to Hough's symbolism at the nine o'clock position where both "theme and image are equally present" but without fusion.[95] However, the thing being substituted by the image is not named in Frye's *symbolism*, which makes it implicit and becomes a major difference with Hough's symbolism.[96] Frye's heraldic symbol that uses emblematic image also matches well with Hough's emblem symbolism at the ten thirty position.[97] In sum, the second half of Frye's Sliding Scale actually covers a variety of symbols matching better with Hough's symbolism at nine and heraldic symbol at the ten thirty position than with realism at the six o'clock position. To visualize Frye's Sliding Scale in Hough's terms, Frye's model starts at the twelve o'clock (naive allegory) and it goes to three (incarnation). From the three o'clock (incarnation), Frye's model jumps to the nine o'clock (symbolism) and returns to the twelve o'clock. That is, Frye arranges his sliding scale from explicit allegory (naive allegory) on the very left and it goes to implicit allegory in the middle. Then, from implicit allegory in the middle, he continues toward the right with implicit symbols.

Realism

From the three (incarnation) to the six o'clock (realism), Hough sees that image dominates over theme increasingly in novel type of literature.[98] At the four thirty position, theme begins to detach from images in literature.[99]

   95. Hough, "The Allegorical Circle," 206.
   96. Frye, *Anatomy of Criticism*, 92. Hough, "The Allegorical Circle," 206.
   97. Frye, *Anatomy of Criticism*, 92. Hough, "The Allegorical Circle," 207.
   98. Ibid., 205.
   99. Ibid., 206.

Hough suggests that novels written by Fielding, Dickens, and Thackeray belong to this type.[100] From the five to six o'clock position, literature moves from "professed" realism to "pure realism."[101] Hough sees that image is taking a dominant role while theme is diminishing in realism, which is the opposite style of naive allegory.[102] Ryken suggests that work at this spot is less about theme but more about reporting "surface detail."[103] Hough finds realism in "direct mimesis of common experience" such as "quasi-documentary fiction" and "descriptive writing."[104] Although Tinsley places the allegorical parables of Jesus mostly at incarnation, he finds that some scholars place the parables of Jesus near realism to consider them as "transcripts of life."[105] Unless there is a parable of Jesus that is completely non-allegorical, telling a story without any meaning behind it, or using images mainly for reporting without thematic intention, finding his parables close to or at realism is very unlikely.

Symbolism

Between realism at six and symbolism at nine, in poetic literature such as *The Waste Land* of Eliot, images are used "atomically and disjunctively" and even appositionally, while theme only appears "surreptitiously."[106] This is especially the case in imagism at the seven thirty position on Hough's Allegorical Circle.[107] Hough suggests that image in imagism usually has "mysterious correspondences" and is related to visionary literature.[108] Theme in imagism is rather "depreciated," "vague and abstract."[109] In other words, between realism and symbolism, image still takes the lead with the appearance of disconnected and mystical in content, while theme is insignificant and imprecise.

---

100. Ibid.
101. Ibid.
102. Ibid., 205.
103. Ryken, *How to Read the Bible as Literature*, 147. Ryken, *Words of Life*, 66.
104. Hough, "The Allegorical Circle," 205.
105. Tinsley, "Parable and Allegory," 39. Tinsley, "Parable, Allegory and Mysticism," 175.
106. Hough, "The Allegorical Circle," 207.
107. Ibid., 206–7.
108. Ibid., 207.
109. Ibid., 206.

Part I: Allegorical Spectrum

Symbolism occurs at the nine o'clock position, where "theme and image have equal weight" such as incarnation.[110] However, their difference is that in symbolism, image and theme are not in "harmonious wholeness" or fused.[111] Tinsley suggests that symbolism focuses on using image to show "the invisible with all the concreteness of sense experience."[112] Tinsley's definition of symbolism is very similar to Lewis, "The attempt to read that something else through its sensible imitations, to see the archtype in the copy."[113] In other words, while both incarnation and symbolism show equal weight on theme and image, theme is fused into image in incarnation but in symbolism, theme is expressed tangibly through image.

According to Tinsley, symbolism can be a metaphor by using concrete image to refer to something invisible.[114] However, symbolism is very different from allegory. Lewis suggests that allegory and symbolism oppose one another in that after leaving what is given, allegory moves into the discussion of less realistic things while symbolism goes on to discuss more real things.[115] Lewis considers symbolism as "a mode of thought" while allegory as "a mode of expression."[116] Thus, the kind of metaphorical image in symbolism is not fictional for making allegory but is for the illustration of thought. Hough describes their difference such that allegory has concept come first and then the concept is visualized with image, while symbolism has image presented first to help in seeing the "immaterial reality" behind it.[117] That is, allegory shapes image into the framework of the theme but symbolism uses image to point to the theme or the thought behind it.

It is hard to find an example of symbolism in the parables of Jesus. However, symbolism occurs in other literary genres. For example, it shows in the gospel narrative such as the bread and cup in the Lord's Supper (Luke 22:19–20), "I am the Light of the world" (John 8:12), and "I am the door of the sheep" (John 10:7). In addition, symbolism can be found in visionary

---

110. Ibid.
111. Ibid.
112. Tinsley, "Parable and Allegory," 39.
113. Lewis, *The Allegory of Love*, 45.
114. Tinsley, "Parable and Allegory," 36.
115. Lewis, *The Allegory of Love*, 45.
116. Ibid., 48.
117. Hough, "The Allegorical Circle," 200.

literature such as OT prophetic books and Revelation.[118] Ryken regards "a pillar in the temple of my God" in Rev 3:12 as an illustration of symbolism.[119]

Between the nine to the twelve o'clock, there is "emblem or hieratic symbolism."[120] Hough suggests that this type of work is not found in literature but in "iconography and religious imagery."[121] He finds that at symbolism on the allegorical circle, image becomes "stereotyped" while theme increases.[122] At emblem or hieratic symbolism, image approaches "limited and inflexible" while theme grows toward naive allegory.[123] In other words, emblem symbolism is a more specific type of symbol, which can be found both outside literature and within literature. Its image is not as flexible as naive allegory. However, as emblem symbolism approaches naive allegory, theme dominates over image. Hough uses "the cross or the marriage ring" as examples of emblems while "baptismal water" or "oil of consecration" as heraldic device.[124]

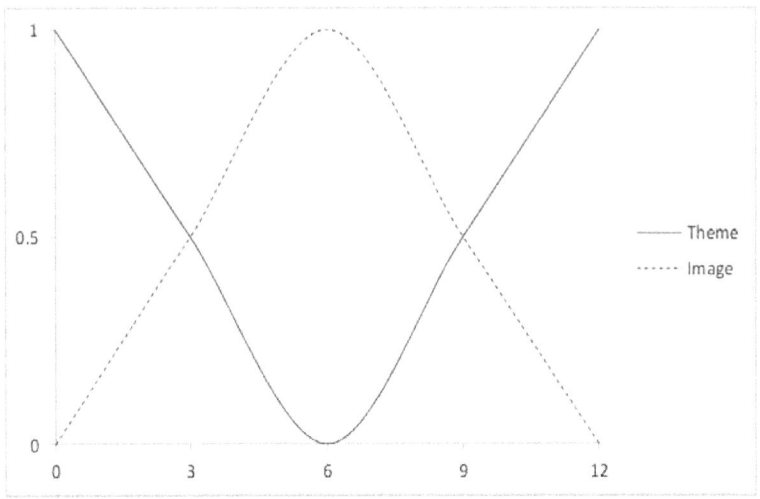

Figure 3. A Modified Expression of Hough's Allegorical Circle on Image and Theme

118. Ryken, *How to Read the Bible as Literature*, 171.
119. Ibid., 172.
120. Hough, "The Allegorical Circle," 207.
121. Ibid.
122. Ibid.
123. Ibid.
124. Ibid.

Part I: Allegorical Spectrum

Figure 3 is an alternative expression of Hough's Allegorical Circle for summarizing the relationship between image and theme. At the twelve o'clock which is also point zero on the graph, theme completely dominates over image in naive allegory. From naive allegory at the twelve o'clock (point zero) to incarnation at three, theme decreases its leading role over image until they are equally weighed and fused. This is the zone of allegory where a gradation of implicitness exhibits from the least to the most. From incarnation at three to realism at six, theme is further fading while image is taking the lead over theme. This is the zone of novel and report.

From realism at six to symbolism at nine, image decreases to be dominant over theme until they are equally weighted but not fused. This is the zone of the mysterious symbol of poetry. From symbolism at nine to naive allegory at twelve, image further decreases while theme increases again until it completely dominates over image. This is the zone of symbols. Current study on allegory is restricted only to the zone between naive allegory and incarnation.

Figure 4 is used to conclude the several allegorical models. Although Frye is the first to put literature on an allegorical sliding scale, Hough expands it into an allegorical circle. The first quarter from naive allegory to incarnation on Hough's Allegorical Circle is almost the same as the first half of Frye's Sliding Scale except for a few terms. At naive allegory, image explicitly reveals the theme but they have poor integration. This is the beginning point of allegorical literature that appears explicitly and briefly in educational material such as classroom morality. At continuous allegory, theme still takes a leading role over image in an explicit relationship, while image is having more development such as in short stories. In freestyle allegory, thematic story is mixed with some unexplained allegories and is seen occasionally in poetic fiction. The next point is poetic style of literature, which has doctrinal interest and uses fiction as example. At incarnation, theme and image are completely implicit in allegory with coherent plot and details for making good drama. In general, this quarter increases toward implicitness in allegory.

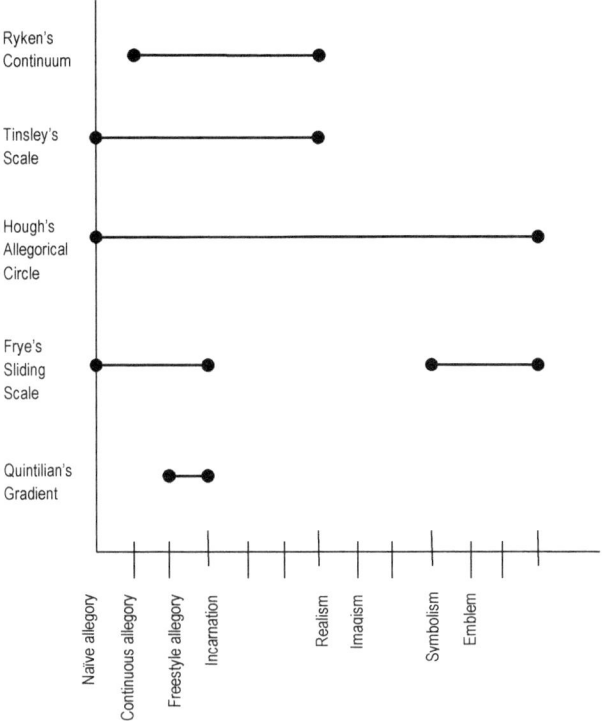

Figure 4. A Comparison of Several Allegorical Models

After incarnation, Frye's Sliding Scale is very different than Hough's Allegorical Circle. From naive allegory at the left moving toward the center at the right, allegory on Frye's model goes from explicitly allegorical to implicitly allegorical. From the center toward the right, Frye's Sliding Scale continues to be implicit but it is anti-allegorical. The second half of Frye's model is ironic symbolism, while Hough has never clearly indicated the location of irony. On the contrary, from incarnation to realism on Hough's Allegorical Circle, literature goes back to explicitness. With reference to Hough's Allegorical Circle, Frye's model is as if jumping from incarnation directly to symbolism skipping realism completely. Frye's Sliding Scale finishes at symbolism. Hough's Allegorical Circle, on the other hand, continues from realism to symbolism and then from symbolism, it goes back to naive allegory.

Part I: Allegorical Spectrum

The models of Tinsley and Ryken are very similar to the first half circle of Hough's Allegorical Circle. Tinsley's model is actually the same as Hough's from naive allegory to realism, which has explicitness at the two extremities while implicitness is found at incarnation at the center. Ryken's model slightly differs from Hough's model in the way that he starts his continuum at continuous allegory instead of naive allegory. Then, Ryken ends his model with realistic and reporting type of literature.

The allegorical terms of Quintilian (Quintilian's Gradient) express a trend of increasing implicitness located densely from freestyle allegory to incarnation on Hough's model. However, Quintilian's Gradient is very different from other allegorical models. Unlike Hough's naive allegory, the use of metaphor is not a concern to Quintilian's "no metaphor" allegory. Though Quintilian's pure allegory and maxim-in-example allegory match well with Hough's incarnation, his enigma allegory and irony are something not found in other allegorical models.

3

A New Allegorical Spectrum

Although there are several allegorical models, they are basically reusing Hough's Allegorical Circle that is modified from Frye's Sliding Scale. The part that is related to allegory mainly falls between naive allegory and incarnation on Hough's model. However, Tinsley and Ryken show a huge difference when they apply their models to the parables of Jesus. Tinsley puts all the parables of Jesus under incarnation.[1] Alternatively, Ryken spreads the parables of Jesus between continuous allegory and incarnation instead of placing them only at incarnation.[2] In other words, it is still unclear where the parables of Jesus should be located on Hough's model when considering their allegorical features. Should the parables of Jesus be arranged from naive allegory to incarnation or from continuous allegory to incarnation? Or, should the incarnation location be expanded to accommodate all parables of Jesus according to their allegorical feature?

Moreover, neither Hough's Allegorical Circle nor Frye's Sliding Scale match well with Quintilian's Gradient. For example, there is not a place for irony on Hough's model. Although the second half of Frye's Sliding Scale has some concern about ironic imagery, he refers only to symbolism, which is something anti-allegorical.[3] However, Quintilian considers irony as a kind of allegory.[4] In fact, Ryken suggests that the Rich Man and Lazarus, and the Pharisee and Tax Collector use satire to develop their main points.[5] That

1. Tinsley, "Parable and Allegory," 39.
2. Ryken, *Words of Life*, 66.
3. Frye, *Anatomy of Criticism*, 91–92.
4. Quintilian *Inst.* 8.6.44, 54.
5. Ryken, *Words of Life*, 64.

Part I: Allegorical Spectrum

is, some parables of Jesus use irony. However, existing allegorical models do not have a place for irony. It appears that a better allegorical spectrum needs to be developed so that all parables of Jesus can be expressed on it.

Screening Questions

The four criteria for indicating allegory from the previous discussion will be used here for developing a new allegorical model for the parables of Jesus. The four criteria are converted into four sets of questions. Each set of questions will be rated from zero to two points if a parable meets a criterion. The points from the four questions for each parable will be summed up to get a final score. Concerning the terms used in these questions, image giver refers to the character, the action, the event, or the whole drama of allegory in a parable, while image receiver is the corresponding theme, concept, or the idea of the image giver.

Question 1: Is there any fusion between image giver and image receiver in a parable? If explanation of the image giver concerning its image receiver is provided in a parable, or there is a clear structural indicator given in a parable such as ὁμοιόω or ὅμοιος, ὡς, ὥσπερ, and "this is that," the parable will be given zero points for question 1. If no explanation is provided in a parable but it can be implied from the context through some hints or partial explanation, the parable will be given one point for question 1. If no explanation can be found at all in the context of a parable, the parable will be given two points for question 1.

Question 2: Is it difficult to detach a metaphor or allegory from the whole drama in a parable? In other words, does the drama maintain a good flow instead of being interrupted by metaphorical details? Or, is it difficult to discover the metaphor or allegory in the drama? If the answer is "yes," the parable will be given two points. If the answer is "no," the parable will be given zero points.

Question 3: Is implicit metaphor or allegory the leading image giver in the parable? That is, is implicit metaphor or allegory used to connect through the whole drama in the parable? If the answer is yes to a parable, the parable will be given two points for question 3. This question can be applied on a parable that contains several implicit metaphors or allegories although only one of them takes lead in the drama. If the answer is no to a parable, the parable will be given zero points for question 3. A negative answer can be a result of having an explicit metaphor or allegory as the

A New Allegorical Spectrum

dominating image giver. If a parable contains both explicit and implicit metaphors, a decision is necessary regarding which one of them takes the lead. In the previous discussion on the Seed (Sower), the unexplained image giver, the sower, is an implicit metaphor but it is not the dominating image. Since the parable is all about the response of the seed in various soil types after sowing, the leading image giver is the seed, which is an explicit metaphor referring to the word of God (Luke 8:11). There are two considerations in the decision process concerning the leading image giver. Although it is easier to discern an explicit image giver than an implicit one, an explicit image giver is not necessarily the leading image in a parable. Another concern is that not all the details in a parable need to be considered as implicit image givers.

Question 4: Is the image giver extended into an allegorical drama? If the dominating image of a parable is very brief, or it is just a metaphor, the parable will be given zero points. If the dominating image develops into a brief allegory in a parable, the parable will be given one point only. If the dominating image of a parable develops into a narrative of some length, the parable will be given two points.

The final score for each parable is relative in nature instead of absolute. This score is used as an indicator of the allegorical level of a parable. By arranging all the final scores from the least to the most in the format of visual analog, a new allegorical spectrum for the parables of Jesus is created. The major focus will be given to the parables in Luke unless the parables occur only in Matthew or Mark. Parallel passages among the Synoptic Gospels are placed together. A square bracket in Table 1 indicates a parable that is possibly a parallel account. In case a parable is too short, a round bracket is used to indicate the extent of the related context. The results are shown in Table 1.

Part I: Allegorical Spectrum

Luke	Matt	Mark	Parables	Questions				Total
				1	2	3	4	
4:23 (vv. 16–30)			Physician	0	0	0	0	0
5:33–35	9:14–15	2:18–20	Bridegroom and Attendants	1	0	2	0	3
5:36	9:16	2:21	Cloth and Garment	1	0	2	0	3
5:37–39	9:17	2:22	Wine and Wineskins	1	0	2	0	3
[6:37–42]	15:14 (vv. 10–20)	[7:15–23]	Blind Guide	1	0	2	0	3
6:46–49	7:24–27		Two Builders	0	0	0	0	0
7:31–35	11:16–19		Market's Children	0	0	0	0	0
7:40–43 (vv. 36–50)			Two Debtors	1	1	2	1	5
8:4–8, 11–15	13:1–9, 18–23	4:1–9, 13–20	Seed (Sower)	0	0	0	2	2
10:25–37			Good Samaritan	1	2	2	2	7
11:5–8 (vv. 1–13)			Friend at Midnight	1	2	2	1	6
11:21–22 (vv. 14–23)	12:29 (vv. 22–30)	3:27 (vv. 20–27)	Strong Man	1	1	2	0	4
12:13–21			Rich Fool	1	2	2	2	7
12:33–34	[6:19–21]		Money Belts	0	0	0	0	0
12:35–38			Watchful Servants	0	0	0	1	1
12:39–48	24:43–51		Thief and Stewardship	1	1	2	2	6
12:57–59	5:25–26		Defendant	1	0	2	1	4
13:6–9			Barren Fig Tree	2	2	2	2	8
13:18–19	13:31–32	4:30–32	Mustard Seed	0	0	0	0	0
13:20–21	13:33		Leaven	0	0	0	0	0
13:23–30			Those outside	1	1	2	2	6
14:7–11			Dinner Guests	0	0	0	1	1
14:12–24			Big Feast	2	2	2	2	8
14:25–33			Tower Builder and Warring King	0	0	0	1	1
[14:34–35]	5:13	9:50	Salt	0	0	0	0	0

A New Allegorical Spectrum

Luke	Matt	Mark	Parables	Questions				Total
				1	2	3	4	
15:3–7 (vv. 1–7)	18:12–14		Lost Sheep	1	2	2	1	6
15:8–10			Lost Coin	1	2	2	1	6
15:11–32			Prodigal Son	1	2	2	2	7
16:1–12			Unjust Steward	1	2	2	2	7
16:19–31			Rich Man and Lazarus	2	2	2	2	8
17:5–6	[17:20]		Mustard Seed's Faith	0	0	0	0	0
17:7–10			Servant's Manner	1	0	2	1	4
18:1–8			Unjust Judge	1	2	2	2	7
18:9–14			Pharisee and Tax Collector	1	1	2	2	6
19:11–27	[25:14–30]		Minas/ Pounds [Talents]	1	2	2	2	7
20:9–19	21:33–46	12:1–12	Wicked Tenants	1	2	2	2	7
21:29–33	24:32–35	13:28–31	New Leaves	0	0	0	1	1
	13:24–30, 13:36–43		Wheat and Weeds	0	0	0	2	2
	13:44		Treasure	0	0	0	0	0
	13:45–46		Pearl	0	0	0	0	0
	13:47–50		Dragnet	0	0	0	0	0
	13:52		New and Old	0	0	0	0	0
	15:10–20	7:14–23	Defilement	0	0	0	0	0
	18:21–35		Unforgiving Servant	0	2	0	2	4
	20:1–16		Wages	0	2	0	2	4
	21:28–32		Two Sons	0	1	0	1	2
	22:1–14		Wedding Feast	0	2	0	2	4
	25:1–13		Ten Virgins	0	2	0	2	4
	25:31–46		Sheep and Goats	0	2	0	2	4
		4:26–29	Growing Seed	0	0	0	0	0

Table 1. Evaluation of the Allegorical Level of the Parables of Jesus

Part I: Allegorical Spectrum

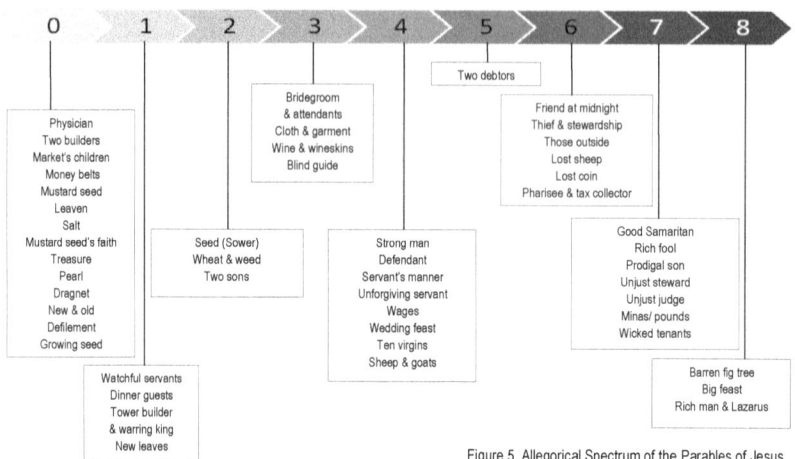

Figure 5. Allegorical Spectrum of the Parables of Jesus

Categories under the New Allegorical Model

I have named the new allegorical model shown in figure 5 as Allegorical Spectrum of the Parables of Jesus. The allegorical level of the parables ranges from zero to eight points on the spectrum. Starting from the least allegorical parables at the left, the spectrum increases to the most allegorical parables at the right.

Parables with zero points are the least allegorical. The allegorical feature in these parables is basically none or minimal. Image (image giver) and theme (image receiver) are in explicit relationship. These parables are usually brief in length. Most of them are similes. They use structural indicators such as ὅμοιος and ὡς to connect theme with image. These parables include the Two Builders, the Market's Children, the Mustard Seed, the Leaven, the Mustard Seed's Faith, the Treasure, the Pearl, the Dragnet, the New and Old, and the Growing Seed. Some parables in this group provide clear explanation such as the Money Belts and the Salt. Other parables in this group are short proverbial sayings such as the Physician and the Defilement. I designate this group of parables with zero points as explanatory-brief.

Parables with one point express explicit relationship between image and theme just as parables with zero points. Allegorical feature begins to develop in these parables but it inclines to be descriptive for illustrating some points rather than making story. For instance, as the thematic point in the Dinner Guests is about whoever exalts oneself will be humbled while

A New Allegorical Spectrum

one who humbles himself will be exalted (Luke 14:11), the parable becomes descriptive around this idea instead of developing into a drama. The parables with one point are slightly longer than parables with zero points. Explanation is readily found in the context of these parables. Apart from the parable just mentioned, this group also includes the Tower Builder and Warring King, and the New Leaves. The use of structural indicator ὅμοιος in the Watchful Servants makes the short story into a similitude. I call this group of parables with one point as explanatory-point.

Parables with two points still express the relationship between image and theme explicitly. Similar to parables with one point, the allegorical feature of parables with two points is descriptive for illustrating some points. However, they are different in that parables with two points are longer in length with a slight amount of story development. For instance, the Seed (Sower) is a brief farming story. However, instead of developing the story, the focus is more about illustrating the metaphorical points concerning the responses after hearing the word of God (Luke 8:11–15). In addition to the Seed (Sower), the Wheat and Weeds also uses extended metaphor in this group. The Two Sons is a short explained story. I name this group of parables with two points as explanatory-illustrative story. In general, although allegorical feature increases from zero to two points, parables in these three groups namely explanatory-brief, explanatory-point, and explanatory-illustrative story, maintain an explicit relationship between image and theme. They are mainly for illustrating points rather than telling stories. The main differences among these three groups can be seen in the length and complexity of the stories.

Parables with three points begin to show implicit relationship between image and theme. Although hints for explanation can be found in the context, indirect expression marks the allegorical feature of these parables. For example, the Cloth and Garment does not provide direct explanation concerning what the parable is about. However, the context shows that the parable is related to the complaint of the religious people against the disciples of Jesus because they do not fast. Jesus responded with three parables (Luke 5:33–39). The new cloth and the old garment in the parable imply the mismatch between the new teaching of Jesus and the old practice of fasting of the religious people. The parables in this group are generally short analogy. Apart from the parable just mentioned, this group also includes the Bridegroom and Attendants, the Wine and Wineskins, and the Blind Guide. I term this group of parables with three points as implicit-short analogy.

Part I: Allegorical Spectrum

Parables with four points show a better development of story than parables with three points. Although both implicit and explicit allegories can be found in this group of parables, their allegorical features are different. Parables that show implicit relationship between image and theme express their allegorical feature in the indirectness of explanation. These parables are short descriptive stories including the Strong Man, the Defendant, and the Servant's Manner. For instance, in the Servant's Manner, the story is flatly descriptive without development for drama (Luke 17:7–10). It indirectly states at the end the proper manner of a servant, which is about considering oneself as unworthy and doing what one should do at work. The other type of parables with four points that show explicit relationship between image and theme is allegorical in the story development. These are mainly similitudes from Matthew. Most of them are longer stories with the use of structural indicator ὁμοιόω. Explanation of their themes can be found in the stories. These include the Unforgiving Servant, the Wages, the Wedding Feast, the Ten Virgins, and the Sheep and Goats. For instance, the Wedding Feast is dramatic in development with the theme explained at the end (Matt 22:1–14). As the original guests declined the invitation, the king invited the unworthy to attend the wedding feast. However, the king found that one of the invited guests in the second round did not wear proper clothing. He ordered his servants to cast out this guest. The explanation of the theme of the parable occurs at the end, "Many are called, but few are chosen" (Matt 22:14). I call this group of parables with four points as implicit-explicit mixed. In general, while allegorical feature increases from three to four points, parables begin to show implicit relationship between image and theme in these two groups, namely implicit-short analogy and implicit-explicit mixed. However, explicit parables can still be found.

The Two Debtors is the only parable scoring five points. Just as parables with four points, the allegorical feature of this parable is shown in the implicit relationship between image and theme. Although explanation of the theme is provided, it is expressed indirectly in the context with a bit more of story development than implicit parables with four points. For instance, the debtors in the parable were never directly referred to the sinful woman or the Pharisee. The debtors needed to be inferred from the context of the interaction between Jesus and the Pharisee. Thus, the theme of the story is implied indirectly from the response of Jesus. He explained to the Pharisee concerning why the sinful woman expressed so much love to Jesus (Luke 7:42–43). I designate this group with five points as implicit medium.

A New Allegorical Spectrum

Parables with six points continue to be implicit in relationship between image and theme. Their allegorical feature is more on drama development than the parable with five points. That is why dialogue or self-talk from the characters are found in these parables. However, these parables are only simple dramas without plot development. In addition, explanation of the theme can still be seen in the context even though it does not make direct referent. For instance, in the Pharisee and Tax Collector, the theme can be found both in the beginning and at the end: the self-righteous will be humbled while the humble will be exalted (Luke 18:9, 14). However, the Pharisee and the Tax Collector in the drama do not have particular referents. Rather, they are generally two types of attitudes carrying contrary outcomes. When the drama continues, the actions of the characters appear straightforward in the explanation of the theme instead of making the parable into a good story. Other parables in this group include the Friend at Midnight, the Thief and Stewardship, Those Outside, the Lost Sheep, and the Lost Coin. I call this group of parables with six points as implicit-simple drama. In general, while allegorical feature increases from five to six points, parables in these two groups, implicit medium and implicit-simple drama, continue to be implicit in relationship between image and theme. However, explanation of theme is more indirect in expression. These parables have more development in the stories, but they remain as simple dramas.

Parables with seven points continue to be implicit in relationship between image and theme. These are longer stories than parables with six points. Their allegorical feature is more on the development of drama having plots, dialogue, and actions of the characters rather than explaining the theme. Hints of explanation about the theme can still be found in the context but very indirectly and at times, incompletely. For instance, in the Prodigal Son, the drama developed around the protagonist, the second son, concerning his initial wayward living, his repentance and return, and the acceptance from his father (Luke 15:11–24). The explanation of the parable was embedded in the conversation of the father with the servants and the older son, "This son of mine was dead and is alive, he was lost and he is found" (Luke 15:24, 32). This group of parables also includes the Good Samaritan, the Rich Fool, the Unjust Steward, the Unjust Judge, the Minas or Pounds, and the Wicked Tenants. I name this group of parables with seven points as implicit-complex drama.

Parables with eight points are the most allegorical. While image in parables with seven points still provides some hints indirectly about the

PART I: ALLEGORICAL SPECTRUM

theme, the allegorical feature of parables with eight points gives no hint about the referent of the image (image giver). That is, theme (image receiver) is completely implicit or unexplained in this group. These parables intend to make good dramas. As a result, images (image givers) are hard to be detached from the narrative. For instance, the Barren Fig Tree is not a very long drama. The two characters in the story, the owner and the vineyard keeper, are discussing a gardening situation. As explanation is absent, the theme becomes uncertain as to whether the parable refers to some people, an event in the future, an action of improvement, or a message from the story as a whole. The Barren Fig Tree turns out to be a complete unit of fluent drama rather than an explanation of metaphorical details. Other parables in this group include the Big Feast and the Rich Man and Lazarus. I term this group of parables with eight points as implicit drama major. In general, allegorical feature increases from seven to eight points. Although they both form very good dramas, the relationship between image and theme grows from partially explained to completely unexplained in these two groups of parables, implicit-complex drama and implicit drama major.

Under the new categorization, Allegorical Spectrum of the Parables of Jesus, parables are grouped in categories according to their allegorical features. They are listed in Table 2.

Points	Categories
0	Explanatory-brief
1	Explanatory-point
2	Explanatory-illustrative story
3	Implicit-short analogy
4	Implicit-explicit mixed
5	Implicit medium
6	Implicit-simple drama
7	Implicit-complex drama
8	Implicit drama major

Table 2. Categories under Allegorical Spectrum of the Parables of Jesus

A New Allegorical Spectrum

Comparison with Former Models

Allegorical Spectrum of the Parables of Jesus is a re-categorization of Hough's model between naive allegory and incarnation. At the explicit terminal, categories such as explanatory-brief, explanatory-point, and explanatory-illustrative story on the new spectrum are similar to Hough's naive allegory but they are increasingly complex in form. Toward the opposite end, the new spectrum is an expansion of Hough's incarnation. It provides more elaboration on the increasing implicitness of allegories including implicit-short analogy, implicit-explicit mixed, implicit medium, implicit-simple drama, implicit-complex drama, and implicit drama major.

Allegorical Spectrum of the Parables of Jesus shares several similar places with Quintilian's Gradient. For example, categories such as explanatory-brief, explanatory-point, and explanatory-illustrative story on the new spectrum is similar to the explicitness of Quintilian's "no metaphor" allegory. The style of having both implicit and explicit elements under the category of implicit-explicit mixed on the new spectrum is also similar to Quintilian's mixed allegory and combined allegory. The increasing implicitness and complexity of story development under categories such as implicit-complex drama and implicit drama major on the new spectrum are also similar to the style of Quintilian's enigma allegory and irony. The new spectrum indeed has a closer match with Quintilian's Gradient than with Hough's Allegorical Circle. A possible explanation is that Hough developed his model around one dimension, the relationship between theme and image. On the other hand, Quintilian arranges the allegorical terms based on their style of complexity.

Apart from that, the four parables in example stories do not appear in the same group on the Allegorical Spectrum of the Parables of Jesus. The Rich Man and Lazarus has eight points, which is found under the most allegorical group, implicit drama major. Another two example stories, the Good Samaritan and the Rich Fool, have seven points. These two parables are placed under implicit-complex drama, which is a less allegorical group than implicit drama major. Still another example story, the Pharisee and Tax Collector, has six points only. It is located under implicit-simple drama and it appears less allegorical than implicit-complex drama. This suggests that the original four example stories under the grouping of Jülicher are not homogenous on the allegorical spectrum. In fact, two other parables, the Barren Fig Tree and the Big Feast, are grouped together with the Rich Man and Lazarus under implicit drama major. Similarly, the Prodigal Son, the

Part I: Allegorical Spectrum

Unjust Steward, the Unjust Judge, the Minas or Pounds, and the Wicked Tenants are now grouped together with the Good Samaritan and the Rich Fool under implicit-complex drama. In addition, the Friend at Midnight, the Thief and Stewardship, Those Outside, the Lost Sheep, and the Lost Coin are found under the group, implicit-simple drama, with the Pharisee and Tax Collector. The result of these new combinations indicate that not just the four example stories, but also the whole categorization of Jülicher on the parables of Jesus does not hold together when rhetorical allegory is put into the consideration of parable study.

To conclude, the new categorization of the parables of Jesus is called Allegorical Spectrum of the Parables of Jesus. The model is built upon several factors for making a good allegory. One of these factors is the fusion between theme (image receiver) and image (image giver), which explores whether or not explanation is provided. Another factor concerns about how fluently an allegorical drama is told, which assesses the difficulty in detaching the metaphorical details from a story. Another factor searches for the leading image giver connected through the whole drama. The last factor relates to the length of the story. These four factors help to spread out all parables of Jesus along the newly developed allegorical spectrum with a new set of categories.

With the consideration of the rhetorical use of allegory, Allegorical Spectrum of the Parables of Jesus impacts the theory of parable categorization of Jülicher in that his four example stories are not found under one category, but several. What leads to the problem of the grouping of Jülicher on the parables of Jesus will be discussed in the following three chapters. We will first review the rise of the categorization theory of Jülicher on example stories.

Part II

On Example Stories

4

"Example Stories" of Jülicher

As discussed in the previous chapter, example stories are not homogeneous enough to form a single group for the parables of Jesus when allegory as rhetorical feature is in view. As a result, "example stories" are unable to form a unique category. Without "example stories," can the categorization of Adolf Jülicher be preserved with the replacement of a new category? Alternatively, should the whole categorization of Jülicher be rejected? Indeed, are example stories misunderstood as examples by their rhetorical expression of allegory? Can other parables be considered generally as examples as well? Are the parables of Jesus used to prove something or to be a kind of decoration in a speech or both? The following three chapters will critically evaluate the parable categorization of Jülicher in particular the term "example stories."

How Jülicher defines the term "example stories" becomes the focus of the discussion in the current chapter. It explores the definitions of each category and the association of his parable categorization with Aristotle's logical proof. Chapter 5 is a quest for the development of the term "example stories" from other scholarly works. Chapter 6 is an exhaustive critique of the term "example stories" and the whole categorization of Jülicher. The search of rhetorical works around biblical times will help to justify a system that better explains the parable teaching of Jesus. The process hopes to affirm the new categorization developed in chapter 3, Allegorical Spectrum of the Parables of Jesus.

The Categorization of Jülicher on the Parables of Jesus

In order to understand the development of the term "example stories," it is necessary to explore how Jülicher defines each category in his theory

PART II: ON EXAMPLE STORIES

about the parables of Jesus. He puts the parables of Jesus into three categories: *Gleichnisse* (parables), *Parabeln* (parables in the narrower sense), and *Beispielerzählungen* (example stories).[1]

Gleichnisse (Parables)

Gleichnisse compares the relationships between two sets of propositions or sentences from one level to another in a parable.[2] A coherent set of terms or concepts is represented by another coherent set of terms or concepts of another area.[3] Jülicher uses the comparison of the terms "Herod" and "fox" as an illustration.[4] By using a mathematical expression a = α to represent these terms, the relationship in a/b is compared with that in α/β.[5] In other words, the relationship represented by "fox" (a/b) is compared with the relationship represented by "Herod" (α/β). Jülicher emphasizes that a parable does not look for the similarity between words but the relationship of concepts.[6] Whether it is a word comparison or a thought, it is indicated with ὅμοιον (like).[7] Instead of several points of comparison, there is only *tertium comparationis* (a point of comparison) in a parable.[8]

Jülicher calls these two propositions or sentences for comparison in a parable as *Sache* (thing/subject matter) and *Bild* (image).[9] In fact, he considers this type of parable (*Gleichnis*) as Aristotle's παραβολή (parable), which is a kind of κοιναὶ πίστεις (common proof or logical proof) along with fable and historical example.[10] He uses the examples of Aristotle for illustration. The *Sache* (thing/subject matter) is "rulers should not be chosen by lot," which is compared with two *Bilder* (images), the choice of an athlete for competition and a sailor to take the rudder should not be made by lot but by their ability and knowledge.[11] However, he suggests that no matter how unimaginable it is

1. Jülicher, *Die Gleichnisreden Jesu*, rev. and combined ed., 1:69, 101, 112.
2. Ibid., 1:69.
3. Ibid., 1:80.
4. Ibid., 1:69.
5. Ibid.
6. Ibid., 1:70.
7. Ibid., 1:70, 80.
8. Ibid., 1:70.
9. Ibid.
10. Ibid., 1:69, 71. Aristotle *Rhet.* 2.20.4.
11. Jülicher, *Die Gleichnisreden Jesu*, rev. and combined ed., 1:70. Aristotle *Rhet.* 2.20.4.

to put the image sentences together for comparison, their differences will not affect the internal character of *Gleichnisses* (parables), namely making comparison under a single point or thesis in each set of them.[12] He illustrates with Mark 13:28–29. The relationship between the arrival of "these things" and Parousia in verse 29 is compared with the relationship between the condition of the leaves on the fig tree and the coming of summer.[13] He elaborates that as the summer shoot announces summer, things described in verses 31–36 declare the close distance of Parousia.[14] He sees the similarity of the two sets of relationships in that when one thing becomes noticeable, the other is near.[15]

Jülicher distinguishes the difference between *Gleichnis* (parable) and allegory. While the *Bild* (image) in the allegory needs to be interpreted, the image in *Gleichnis* (parable) makes the parallel clear.[16] He explains that the image in *Gleichnis* (parable) must be clearly indicated or it is just a waste.[17] On the other hand, allegory looks for the "dark light" to amaze the reader by the spiritual thing behind the wording.[18] He suggests that on approaching *Gleichnis* (parable), its exact thought should be seen, while in case of allegory, a new interpretation will be found on every instance of encountering it.[19] Because of these differences, he recommends that parable and allegory cannot be mixed.[20] He explains that image in the *Gleichnis* (parable) must be understood literally while image in allegory is read figuratively.[21] Table 3 displays Jülicher's category on *Gleichnisse* (parables).[22]

In general, Jülicher's *Gleichnisse* are parables that make obvious comparison between two sets of propositions, namely *Sache* (thing/subject matter) and *Bild* (image). It is indicated with a comparison particle and it allows only one point of comparison in each *Gleichnis*. This kind of comparison can occur between concepts, thoughts, or words. Unlike allegory, the comparison in *Gleichnis* is so clear that it can be understood literally.

12. Jülicher, *Die Gleichnisreden Jesu*, 1:70–71.
13. Ibid., 1:83.
14. Ibid.
15. Ibid.
16. Ibid., 1:73.
17. Ibid., 1:74.
18. Ibid.
19. Ibid.
20. Ibid.
21. Ibid., 1:76.
22. Ibid., 2:vii.

Part II: On Example Stories

Gleichnisse (Parables)	Passages
Precursors of Fig Tree	Matt 24:32; Mark 13:28; Luke 21:29–31
Slaves Committed to Work at Anytime	Luke 17:7–10
Playing Children	Matt 11:16–19; Luke 7:31–35
Pleading Son	Matt 7:9–11; Luke 11:11–13
Students and Teachers	Matt 10:24; Luke 6:40
Blind Guides of Blinds	Matt 15:14; Luke 6:39
True Impurity	Mark 7:14–23; Matt 15:10–20
Salt	Matt 5:13; Mark 9:49; Luke 14:34
Light on the Lampstand	Mark 4:21; Matt 5:14–15; Luke 8:16, 11:33
Mountain	Matt 5:14
Unveiling of the Concealed	Mark 4:22; Matt 10:26; Luke 8:17, 12:2
Eye as Lamp of the Body	Matt 6:22; Luke 11:34–36
Two Services	Matt 6:24; Luke 16:13
Tree and its Fruits	Matt 7:16–20, 12:33–37; Luke 6:43–46
Right Scribes	Matt 13:52
Carcass and the Eagles	Matt 24:28; Luke 17:37
Thief	Matt 24:43; Luke 12:39
Faithful and Unfaithful Stewards	Matt 24:45–51; Luke 12:41–48
Late Returning of Landlord	Luke 12:35–38; Mark 13:33–37
Doctor Save Yourself	Luke 4:23
Physician and Patient	Mark 2:17; Matt 9:12; Luke 5:31
Bridegroom	Mark 2:18–20; Matt 9:14; Luke 5:33–35
Old Garment, Old Tubes, Old Wine	Mark 2:21; Matt 9:16; Luke 5:36–39
Tower and Waging War	Luke 14:28–33
Beelzebul	Mark 3:22–27; Matt 12:22–30, 43–45; Luke 11:14–26
Going to the Judge	Matt 5:25; Luke 12:57–59
Hierarchy at Feast and the Right Guests	Luke 14:7–11, 12–14
Children and Dogs	Mark 7:27; Matt 15:26

Table 3. Parables under *Gleichnisse* (**Parables**) of Jülicher

"Example Stories" of Jülicher

Parabeln (Parables in the Narrower Sense)

Another category is *Parabeln* (parables in the narrower sense). Jülicher identifies about 20 parables in the synoptic gospels that are in narrative form.[23] Unlike *Gleichnis* (parable), the *Bild* in *Parabeln* (parables in the narrower sense) is always in the past while the *Sache* is not so.[24] The *Bild* in *Gleichnis* can use everyday things to describe the comparison relationship.[25] Rather, a story in *Parabeln* is something freely invented by Jesus telling what someone has once done.[26] Jülicher calls this type of parable as *Gleichniserzählung* (parable story), or a more familiar speech form, fable.[27]

As in *Gleichnis* (parable), the fable type of parable also makes *tertium comparationis* (a point of comparison).[28] Jülicher illustrates with the fables from Aristotle.[29] He uses the example about an avenging horse from Stesichorus.[30] The implication of the fable of Stesichorus is that one's desire for revenge on an enemy will turn oneself into a slave just as the horse in the story.[31] However, Jülicher recommends that instead of looking for the correspondence of the details in the fable, it is indeed the whole story that is compared to the situation.[32] The way that the people of Himera behave toward Phalaris is like the horse toward the man in the story.[33] That is, by seeking help from a dictator like Phalaris, the people of Himera become slaves to him like the horse to the man in the fable.[34] Thus, *Parabeln*, the fable style of parables, make one point of comparison in each story like *Gleichnisse*. Jülicher considers fable as a kind of figure of speech in that a proposition is secured by a fictional story with similar frame of thought in

---

23. Ibid., 1:92.
24. Ibid., 1:93.
25. Ibid.
26. Ibid.
27. Ibid., 1:94.
28. Ibid., 1:95.
29. Ibid., 1:94. Aristotle *Rhet.* 2.20.5.
30. Jülicher, *Die Gleichnisreden Jesu*, rev. and combined ed., 1:94. Aristotle *Rhet.* 2.20.5.
31. Ibid. Jülicher, *Die Gleichnisreden Jesu*, rev. and combined ed., 1:94.
32. Ibid., 1:95.
33. Ibid.
34. Aristotle *Rhet.* 2.20.5.

another area.[35] In general, it is the whole fable or story instead of the details that is compared with the proposition or subject matter.

In fact, fable is also used as κοιναὶ πίστεις (common proof or logical proof) like *Gleichnis*.[36] A fable helps to bring clarity to the subject matter.[37] Jülicher recommends to look into the resemblance between the subject matter and the fable first.[38] Usually, a single case will be invented in a fable that is similar to the situation being described.[39] He explains that as reality is always comprised of multiple factors, it will be hard to present it by way of a single principle.[40] This is why by inventing a single case, it gives more clarity to the *Sache* (subject matter/ thing) and the interest becomes more intense.[41] As a result, the fable brings the subject matter step by step closer to the audience with overwhelming power.[42] Jülicher suggests that if *Gleichnis* (parable) gives the idea such as "no one sews a piece of cloth on an old garment," fable emphasizes on both the thought and the visual effect.[43] In other words, not only does a fable present a subject matter, but it also visualizes the subject matter to give clarity. While *Gleichnis* (parable) refers to what is universally valid, fable creates a reality telling what has once occurred.[44]

Jülicher points out that there are several kinds of fables, which can be distinguished by their tone.[45] Fables are usually comedies but those in the parables of Jesus (*Parabeln*) are more elegant and serious.[46] Having the relationships of the higher areas in view such as religious-moral life, conditions that are similar to the lower areas of relationships such as earthly-social life are created in *Parabeln*.[47] He suggests that if *Parabeln* only make comparison between the higher and the lower areas, they can just keep the name

35. Jülicher, *Die Gleichnisreden Jesu*, rev. and combined ed., 1:98.
36. Ibid., 1:96.
37. Ibid.
38. Ibid.
39. Ibid.
40. Ibid.
41. Ibid.
42. Ibid.
43. Ibid., 1:96–97.
44. Ibid., 1:97.
45. Ibid., 1:100.
46. Ibid., 1:101.
47. Ibid.

fables. However, they are more than that. They are *Gleichniserzählungen* (parable stories).⁴⁸ Therefore, he uses the term *Parabeln* (parables in the narrower sense) as the second category of the parables of Jesus.⁴⁹ That is, *Parabeln* are not just about making comparison of relationships between the higher and the lower areas, but they are also stories. Jülicher points out that Jesus uses fictional stories to correct the ignorance of the kingdom citizens.⁵⁰ These fictional stories are taken from lower life such as a sower (Matt 13:24).⁵¹ The particular case being presented through the life of a sower is that no work, nor effort, nor possession is going to receive the same amount of success.⁵² In spite of how much work is done, there is always a lot of loss.⁵³ Jülicher suggests that this is also the law for the kingdom of heaven.⁵⁴ It is no shame to count the loss in gospel work.⁵⁵ Rather, it is common that the gospel encounters deaf ears and no applause.⁵⁶ Just as the three types of soil yield no success, the word of God is labored in vain to these three types of hearts.⁵⁷ Table 4 displays the parables that Jülicher groups under *Parabeln*.⁵⁸

To summarize, the second category of Jülicher refers to a group of fable-like parables. As these parables emphasize visualizing the subject matters with specific stories, they are also known as *Parabeln*, parables in the narrower sense. Images in these parables are freely invented about things or actions in the past to affirm present subject matters. *Parabeln* also make one point of comparison just as *Gleichnisse*. However, the comparison in *Parabeln* occurs between the higher and the lower areas. Instead of the details, the whole story of each of these parables is compared with the subject matter.

48. Ibid.
49. Ibid.
50. Ibid., 1:104.
51. Ibid.
52. Ibid., 1:110.
53. Ibid.
54. Ibid.
55. Ibid.
56. Ibid.
57. Ibid., 1:110–111.
58. Ibid., 2:viii.

Part II: On Example Stories

Parabeln (Parables in the narrower sense)	Passages
Building on Rock or Sand	Matt 7:24–27; Luke 6:47–49
The Pleading Friend	Luke 11:5–8
The Widow and the Unjust Judge	Luke 18:1–8
The Money Lender and the Two Debtors	Luke 7:36–50
The Merciless Servant	Matt 18:21–35
The Lost Sheep and Lost Coin	Matt 18:10–14; Luke 15:1–10
The Lost Son	Luke 15:11–32
The Two Dissimilar Brothers	Matt 21:28–32 (Luke 7:29)
The Evil Vine Dressers	Mark 12:1–12; Matt 21:33–46; Luke 20:9–19
The Reluctant Guests	Matt 22:1–14; Luke 14:15–24
The Barren Fig Tree	Luke 13:6–9
The Ten Virgins	Matt 25:1–13 (Luke 13:23–30)
Equal Pay for Various Workers	Matt 20:1–16
The Entrusted Funds	Matt 25:14–30; Luke 19:11–27
Unjust Steward	Luke 16:1–12
Four kinds of Farmlands	Mark 4:3–9, 14–20; Matt 13:3–9, 18–23; Luke 8:5–8, 11–15
The Autonomous Growing Seed	Mark 4:26–29
Weed among the Wheat	Matt 13:24–30, 36–43
Fishnet	Matt 13:47–50
Mustard Seed and Leaven	Mark 4:30–32; Matt 13:31–33; Luke 13:18–21
Treasure and Pearl	Matt 13:44–46

Table 4. Parables under *Parabeln* of Jülicher

Beispielerzählungen (Example Stories)

As some parable stories look neither like *Gleichnisse* (parables) nor *Parabeln* (parables in the narrower sense), Jülicher calls them *Beispielerzählungen* (example stories).⁵⁹ These parables include the Good Samaritan, the Rich Fool, the Rich Man and Lazarus, and the Pharisee and Tax Collector. Like the previous two categories of the parables of Jesus, example stories are also invented freely for religious-moral purpose for promoting the kingdom of heaven.⁶⁰ However, what distinguishes example stories from the other two categories of parables is that while *Gleichnisse* and *Parabeln* lead readers to earthly situations, example stories have already moved to the higher area.⁶¹ Instead of being used for making comparison with the higher area, these four example stories readily belong to religious-moral matters.⁶² He explains that these stories do not run from one area into other areas as the way a parable is defined, but they belong to the same area to secure the proposition of the same area.⁶³ These stories are examples for propositions to be asserted.⁶⁴ Therefore, he names this category of the parables of Jesus as *Beispielerzählungen* (example stories) since his first edition.⁶⁵ In his later editions, he adds a reference from Immanuel Stockmeyer to give further support about these parables as examples.⁶⁶

Jeffrey T. Tucker points out that Jülicher makes modification between editions concerning the conceptual idea of *Beispielerzählungen* (example stories) though he keeps the same definition for the term.⁶⁷ In the first edition, Jülicher suggests that the law of comparison in example stories is meaningless.⁶⁸ He explains that the referents of the foolish rich man and the tax collector cannot be found.⁶⁹ He states, "The bottom line of ὅμοιον (like) is actually abandoned."⁷⁰ His implication is that as the narrator has

59. Jülicher, *Die Gleichnisreden Jesu*, 1st ed., 117.
60. Jülicher, *Die Gleichnisreden Jesu*, 1st ed., 117.
61. Ibid., 117. Jülicher, *Die Gleichnisreden Jesu*, rev. and combined ed., 1:112.
62. Jülicher, *Die Gleichnisreden Jesu*, 1st ed., 117. Jülicher, *Die Gleichnisreden Jesu*, rev. and combined ed., 1:112.
63. Jülicher, *Die Gleichnisreden Jesu*, 1st ed., 117. Jülicher, *Die Gleichnisreden Jesu*, rev. and combined ed., 1:112.
64. Jülicher, *Die Gleichnisreden Jesu*, 1st ed., 117. Jülicher, *Die Gleichnisreden Jesu*, rev. and combined ed., 1:112.
65. Jülicher, *Die Gleichnisreden Jesu*, 1st ed., 117.
66. Jülicher, *Die Gleichnisreden Jesu*, rev. ed., 112. Jülicher, *Die Gleichnisreden Jesu*, rev. and combined ed., 1:112. Stockmeyer, *Exegetische und praktische Erklärung*, 7.
67. Tucker, *Example Stories*, 60–61.
68. Jülicher, *Die Gleichnisreden Jesu*, 1st ed., 117.
69. Ibid.
70. Ibid. Tucker, *Example Stories*, 62.

not done any comparison activity in the example stories, neither should the hearer do.[71] Instead, the hearer should find general rules expressed by the example stories and submit his life to them.[72] Thus, he prefers other categories of the parables of Jesus than example stories.[73] He explains that, as an object cannot illuminate itself unless lightened up by a foreign body, "the κοιναὶ πίστεις (common proof or logical proof) must be borrowed from other area."[74] Therefore, he removes example stories from *Mashal* owing to the lack of comparative feature.[75] He then defines *Beispielerzählungen* (example stories) as stories in which general propositions are shown in particular cases of the religious-moral characters so that their actions confirm these general principles.[76] The initial idea of Jülicher about example stories is that they have no comparative feature because they do not refer to the other field but the same field to prove the propositions. In this way, what a religious-moral character does under a specific situation in a story affirms a general truth.

Without changing the definition, Jülicher significantly modifies the conceptual idea of example stories in the later edition.[77] Instead of saying "the bottom line of ὅμοιον (like) is actually abandoned," he amends that "the bottom line of ὅμοιον (like) is almost abandoned."[78] By affirming some comparison in example stories, he further changes his implication about it. While he previously states, "neither the narrator has practiced a comparison activity nor the hearer should [do] so," he later alters it to be "the hearer should practice it" even though the narrator has not made any comparison.[79] In other words, the comparison in example stories does not come from the narrator but from the hearer who makes it between oneself with the characters in the story.[80] As a result, the characters either become role

71. Jülicher, *Die Gleichnisreden Jesu*, 1st ed., 118.

72. Ibid.

73. Ibid.

74. Ibid. Tucker, *Example Stories*, 62.

75. Ibid. Tucker, *Example Stories*, 62–63.

76. Jülicher, *Die Gleichnisreden Jesu*, 1st ed., 119. Tucker, *Example Stories*, 61.

77. Jülicher, *Die Gleichnisreden Jesu*, rev. ed., 114. Tucker, *Example Stories*, 60–61.

78. Jülicher, *Die Gleichnisreden Jesu*, 1st ed., 117–18. Jülicher, *Die Gleichnisreden Jesu*, rev. ed., 113. Jülicher, *Die Gleichnisreden Jesu*, rev. and combined ed., 1:113.

79. Jülicher, *Die Gleichnisreden Jesu*, 1st ed., 118. Jülicher, *Die Gleichnisreden Jesu*, rev. ed., 113.

80. Jülicher, *Die Gleichnisreden Jesu*, 1st ed., 118. Jülicher, *Die Gleichnisreden Jesu*, rev. ed., 113.

"Example Stories" of Jülicher

models of life or patterns to avoid to the hearer.[81] From refusing to consider example stories as מָשָׁל, he embraces them back to be parables assuming מָשָׁל is correctly defined as either containing a comparison or provoking one.[82] Like his previous definition, he again affirms that example stories are general statements being demonstrated with specific cases in the clothes of religious-moral characters.[83] However, in the later edition he suggests that example stories are so clear that instead of further explanation, they just need practical application.[84] In other words, he is saying that example stories are also parables for making comparison.

However, Jülicher still insists that there is neither comparison nor allegory in the four example stories.[85] When the comparisons with higher reality that are done by the readers' imagination of the parable stories are in close juxtaposition to the illustrations, one "might very easily regard the two sorts as identical."[86] He suggests that if the term "parable" is to be avoided for these four passages, they should be called illustrative instances.[87] That is, Jülicher finds no comparative feature or allegory in example stories. The comparison in these four passages that Jülicher counts comes purely from the readers.

In general, example stories are particular cases used to illustrate the general propositions or religious-moral propositions of the same area as a way to secure them. However, Jülicher makes significant amendment between editions about the conceptual idea of example stories. From disregarding any comparative feature in example stories to the acceptance of some comparison, Jülicher puts them back in the category of parables. However, he embraces a reader approach comparison in these parables. He also recommends calling example stories as illustrative instances.

Wolfgang Harnisch observes that the three categories of Jülicher on the parables of Jesus carry the key components of paradigmatic function.[88]

---

81. Jülicher, *Die Gleichnisreden Jesu*, rev. ed., 113.

82. Jülicher, *Die Gleichnisreden Jesu*, 1st ed., 118. Jülicher, *Die Gleichnisreden Jesu*, rev. ed., 113. Tucker, *Example Stories*, 124.

83. Jülicher, *Die Gleichnisreden Jesu*, 1st ed., 119. Jülicher, *Die Gleichnisreden Jesu*, rev. ed., 114.

84. Ibid.

85. Jülicher, "Parables," 3566. Tucker, *Example Stories*, 124n209.

86. Jülicher, "Parables," 3566. Tucker, *Example Stories*, 124n209.

87. Jülicher, "Parables," 3566.

88. Wolfgang Harnisch, "Language of the Possible," 46.

Part II: On Example Stories

In fact, he suggests that the parables of Jesus can all be considered as example stories under the exegetical approach of Jülicher.[89] The comment of Harnisch indeed raises some concerns about the categorization of Jülicher on the parables of Jesus. Do all three categories of Jülicher follow the model of Aristotle on logical proof? If all parables of Jesus are indeed example stories, does this mean that the category "example stories" really means nothing and the whole parable categorization of Jülicher needs to be discarded or modified? Before providing an in-depth critique of the categorization of Jülicher on the parables of Jesus, the following will examine the use of Aristotle's theory by Jülicher.

The Use of Aristotle's Theory

As Jülicher uses the logical proof of Aristotle to explain two categories, *Gleichnisse* (parables) and *Parabeln* (parables in the narrower sense), a review of the rhetoric of Aristotle can help to see how it supports the theory in parable categorization of Jülicher. The rhetoric of Aristotle is defined as "the faculty of discerning the possible means of persuasion in each particular case," which are either inartificial or artificial proofs.[90] There are three kinds of artificial proof, namely ethical, emotional, and logical.[91] Logical proof refers to a speech in which "a real or apparent truth is demonstrated."[92] There are two kinds of logical proof: ἐνθύμημα (syllogism) and παράδειγμα (example). Ἐνθύμημα presents logical proof deductively, while παράδειγμα makes logical proof inductively.[93] There are two kinds of examples. One of them is historical example, which refers to "things that have happened before." Another type of example is created under the invention of the speaker, which is further divided into παραβολή (comparison) and λόγοι (fables).[94]

---

89. Ibid.
90. Aristotle *Rhet.* xxxvi.
91. Aristotle *Rhet.* xxxvi.
92. Aristotle *Rhet.* xxxvi.
93. Aristotle *Rhet.* xxxvi.
94. Aristotle *Rhet.* xlii, 2.20.2–3.

Historical Examples

Aristotle uses two actual incidents as illustration for historical example. After Darius took Egypt, he proceeded to attack Greece.[95] A similar one was found with Xerxes.[96] The point of Aristotle is that the stability of Greece depends on who gains control over Egypt. Once Egypt is taken, anyone can cross over to get Greece. This kind of logical proof uses what really happened in history for making examples.

Comparison

Under invented examples for making logical proof, Aristotle includes παραβολή (comparison) and λόγος (fable).[97] Concerning comparison, Aristotle uses two illustrations from Socrates. Socrates does not recommend choosing rulers by lot.[98] One of his examples that Socrates gives is about choosing representative athletes. The other is about looking for someone to take the helm on a ship.[99] While the requirement of athletes is competency, it demands knowledge from sailors who take control of a ship. Both instances suggest that selecting a person for a position by using lot is not a good method. Similarly, magistrates should not be chosen by lot. Particles such as ὅμοιον (like), ὥσπερ (as), and ὡς (as) are used in παραβολή (comparison).[100] This type of example is usually straightforward showing the similarity between the idea and illustration clearly.

Fables

Aristotle illustrates the other kind of logical proof with a fable from Stesichorus. While the people of Himera discussed about getting Phalaris the dictator a body guard, Stesichorus told them a fable.[101] A horse wanted revenge on a deer for damaging the pasture.[102] The horse asked a man for

---

95. Aristotle *Rhet.* 2.20.3.
96. Aristotle *Rhet.* 2.20.3.
97. Aristotle *Rhet.* 2.20.4–5.
98. Aristotle *Rhet.* 2.20.4.
99. Aristotle *Rhet.* 2.20.4.
100. Aristotle *Rhet.* 2.20.4.
101. Aristotle *Rhet.* 2.20.5.
102. Aristotle *Rhet.* 2.20.5.

help.¹⁰³ The man agreed but the horse needed to submit to his control by mounting javelins on it.¹⁰⁴ Stesichorus suggests that a similar situation like the horse will be the result if the people choose a dictator to satisfy the desire of revenge on their enemy.¹⁰⁵ If they give a dictator a body guard and allow him to control them, they will turn themselves into the slaves of Phalaris.¹⁰⁶ In this way, a fictitious story is used to illustrate a principle for choosing a ruler. Aristotle uses another fable from Aesop to make an illustration. A fox that was trapped in a ravine was disturbed by dog fleas.¹⁰⁷ A hedgehog passed by and wanted to help but was refused by the fox.¹⁰⁸ The fox explained that by removing the fleas that had sucked a little of her blood, other hungry fleas would come and drain the remaining blood from her.¹⁰⁹ Aesop gives the explanation. Although a demagogue at Samos was tried, the people would not experience more suffering from the same man since he was wealthy.¹¹⁰ However, if the man is put to death and is replaced with poor men, public funds would be stolen and wasted.¹¹¹ The second story illustrates why switching leaders may not bring a better situation. In general, both fable and comparison are invented examples for making logical proofs. However, the use of fable is more for storytelling, while the approach of comparison is more simple and direct in presenting the point.

An Odd Category

Jülicher associates his first two categories of parables with two categories of Aristotle on logical proof. He considers *Gleichnis* (parable) as Aristotle's παραβολή (comparison).¹¹² In *Gleichnis,* he looks for the comparison between two sets of relationships connected by a comparison particle.¹¹³ The relationship in *Sache* (thing) is compared with the relationship in *Bild*

---

103. Aristotle *Rhet.* 2.20.5.
104. Aristotle *Rhet.* 2.20.5.
105. Aristotle *Rhet.* 2.20.5.
106. Aristotle *Rhet.* 2.20.5.
107. Aristotle *Rhet.* 2.20.6.
108. Aristotle *Rhet.* 2.20.6.
109. Aristotle *Rhet.* 2.20.6.
110. Aristotle *Rhet.* 2.20.6.
111. Aristotle *Rhet.* 2.20.6.
112. Jülicher, *Die Gleichnisreden Jesu*, rev. and combined ed., 1:69.
113. Ibid., 1:70.

(image).¹¹⁴ Jülicher suggests that in the examples of Aristotle for παραβολή (comparison), the main concept concerning rulers should not be chosen by lot (thing) is similar in concept to the other fields, namely neither selecting athletes nor sailors to take the helm (images) should be done by lot.¹¹⁵ Jülicher's *Gleichnis* (parable) and Aristotle's παραβολή (comparison) are basically similar. The "parable" they both refer to is a kind of explicit comparison with the use of a comparison particle. Simile is a more common term for Aristotle's παραβολή and Jülicher's *Gleichnis*.

Jülicher also refers his *Parabeln* (parables in the narrower sense) to another category of Aristotle on logical proof, λόγος (fable).¹¹⁶ He finds that *Parabeln* are invented narratives describing what someone has once done, which are similar to the fables of Aristotle.¹¹⁷ He also uses Aristotle's illustrations for fables, the horse and the fox, as mentioned above.¹¹⁸ Jülicher emphasizes that it is not the details but the whole fable that is similar to the contemporary situation.¹¹⁹ He suggests that the narrative parables of Jesus are mostly fables just like the style of Stesichorus and Aesop.¹²⁰ He defines this type of fable as a statement of thought secured by a fictional story with a similar frame of thought from another area.¹²¹ However, he emphasizes the seriousness and elegance of the parables of Jesus as opposed to the comedy style usually found in fable.¹²² These narrative parables are fictional stories taken from lower life such as lord and servants (Matt 18:23) and father and children (Matt 21:28) for making comparison with the higher life, namely the religious and moral life.¹²³ Therefore, he calls this type of fables *Parabeln* (parables in the narrower sense).¹²⁴ It thus says that *Parabeln* (parables in the narrower sense) of Jülicher are similar to the fables of Aristotle but are more specific about making comparison between the higher and the lower areas through stories.

---

114. Ibid.
115. Ibid., 1:70, 75. Aristotle *Rhet.* 2.20.4.
116. Jülicher, *Die Gleichnisreden Jesu*, rev. and combined ed., 1:94, 96.
117. Ibid., 1:93–94.
118. Ibid., 1:94–96.
119. Ibid., 1:95.
120. Ibid., 1:98.
121. Ibid.
122. Ibid., 1:100–101.
123. Ibid., 1:101, 104.
124. Ibid., 1:101.

Part II: On Example Stories

Concerning *Beispielerzählungen* (example stories), Jülicher has nothing to cite from Aristotle. Instead, he adds Stockmeyer in his revised edition to support that the four parables in example stories are just examples.[125] As Jülicher has two parable categories that are closely related to the categories of Aristotle under παράδειγμα (example), are *Beispielerzählungen* (example stories) also similar to the historical examples of Aristotle under the same system for making inductive proof? However, Jülicher does not consider example stories to be used for enrichment of historical knowledge.[126] Indeed, the historical example of Aristotle needs to be something that actually happened in history.[127] Jülicher rather defines example stories as specially designed narratives using religious-moral characters to secure general propositions of the same field instead of a different field.[128] That is, example stories are also created for proving some propositions but they are not for enrichment of historical events. Thus, example stories are not the same as the historical examples of Aristotle. This leads to more thinking concerning what example stories are and where they should be located in a categorization for parables. There are several possibilities if one stays with the system of Aristotle's logical proof.

Can example stories be a kind of fable? As example stories are also narratives, this option is possible. Jülicher intentionally distinguishes example stories from *Parabeln* and *Gleichnis* because example stories illustrate their narratives from the same field instead of different fields to secure the propositions.[129] As Jülicher still considers example stories as narrative parables just like *Parabeln*, he may regard example stories as a kind of fable.

Can example stories be another type of invented example of Aristotle along with fables and παραβολή (comparison)? This is consistent with the whole categorization of Jülicher. However, as Tucker points out, it is still a concern as to whether example stories are different from *Parabeln*.[130] If example stories cannot be distinguished from *Parabeln*, it may be easier to set example stories as a kind of fable instead of a kind of invented example. It all depends on whether or not example stories are unique enough to form

---

125. Ibid., 1:112.

126. Ibid.

127. Aristotle *Rhet.* 2.20.4.

128. Jülicher, *Die Gleichnisreden Jesu*, rev. and combined ed., 1:112, 114.

129. Ibid., 1:112.

130. Tucker, *Example Stories*, 265, 273.

a group. There will be further discussion on that during the critical evaluation of example stories in chapter 6.

Can example stories be a kind of παράδειγμα (example) for inductive proof such that the whole group is placed next to the historical examples of Aristotle and invented examples? As before, if these four parables really can be distinguished from the rest of the parables of Jesus and are making inductive proof, it could be the case. However, as example stories are narratives invented for proving a proposition in the same field, they are better placed under invented examples. Harnisch indeed suggests that the three categories of Jülicher, *Gleichnisse* (parables), *Parabeln* (parables in the narrower sense), and *Beispielerzählungen* (example stories), should be considered example stories.[131] Like Tucker, the comment of Harnisch indeed highlights the vagueness of the category of example stories. If Harnisch is correct, the four example stories will need to have a new definition that can explain their features as a group to list with *Gleichnisse* and *Parabeln*. Otherwise, the category of example stories is unnecessary. At best, it is a general term covering *Gleichnisse* and *Parabeln* and the four parables. That is, the category of example stories is more general than *Gleichnisse* and *Parabeln*. However, why is it necessary to put all parables of Jesus under the logical proof of Aristotle? Indeed, παράδειγμα (example) of Aristotle for inductive proof may not be inclusive enough to be the foundational model for shaping the categorization of the parables of Jesus. The reason is that Aristotle's model is really about kinds of examples that can be used in making inductive proof during a persuasive speech.[132] It is hard to stretch the model of Aristotle in order to include the different rhetorical features found in parables even though these parables are all used as examples. If Jülicher is correct about example stories, this group may still be considered as an additional branch under invented examples or under fables in Aristotle's model of logical proof. However, if Jülicher is incorrect about example stories, the parables in example stories may need either a better definition in order to distinguish them from *Parabeln* and *Gleichnisse,* or a regrouping of categories for all parables of Jesus. Consequently, it is uncertain if the model of Aristotle for logical proof can still be used for the categorization of the parables of Jesus. Replacing the whole categorization of Jülicher for the parables of Jesus with a new model may be a better solution.

131. Harnisch, "Language of the Possible," 46.
132. Aristotle *Rhet.* xxxvi.

5

Precursors of Jülicher's Parable Categorization

JEFFREY T. TUCKER FINDS some scholarly works before Adolf Jülicher that contain discussion about the four parables, which are later known as example stories.[1] Though Immanuel Stockmeyer publishes *Exegetische und Praktische Erklärung Ausgewählter Gleichnisse Jesu* after the first edition of Jülicher, Jülicher uses it to support his argument about example stories in his revised edition.[2] This chapter focuses on how these scholarly works shape the development of example stories in the parable categorization of Jülicher.

Bernhard Weiss

In a public speech about the use of image in the New Testament, Weiss identifies eighteen to twenty *Gleichniserzählungen* (narrative parables) in the speech of Christ, which are different from *Gleichnisse* (parables) and are usually called *Parabeln* (parables in the narrower sense).[3] The difference between *Parabeln* from *Gleichnis* is that while *Gleichnis* is based upon a standing relationship that exists at all times and in every place, *Parabel* uses a single event that occurs once concretely under certain situation for the representation of a higher wisdom.[4]

---

1. Tucker, *Example Stories*, 47.

2. Jülicher, *Die Gleichnisreden Jesu*, rev. and combined ed., 1:112. Stockmeyer, *Exegetische und praktische Erklärung*, 7.

3. Weiss, "Ueber das Bildliche," 324.

4. Ibid., 324. Tucker, *Example Stories*, 54–55.

Precursors of Jülicher's Parable Categorization

Weiss suggests that the meanings of narrative parables are mainly indicated by Christ except for two parables.[5] He finds interpretative hints in several places such as a general claim at the end of the Workers in the Vineyards, or an immediate instruction from Christ in the Rich Fool, or a conclusion in the Poor Widow, or an answer to a question in the Good Samaritan, or an application to a non-specified audience in the Two Debtors.[6] Weiss identifies some other narrative parables even though hints for explanation in them are insufficient.[7]

The two parables in which Weiss cannot find hints for explanation are the Lost Son and the Rich Man and Poor Lazarus.[8] He explains that this is due to their double applications.[9] In the Lost Son, not only does the parable show the merciful love of God, but it also warns against self-righteousness before grace.[10] The Rich Man and Poor Lazarus reminds the audience about the danger of wealth as well as the demanding of new signs before the judgment of God.[11] Although these two parables are difficult to interpret, Weiss identifies two themes in each of them.

Apart from that, he mentions two kinds of *Parabeln* that are different from the majority. One of them is the allegorical speech of the Rebellious Tenants. He finds that in this parable, living reality and intentional invention are in analogy referring to the concrete circumstance.[12] He points out that the background of this parable is obviously from Isa 5, while the allegorical significant is about the Son of God.[13] Jesus applied the parable story to his own situation.

---

5. Weiss, "Ueber das Bildliche," 324.

6. Ibid., 324–25.

7. Ibid. Parables that are grouped under *Gleichniserzählungen* or "parables in the narrower sense" including Lost Son (Luke 15:11–32), Rich Man and Poor Lazarus (Luke 16:19–31), Royal Wedding Feast (Matt 22:1–14), the Pearl of Great Price (Matt 13:44–46), Barren Fig Tree (Luke 13:6–9), the Workers in the Vineyards (Matt 20:1–16), the Entrusted Talents (Matt 25:14–28), Rich Fool (Luke 12:16–21), Pharisee and Tax Collector (Luke 18:9–14), the Poor Widow (Luke 18:2–8), the Friends (Luke 11:5–8), Evil Servant (Matt 18:23–35), Good Samaritan (Luke 10:30–37), the Two Debtors (Luke 7:41–43), the Two Different Brothers (Matt 21:28–31), the Rebellious Tenants (Matt 21:33–46), and some others.

8. Ibid., 324.

9. Ibid.

10. Ibid.

11. Ibid.

12. Ibid., 326.

13. Ibid.

Part II: On Example Stories

Another kind of *Parabeln* is also difficult to interpret. Weiss points out that some parables "borrow their material from so closely related areas that appear to be merely examples for truth so meant."[14] He illustrates with four parables,

> In the Pharisee and Tax Collector, it is about humility and arrogance in front of God. The Good Samaritan is about a living example of love. The stories of the Rich Man and Poor Lazarus and the Rich Fool are directly about the fraud of wealth.[15]

However, Weiss elaborates further in his later work. Instead of considering these four parables as merely examples, he suggests that they represent certain general truth.[16] Rather than being an example (*Beispiel*), he finds the statement of truth at the end of the Pharisee and Tax Collector: only repentant humility instead of self-righteous pride will attain the grace of God.[17]

Similarly, he suggests that the Rich Man and Poor Lazarus is not an example story (*Beispielerzählung*) about the teaching of Moses and the Prophets concerning repentance from worldly living, waiting upon a miracle, or warning to the living by the deceased.[18] Weiss proposes that Jesus sees the inadequacy of the repentance of OT and the need of his repentance that would be affirmed by his miracles and resurrection.[19] Therefore, the parable is rather an example story (*Beispielerzählung*) concerning the continuation of the Law and prophets in the Messianic time for the repentance of the worldly and the proclamation of the gospel.[20] He finds that the theme of the Rich Man and Poor Lazarus is not about the reversal of position after death.[21] At best, considering its theme as irreversible change of one's lot after death is only preparation for the ending of the story.[22] The theme of the Rich Man and Poor Lazarus is that if the brothers of the Rich Man do not listen to Moses and the Prophets, they will not be convinced by any method

---

14. Ibid., 327. Tucker, *Example Stories*, 55.
15. Weiss, "Ueber das Bildliche," 327.
16. Weiss, *Das Leben Jesu*, 1:513; 2:64–65, 106, 174. Tucker, *Example Stories*, 55n39.
17. Weiss, *Das Leben Jesu*, 1:512–13.
18. Ibid., 2:64–65n1.
19. Ibid.
20. Ibid., 2:65n1.
21. Ibid., 2:62.
22. Ibid., 2:64.

including a warning message from the dead (Luke 16:27–31).[23] Weiss has made a change here. While he previously finds no hint for interpreting this parable, he confirms the theme of the Rich Man and Poor Lazarus in his later work. He also begins to use the term *Beispielerzählung* (example story) for this parable although he uses the terms example and example story interchangeably in these two parables and the following two parables.

Weiss proposes that the Good Samaritan is not merely an example story (*Beispielerzählung*) about loving one's enemies.[24] He finds the interpretative hint at the end of the parable.[25] Jesus asked who the neighbor of this man being robbed was (Luke 10:36). The lawyer answered that it was the one who showed mercy to the man (Luke 10:37). Similarly, he suggests that the Rich Fool is not just an example (*Beispiel*) of elementary truth.[26] He finds the explanation provided by Jesus: whoever has possessions without seeing oneself as rich is what God considers as rich (Luke 12:21).[27]

More Than Examples

There are several observations from the works of Weiss. First, within the group of *Parabeln*, he indeed identifies more than four parables that are difficult to look for interpretative hints. Second, though he originally calls the Pharisee and Tax Collector, the Good Samaritan, the Rich Man and Poor Lazarus, and the Rich Fool as example stories, he makes an amendment later that they are more than just examples or example stories. The reason is that he finds interpretative hints to explain each of them. In fact, he uses the terms "example" and "example stories" interchangeably, which suggests that he has not specified the meaning for the term example stories. Indeed, he has never set up a particular group for the four example stories either. The real issue with these four to five parables is that their interpretative style is different from the rest of the *Parabeln* as opposed to whether or not they are example. While *Parabeln* represent certain higher wisdom with events or narratives, the example-like parables express some truths with illustrations from closely related areas. Indeed, both *Parabeln* and example-like parables refer to something with their stories, whether they are the

23. Ibid.
24. Ibid., 2:106.
25. Ibid.
26. Ibid., 2:174.
27. Ibid.

higher spiritual messages or the lower living truths. However, the way of presenting these messages differs between *Parabeln* and example stories. Apparently, the representational relationships between the stories and the messages in *Parabeln* are more obvious, whereas the referential messages of the narratives in example-like parables are either implicit or without explanation. Unfortunately, except for considering that example-like parables are difficult to interpret, his assertion that these parables borrow illustrations from closely related areas does not help in understanding this term.

Tucker points out that Weiss is Jülicher's teacher.[28] No wonder terms like *Parabeln* and *Beispielerzählung* are found in the written works of Weiss.[29] It does say that the term *Beispielerzählung* (example story) does not originate with Jülicher. It is only that Weiss does not make it into a parable group. However, Jülicher mentions nothing about Weiss in his definition of example stories. Although Weiss and Jülicher both use the term *Parabeln* (parables in the narrower sense), Weiss uses it to refer to any parable representing a higher wisdom with a single event that has concretely occurred, while Jülicher applies the same term to an invented story about what someone has once done and he calls this a fable.[30] Weiss and Jülicher use the term *Beispielerzählung* (example stories) very differently as well. Weiss uses this term on parables that borrow materials from closely related areas for the illustration of some truths as if examples but they are truly more than examples.[31] Jülicher rather describes the term as a parable story that runs from the same area to assert a proposition within the same area. As a result, what Jülicher considers as comparison in these example parables does not come from the speaker but from the hearers who make personal application from these parables.[32] The elaboration of Jülicher on the term example story tells the difference from Weiss though they both regard these parable stories as borrowing examples either from closely related areas or from the same area.

---

28. Tucker, *Example Stories*, 54.
29. Weiss, "Ueber das Bildliche," 324. Weiss, *Das Leben Jesu*, 2:64–65n1.
30. Weiss, "Ueber das Bildliche," 324. Jülicher, *Die Gleichnisreden Jesu*, 1:93.
31. Weiss, "Ueber das Bildliche," 327. Weiss, *Das Leben Jesu*, 1:513; 2:64–65, 106, 174.
32. Jülicher, *Die Gleichnisreden Jesu*, rev. and combined ed., 1:112–13.

Cornelius Elisa van Koetsveld

Van Koetsveld defines the parables of Jesus by the characteristic of his doctrine.[33] He uses Matt 24:14 as the key verse for the theme of the message of Jesus, "This gospel of the kingdom shall be preached in the whole world as a testimony to all the nations."[34] He finds that the contents of parables focus on two areas, the kingdom of heaven and the gospel of the parables.[35] He uses these to set up two main groups for the parables of Jesus.[36] Having reviewed the nature of parables, he chooses the shortest definition: a parable is an earthly story with a heavenly intention.[37]

Parables in his first category that are mostly found in Matthew are explicit about the kingdom of heaven.[38] He suggests that parables being common to Matthew, Mark, and Luke are clearly symbolic with details provided by Jesus.[39] However, he finds that some peculiar parables in Luke are not symbolic but are more like ordinary moral stories.[40] In the Lost Son (Luke 15:11–32), the images are less about symbols but more about making the parable an example to sketch the manner of God and the vocation of human.[41] He also identifies other parables that are uncertain as to whether or not they are symbolic. They are the Rich Fool (Luke 12:16b-21), the Rich Man and Poor Lazarus (Luke 16:19–31), the Pharisee and Tax Collector (Luke 18:10–13), the Good Samaritan (Luke 10:30–35), and the Judge and Widow (Luke 18:2–5).[42] In fact, he considers these moral parables in Luke as having nothing to do with the kingdom of God.[43] In his second book, he puts these moral parables in Luke together with other parables under the second category of parables, which is called "the gospel of the kingdom."[44]

---

33. Van Koetsveld, *De Gelijkenissen van den Zaligmaker*, 1:vi.

34. Ibid., 1:vi-vii.

35. Ibid., 1:vii.

36. Ibid.

37. Ibid., 1:xxx-xxxii.

38. Ibid., 1:xliii.

39. Ibid., 1:xxxii.

40. Ibid.

41. Ibid. Tucker, *Example Stories*, 51.

42. Van Koetsveld, *De Gelijkenissen van den Zaligmaker*, 1:xxxiv. Tucker, *Example Stories*, 51.

43. Van Koetsveld, *De Gelijkenissen van den Zaligmaker*, 1:xliii. Tucker, *Example Stories*, 51.

44. Van Koetsveld, *De Gelijkenissen van den Zaligmaker*, 2:1; 1:vii. He changes the

Among them, he identifies three parables that are completely unexplained with unclear symbolic connection with the kingdom of God. They are the Rich Man and Poor Lazarus, the Barren Fig Tree, and the Way to the Judge (Luke 12:58–59; Matt 5:25–26).[45]

The second category, the gospel of the kingdom, is subdivided into groups under four topics.[46] The first group, sin and grace, contains the Rich Fool, the Rich Man and Poor Lazarus, and the Lost Son.[47] In the second group, Christ and his, van Koetsveld does not put any moral or example-like parable. In the third group, Christian life, he includes the Good Samaritan.[48] The Judge and Widow and the Pharisee and Tax Collector are found in the fourth group, prayer.[49]

Behind Grouping by Topics

The grouping of van Koetsveld's second category is indeed disorganized. First, parables from Matthew and even the saying of Jesus in John can be found in this category.[50] That is, his second category does not limit to the parables in Luke or the moral-example parables that he identifies. Second, instead of putting all the moral or example-like parables in one group, van Koetsveld scatters them among the subgroups in the second category. Tucker observes that van Koetsveld does not put the four parables together like the grouping of example stories.[51] That is, there is no indication that van Koetsveld wants to put the moral-example parables into one group though these parables are contained in his second category. He uses topics instead of literary terms for categorization, which is different from the other three scholars. Third, in addition to the four parables that are later known as example stories, van Koetsveld includes two more moral or example-like

---

second category from *het Evangelie in Gelijkeniseen* (the gospel in the parables) to *het Evangelie des Koningrijks* (the gospel of the kingdom) in the second book.

45. Ibid., 2:487. Tucker, *Example Stories*, 53n30. In fact, he includes the Way to the Judge among the group of unexplained parables but this one is not unique to Luke. It can be found in Matthew as well (Luke 12:58–59; Matt 5:25–26).

46. Van Koetsveld, *De Gelijkenissen van den Zaligmaker*, 2:3, 169, 253, 406.

47. Ibid., 2:11–53, 113–157.

48. Ibid., 2:278–296.

49. Ibid., 2:422–454.

50. Ibid., 2:3, 169, 179.

51. Tucker, *Example Stories*, 53n29.

parables, which are the Lost Son and the Judge and Widow. The parables of Barren Fig Tree and the Way to the Judge are also put together with Rich Man and Pool Lazarus as unexplained parables. That is, more than four parables can be considered as moral or example-like. In other words, parables that appear similar to the style of the four example stories of Jülicher are more than what people usually think.

When van Koetsveld considers these six to eight parables as moral or example-like, he does not find any symbolic feature in them.[52] In addition, these parables do not show explicit connections to the concept of the kingdom of heaven.[53] If indeed all parables are examples and at times, convey moral messages, why is it necessary to call some parables as moral or example-like? The real problem is that van Koetsveld looks for symbolic references from these parables. Just because he cannot identify what these parables are referring to does not mean that they do not have their referents. Explicit comparison between two things may not be the concern of some of the parables in Luke. Any implicit metaphor or allegorical element in the parables of Luke can appear to be unexplained.

Another explanation is that referential explanation in a parable can be intentionally omitted at times for the purpose of stylish expression in a speech. In addition, the major concern of van Koetsveld is whether a parable makes emblematic reference to the kingdom of heaven.[54] If he cannot find this kind of kingdom expression in parables like those unique to Luke, it may simply be that the gospel writers have different editorial concerns. The term "kingdom of heaven" occurs thirty-one times in Matthew but it never appears in Luke. Furthermore, twelve of the thirty-one parables in Matthew are found to use the term "kingdom of heaven," among which nine parables are unique to Matthew. They are the Wheat and Weeds (Matt 13:24), the Treasure in the Field (Matt 13:44), the Pearl (Matt 13:45), the Dragnet (Matt 13:47), the New and Old (Matt 13:52), the Unforgiving Servant (Matt 18:23), the Wages (Matt 20:1), the Wedding Feast (Matt 22:2), and the Ten Virgins (Matt 25:1). In contrast, Luke uses the term "kingdom of God" thirty-one times. Seven of the thirty-seven parables in Luke carry the term "kingdom of God," but only two of them are unique to Luke, namely the Big Feast (Luke 14:16) and Those Outside the Door (Luke

---

52. Van Koetsveld, *De Gelijkenissen van den Zaligmaker*, 1:xxxii, xxxiv.
53. Ibid., 2:487.
54. Ibid., 1:xxxii. Tucker, *Example Stories*, 53.

13:28–29).⁵⁵ That is, no matter whether "kingdom of heaven," "kingdom of God," or "kingdom" theme is used as a guideline for grouping parables, many parables will not be able to fit in, particularly those parables in Luke.

Although Jülicher cites from van Koetsveld, he does not refer to the written work of van Koetsveld in his discussion on example stories, *Gleichnisse* (parables), or *Parabeln* (parables in the narrower sense). Thus, it is hard to make any connection between the categorizations of the two scholars. In spite of the problem of the categorization of van Koetsveld, his discussion about several moral or example-like parables concurs with Weiss in that they are difficult to interpret. The frustrations of van Koetsveld with these parables are that their symbolic comparison to the kingdom of heaven is uncertain and no explanation is available.

Siegfried Goebel

Goebel observes that the term παραβολή (parable) in the speech of Jesus carries a wide range of meaning.⁵⁶ However, he highlights that parables are not all about detailed comparison.⁵⁷ He suggests that no one will consider the details in the speech of John 10:1–6 as a parable.⁵⁸ Yet the briefness of the Costly Pearl in Matt 13:45–46 will not disqualify it as a parable.⁵⁹ As a result, he looks for specific elements to narrow down the definition of a parable.⁶⁰ He suggests that the distinguishing feature of *Parabeln* (parables in the narrower sense) is the whole narrative, which is created to represent the religious field.⁶¹ Goebel defines *Parabel* (parable) in this way,

> Coming from the field of nature or human life, *Parabel* is not for telling an event that really happened but for illustrating truth in the religious area, either about relationship between humans or between humanity and God.⁶²

---

55. The other five parables that contain the kingdom idea and occur in Luke, Matthew, and Mark, or just between Luke and Matthew are the Seed (Sower), the Mustard Seed, the Leaven, the Pounds, and the New Leaves from Fig Tree.

56. Goebel, *Die Parabeln Jesu*, 1:1–3.

57. Ibid., 1:3.

58. Ibid.

59. Ibid.

60. Ibid., 1:3–4.

61. Ibid., 1:4.

62. Ibid., 1:5. Tucker, *Example Stories*, 57.

Goebel has two types of *Parabeln*, symbolic and typical.[63] He identifies most parables of Jesus as symbolic *Parabeln* while only four parables of Jesus are typical *Parabeln*.[64] The four typical *Parabeln* are the Good Samaritan (Luke 10:25–37), the Rich Fool (Luke 12:16–21), the Rich Man (Luke 16:19–31), and the Pharisee and Tax Collector (Luke 18:9–14).[65] In a later section, Goebel categorizes parables into two large groups. One group is about the essence of the kingdom of God. The other group deals with the right behavior for the kingdom, which includes both the four typical *Parabeln* and some symbolic *Parabeln*.[66]

Goebel defines symbolic *Parabeln* as a presupposition of harmony between two spheres, namely the visible world and human life on one level, and the relationship between human and God on a higher level.[67] In this way, the former sphere is a reflection of the latter.[68] The resemblance found in symbolic *Parabeln* is not by chance but by prevailing internal connection such that the visible becomes a symbol of the invisible, the earthly for the heavenly, and the temporal for the eternal.[69] In this way, the religious truth is illustrated symbolically through significant relations, events, and actions in the freely composed narratives about nature and human life.[70] He suggests that the symbols need to be interpreted, and hints regarding these symbols are mostly found in the wording of the narrator.[71] However, Goebel finds that sometimes allegory is mixed into these symbolic *Para-*

---

63. Goebel, *Die Parabeln Jesu*, 1:5.

64. Ibid., 1:ix-x, 5, 7. Goebel, *Die Parabeln Jesu*, 2:ix. The symbolic *Parabeln* of Jesus are the Various Soils (Matt 13:3–8, 18–23), the Weeds in the Wheat (Matt 13:24–30, 36–43), the Fruitful Earth (Mark 4:26–29), the Mustard Seed (Matt 13:31–32), the Leaven (Matt 13:33; Luke 13:20–21), the Hidden Treasure (Matt 13:44), Pearl of Great Price (Matt 13:45–46), the Fishnet (Matt 13:47–50), the Pleading Friend (Luke 11:5–10), the Fig Tree (Luke 13:6–9), the Big Feast (Luke 14:16–24), the Lost Sheep (Luke 15:4–7), the Lost Coin (Luke 15:8–10), the Prodigal Son (Luke 15:11–32), the Unjust Steward (Luke 16:1–9), the Unjust Judge (Luke 18:1–8), the Merciless Servant (Matt 18:21–35), the Workers in the Vineyard (Matt 20:1–16), the Evil Gardeners (Matt 21:33–41), the Royal Wedding Feast (Matt 22:1–14), the Ten Virgins (Matt 25:1–13), the Entrusted Talents (Matt 25:14–30), and the Entrusted Pounds (Luke 19:11–27).

65. Ibid., 1:7.

66. Ibid., 1:26–27. Tucker, *Example Stories*, 59.

67. Goebel, *Die Parabeln Jesu*, 1:5–6.

68. Ibid., 1:6.

69. Ibid.

70. Ibid. Tucker, *Example Stories*, 58.

71. Goebel, *Die Parabeln Jesu*, 1:6.

beln.[72] Some examples of symbols include the use of sowing and reaping for referring to the action in the kingdom of God, earthly feast for representing spiritual happiness, and the relation of father and son as an image of the relationship between God and humanity.[73] In fact, allegory is found in some of the symbolic *Parabeln* such as the interpretation of the birds of heaven eating up the seed in the Sower, and the birds dwelling on the branches in the Mustard Seed.[74] However, he has no suggestion about the interpretation of the allegory in symbolic *Parabeln*.

On the other hand, Goebel does not use the term "type" in typical *Parabel* in a specific sense but in an ordinary sense as an exemplum either for imitation, warning, or threat(1 Tim 4:12; 1 Cor 10:6).[75] He suggests that these parables illustrate teaching by direct examples instead of in symbolic clothing.[76] He defines typical *Parabeln* as parables in which the author invents stories in particular cases for making side-by-side comparison with the general truth.[77] In this way, these particularly designed fictional stories help to elucidate the religious truth being taught.[78] Goebel emphasizes that although some characters are named in the stories, they are not symbolic but typical representatives of moral-religious attitudes.[79] He has some illustrations from the Rich Fool and the Pharisee and Tax Collector. The name and person of God can appear directly in the stories without symbolic clothing making the unseen divine acts to be the essential components of action.[80] What is impossible to symbolic *Parabel* can occur in typical *Parabeln*, such as the characters in the Rich Man going to another world.[81] Therefore, he proposes that the focus of typical *Parabeln* is not about interpreting the symbols in these narratives, but looking for general application of these narratives in order to trace them back to universal laws and truths.[82]

---

72. Ibid.
73. Ibid., 1:6–7.
74. Ibid.
75. Goebel, *Die Parabeln Jesu*, 1:7.
76. Ibid.
77. Ibid.
78. Ibid. Tucker, *Example Stories*, 58.
79. Goebel, *Die Parabeln Jesu*, 1:7–8.
80. Ibid., 1:8.
81. Ibid.
82. Ibid. Tucker, *Example Stories*, 59.

Precursors of Jülicher's Parable Categorization

In general, the narrower feature of *Parabeln* is essentially narrative instead of detailed comparison. They are invented stories with the use of nature or human life for illustrating religious truth. Goebel identifies two types of *Parabeln*. While symbolic *Parabeln* symbolize religious truth with visible things, typical *Parabeln* make invented stories into direct examples. Only symbolic *Parabeln* require interpretation. However, it is unnecessary to interpret the details of typical *Parabeln* and they only need general application of the universal truth they represent.

Confusion

The difference between symbolic *Parabeln* and typical *Parabeln* indeed is not huge. Both symbolic *Parabeln* and typical *Parabeln* are narratives making comparison and teaching through their stories. However, the difference is found in the way of presenting the comparison in these two types of narratives. Symbolic *Parabeln* make comparison emblematically between the visible layer of earthly matter and the invisible layer of religious truth. Thus, the comparison in symbolic *Parabeln* is explicit. On the other hand, typical *Parabeln* compare invented narratives in particular cases with the general truth to be taught. The comparison in typical *Parabeln* is never in the details but in the stories as a whole with the religious truth that they are teaching.

Goebel's definition of typical *Parabeln* is also confusing. While confirming typical *Parabeln* as comparison between narratives and religious truth, Goebel also claims that these stories are direct examples for application. However, Goebel does not talk about a hearer making application from a parable. Rather, the application that he refers to is the religious truth being presented by the narrator through the parable. Normally, we call it illustration instead of application. His definition of typical *Parabeln* becomes circular in reasoning when he also regards such application as a comparison with the parable.

Apart from that, how to interpret typical *Parabeln* remains unclear. Goebel recommends that the details in the narratives of typical *Parabeln* do not require interpretation. His explanation is that the narrative goes directly into the application of the religious truth being taught. He also does not provide any suggestion on how to interpret this type of parable as a whole. It is as if the interpretation of typical *Parabeln* is a process that can be skipped. If he agrees that typical *Parabeln* make comparison with the religious truth, they need to be interpreted with respect to the truth being referred to from the perspective of the speaker, whether or not they are explained in the parables. Calling these parables as direct examples or direct applications of the religious truth can never be used to replace the necessity for interpretation. The real difficulty in interpreting these parables is that the general principles of these four parables are not as obvious as they seem owing to insufficient hints. That is why these four parables are difficult to interpret. Unfortunately, Goebel leaves the interpretation of these parables hanging. If other parables can also be used as examples in the speech, it is insignificant to consider typical *Parabeln* as examples. Rather, in typical *Parabeln*, the absence of obvious comparison between the lower and the higher levels as in symbolic *Parabeln* makes them relatively atypical for interpretation. However, typical *Parabeln* do use their stories to compare with the religious truth though the comparison is not as explicit as in symbolic *Parabeln*. Thus, interpreting the implicit comparison in this type of parable is necessary.

Combination

As the term *Parabeln* appears in both the parable discussions of Weiss and Goebel, it is helpful to see how the definition of *Parabeln* of Jülicher comes into shape. Indeed, Weiss and Goebel have both similarities and differences in their use of the same term. Both Weiss and Goebel use the term *Parabeln* to refer to narratives that represent some principles of higher level or religious truth. *Parabeln* of Weiss are single and concrete events once occurred for representing higher wisdom, while *Parabeln* of Goebel are invented narratives not for telling any event that really happened, but for illustrating religious truth through nature or human life.[83] Their difference is mainly that Weiss considers these narrative parables as events that have once occurred, while Goebel regards them as invented stories instead of real events. *Parabeln* of Jülicher carries some similarity to both Goebel and Weiss though he does not cite either of them in his discussion of the category. Jülicher considers *Parabeln* as freely invented stories or fables telling what someone has once done.[84] The emphasis on "what someone has once done" is similar to the idea of Weiss about *Parabeln* that these are single and

---

83. Weiss, "Ueber das Bildliche," 324. Goebel, *Die Parabeln Jesu*, 1:5.
84. Jülicher, *Die Gleichnisreden Jesu*, rev. and combined ed., 1:93.

concrete events once happened.[85] On the other hand, the focus of Jülicher on "freely invented stories or fables" is consistent with the idea of Goebel that *Parabeln* are invented pictorial stories or fables.[86] Jülicher's definition of *Parabeln* may be a combination of the concepts of *Parabeln* from Weiss and Goebel.

Additionally, the discussion of Weiss and Goebel concerning a special group of parables shows how Jülicher's category, example stories, comes into shape. As mentioned above, Weiss considers these parables to be examples or example stories though more than merely examples.[87] However, he does not give a name to this group of parables. Goebel rather regards these parables as direct examples and he calls them typical *Parabeln*.[88] Like Goebel, Jülicher also considers these parables as examples and he creates a category for them called example stories.[89] Thus, Jülicher has established the term "example stories."

Jülicher's definition of example stories carries some similarity to both the description of Weiss and Goebel though he again does not cite them. Weiss finds that these four parables appear to be examples containing borrowed material from closely related areas for presenting some truths.[90] Though Weiss looks for the referent of higher wisdom presented through the events in *Parabeln*, he does not explain whether the "closely related areas" from which the four example-like parables are borrowing come from things belonging to the lower or higher level.[91] Goebel, on the other hand, defines typical *Parabeln* as invented stories in particular cases or direct examples for comparison with the general truth being taught.[92] He makes it clear that these parables are direct examples instead of being symbolic.[93] However, while the direct nature of typical *Parabeln* is non-symbolic in presentation, it does not mean that they do not have referents. Jülicher defines *Beispielerzählungen* (example stories) as stories that are examples

---

85. Ibid.; cf. Weiss, "Ueber das Bildliche," 324.

86. Jülicher, *Die Gleichnisreden Jesu*, rev. and combined ed., 1:93. Goebel, *Die Parabeln Jesu*, 1:4.

87. Weiss, "Ueber das Bildliche," 327. Weiss, *Das Leben Jesu*, 1:513; 2:64–65, 106, 174.

88. Goebel, *Die Parabeln Jesu*, 1:7.

89. Jülicher, *Die Gleichnisreden Jesu*, rev. and combined ed., 1:112.

90. Weiss, "Ueber das Bildliche im Neuen Testament," 327.

91. Ibid., 324, 327.

92. Goebel, *Die Parabeln Jesu*, 1:7.

93. Ibid., 1:7.

in religious moral areas for making assertions to some propositions of the same area.[94] The "same area" which Jülicher refers to is really that both the example stories and the religious-moral propositions being asserted belong to the higher areas instead of one from the higher and one from the earthly area like those of fables.[95] The idea of Jülicher that example stories use the "same area" to affirm propositions in the same area is similar to the description of "borrowed material from closely related areas as examples" of Weiss. However, comparing with the idea of "closely related areas" of Weiss, Jülicher's concept of the "same area" in example stories concerning the use of examples from higher level to represent religious teaching of the higher level provides a more specific definition. In fact, what is considered as using the "same area" in any of these example stories for supporting a proposition is really about whether or not an obvious difference is shown between earthly level of things with higher level of things such as the kingdom of God. In other words, based on the underlying assumption of Jülicher about the higher and the lower level of things, if a parabolic illustration and the truth being presented are both from earthly things, or they are both from heavenly things, such a parable will be considered as an example story. However, a parable showing the same level of illustration as the teaching principle that it presents is making referent to something though the referent may not be explicitly indicated. The idea of the "same area" creates confusion regarding example stories as if they referred to nothing. In fact, not every parable needs to touch on the topic of the kingdom of God or heavenly teaching. It is also doubtful that there is any legitimacy in using an earthly-heavenly framework for distinguishing *Parabeln* from example stories. Unfortunately, Goebel also differentiates symbolic *Parabeln* from typical *Parabeln* based upon whether or not the symbolic two levels between the earthly and the heavenly can be found. As a result, whether they are called typical *Parabeln* or example stories, they are not considered to be making referents to anything owing to their lack of explicit comparison between the earthly-heavenly levels. Without understanding the context of wordings such as "closely related area" of Weiss, "direct example" of Goebel, or "same area" of Jülicher, typical *Parabeln* or example stories can be misunderstood as just several examples without making referential relationship with anything. However, this is not what Weiss has tried to present.

---

94. Jülicher, *Die Gleichnisreden Jesu*, rev. and combined ed., 1:112.
95. Ibid.

On the other hand, Jülicher seems to side with Goebel in regarding these four parables as examples, while Weiss emphasizes that these parables are more than examples. Both Goebel and Jülicher agree that typical *Parabeln* or example stories are examples, which require no interpretation or explanation of the details contained in the stories.[96] However, the elaboration of Jülicher on example stories is not completely in line with Goebel. Suggesting that no interpretation of the details of these four parables is required, both Goebel and Jülicher jump into "application." Goebel refers the "application" to the illustration of the general truth presented through the invented stories. Thus, Goebel sees that comparison occurs between the narrative and the truth being taught.[97] On the other hand, Jülicher argues that the comparison in example stories is found in the practical application by the hearers when they compare themselves with the characters in the stories.[98] This is quite different from the application of Goebel's typical *Parabeln*. In Goebel's case, the author's intention is still kept as his "application" is indeed about making use of the religious truth through the narrative of a typical *Parabel*. However, the "application" of Jülicher occurs in an example story when a hearer makes application by comparing oneself with what is taught through a character in the parable. This kind of comparison or application of Jülicher is indeed reading into what the author has said. The example stories of Jülicher seem to be a combination of definitions of Weiss and Goebel regarding this type of parable.

Immanuel Stockmeyer

Stockmeyer places NT parables under three categories. He calls the first *Hypotypose* (prototype or standard), which is a parable using an example in place of comparison to make abstract teaching concrete, vivid, and forceful.[99] Teaching is illustrated through a sketch that is not taken from any area analogically but from a concrete example.[100] He suggests that *Hypotypose* is not an actual parable but a sketch being used as a role model for

---

96. Jülicher, *Die Gleichnisreden Jesu*, rev. and combined ed., 1:114. Goebel, *Die Parabeln Jesu*, 1:8.

97. Ibid., 1:7–8.

98. Jülicher, *Die Gleichnisreden Jesu*, rev. and combined ed., 1:113.

99. Stockmeyer, *Exegetische und praktische Erklärung*, 2.

100. Ibid., 2.

imitation or warning.[101] Parables in this group include the Pharisee and Tax Collector, the Good Samaritan, the Rich Man and Poor Lazarus, and the Rich Fool.[102] In the illustration of the Rich Fool, he finds no comparison in the parable. Rather, the parable goes directly into the religious-ethical area to be a living example.[103] Instead of being analogically compared with another thing, the parable is an example using thing or anonymous from a relevant area in a real world.[104] He suggests that if the parable were about losing everything after the rich man made bad use of good thing, the parable would be a comparison though it was not what the parable said.[105]

The second category of Stockmeyer is *Parabel*, which refers to a fictitious narrative using material from a relationship of natural or ordinary life to illustrate analogically a relationship of higher or supernatural area.[106] He suggests that the Unjust Steward belongs to this group.[107] The third category is called *Allegorische Schilderung* (allegorical or analogized description), which is a parable making comparison not from an individualized thing in a narrative but it is a general description of analogical relationship to the higher area.[108] He illustrates with Matt 7:9–11, "Which one of you if his son asks him for bread will offer him a stone? How much more your Father in heaven will give good gifts to those who ask him?"[109] Apart from making illustration, *Allegorische Schilderung* at times is used for making induction.[110] He finds both *Parabel* and *Allegorische Schilderung* in Luke 15. He suggests that the Prodigal Son is an actual *Parabel* illustrating the heavenly truth about rejoicing at the repentance of a sinner and showing mercy.[111] The self-righteousness of the older son produces a background contrast.[112] On the other hand, the Lost Sheep and the Lost Coin are both *Allegorische Schilderungen*. Induction is found in the reaction of the own-

---

101. Ibid., 2–3.
102. Ibid., 3.
103. Ibid., 2.
104. Ibid.
105. Ibid.
106. Ibid., 3.
107. Ibid.
108. Ibid., 3–4.
109. Ibid., 3.
110. Ibid., 4.
111. Ibid.
112. Ibid.

Precursors of Jülicher's Parable Categorization

ers. Upon recovering from their loss, the owners demonstrate great joy at the lower level, which reaction is compared analogically with the reaction at the higher level.[113] In summary, Stockmeyer identifies three categories for the parables in NT: *Hypotypose*, *Parabel*, and *Allegorische Schilderung* (allegorical or analogized description).

Contradiction

There are some notable observations about the parable model of Stockmeyer. First, he rejects *Hypotypose* as parable. Among the three categories of Stockmeyer, he only considers *Parabel* and *Allegorische Schilderung* as parables. He suggests that though *Hypotypose* is called a parable etymologically, it is not an actual parable in that no comparison can be found.[114] The illustration of the teaching is rather replaced by a concrete example, which appears as a sketch.[115] What he considers as comparison like those being found in *Parabel* and *Allegorische Schilderung* are parables that have correspondence to or analogical relationship with the higher level of things.[116] According to Stockmeyer, the religious teaching of the Rich Fool is about "one who collects treasure but is not rich toward God."[117] However, since the Rich Fool contains no comparison, he concludes that it is just an example and not a parable.[118] Even though a side-by-side comparison is found between the example and the religious-ethical area in the Rich Fool, Stockmeyer does not consider it as a comparison or a parable. This is how he contradicts himself. Although he finds that the story of the Rich Fool is compared to the religious-ethical area, he refuses to regard it as a comparison and he labels it an "example." What he looks for is a really specific area of comparison, namely from the lower or earthly area to the higher or heavenly area. In other words, without referring to the higher level, parables are just examples to Stockmeyer. However, it is truly doubtful why a parable needs to show comparison with heavenly things in order to be called a parable. In some parables, Jesus does not refer to heavenly things but they are still called parables such as "Physician, heal yourself"

113. Ibid.
114. Ibid., 2.
115. Ibid., 2.
116. Ibid., 2–3.
117. Ibid., 2.
118. Ibid.

Part II: On Example Stories

in Luke 4:23. On the other hand, there are parables that refer to heavenly things but they are used simply as examples to elaborate some teachings. In the Big Feast in Luke 14:12–24, while a dinner guest said, "Blessed is everyone who will eat bread in the kingdom of God," Jesus responded at the end of the parable, "For I tell you, none of those men who were invited shall taste my feast." Jesus used the parable as an example to address the saying of the dinner guest in a contrary way. That is, even though dinner guests are invited, they will not taste anything from the kingdom of God if they refuse to attend the feast. Thus, calling any parable as an example because it does not show a comparison with the heavenly level of things may not be an accurate description for this type of "parable."

One of the reasons is that "example" is not a term fit for distinguishing different types of parables. While some parables make obvious comparison between earthly and heavenly areas, other parables may not have anything to refer to the higher level of things but they are still making referents. If the comparison between a parable and its teaching concept is implicit, it will be difficult to understand but such a relationship between a parable and its referent cannot be denied. If those parables are called examples simply because they are not clear in showing their referents, they would be better called "lacking of heavenly realm" parables instead of "examples." Otherwise, it will just stop hearers from exploring carefully what the referents are in the teachings of these parables. Whether the comparison is between the earthly and the heavenly, or between an earthly picture and any teaching principle in life, it can equally be called a parable.

Second, as illustrated with the Big Feast, parables that show comparison with heavenly things can also be used as examples. When some parables are called examples owing to lacking of comparison with the heavenly realm while other parables that refer to the higher level are also used as examples, "example" becomes a confusing term regarding which parable category is being referred.

The other reason that the definition of parable is broader than just a comparison between heavenly and earthly things as mentioned in chapter 1. "Parable" is a term covering a variety of styles including proverb, wisdom saying, simile or similitude, parable, comparison, aphorism, symbol, riddle, mockery song, example, allegory, fable, prophetic statement, simple rule, metaphor, and illustration. Actually, Jesus calls "Physician, heal yourself" as παραβολή (Luke 4:23). Jesus also refers the Rich Fool and the Pharisee and Tax Collector as parables (Luke 12:16; 18:9). Thus, what does not fit the

Precursors of Jülicher's Parable Categorization

definition of Stockmeyer concerning a "parable," namely a parable without comparison with heavenly realm is not really the case. Stockmeyer cannot override the author's intention by denying some passages as parables and calling them as "examples" if the author considers them as parables. Reading a later concept of "parable" into the time of Jesus is anachronism.

Relationship between Jülicher's and Stockmeyer's Parable Models

Another issue is related to Jülicher's citation from Stockmeyer in the revised edition regarding the term "example stories."[119] Tucker points out the stunning similarities between parable categories of Stockmeyer and Jülicher such as Stockmeyer's *Allegorische Schilderung* (analogized description) and Jülicher's *Gleichnis, Parabel* in both, and Stockmeyer's *Hypotypose* and Jülicher's *Beispielerzählung* (example story).[120] Regarding the citation of Jülicher from Stockmeyer in the revised edition, Tucker explains that it is possibly related to their resemblance in categorization.[121] As Stockmeyer does not cite from Jülicher regarding parable categories, Tucker suggests that "a mediating figure" is possible even though nothing is found.[122] The comments of Tucker lead to some questions about the relationship between the parable models of Stockmeyer and Jülicher.

First, how similar are the parable categories between Stockmeyer and Jülicher? The *Hypotypose* of Stockmeyer is not a parable. It is indeed an example being used in place of comparison to illustrate abstract teaching so that it becomes a role model for imitation or warning.[123] On the other hand, the example story of Jülicher is a story being used as an example for asserting a general proposition of the same area.[124] Comparison occurs in an example story when a hearer compares oneself with the behavior of the characters in the story as models for learning or avoiding.[125] Jülicher also affirms example stories as parables in his revised edition.[126] Both *Hy-*

---

119. Jülicher, *Die Gleichnisreden Jesu*, rev. ed., 112.
120. Tucker, *Example Stories*, 64.
121. Ibid., 64.
122. Ibid., 64n77.
123. Stockmeyer, *Exegetische und praktische Erklärung*, 2–3.
124. Jülicher, *Die Gleichnisreden Jesu*, rev. and combined ed., 1:112.
125. Ibid., 1:113.
126. Ibid.

potypose and example story are similar terms, which are used as examples of role models. However, Jülicher considers an example story as a parable containing comparative feature. On the other hand, Stockmeyer does not place *Hypotypose* among parables as he finds no comparison in it. Thus, the two terms, *Hypotypose* of Stockmeyer and example story of Jülicher, are not completely similar. Apart from that, both Stockmeyer and Jülicher have the category *Parabel*. Stockmeyer refers it to a fictitious narrative illustrating analogically things of higher area with those of lower area.[127] Jülicher's *Parabel* is a freely invented narrative from the lower realm about what someone has once done to secure a subject matter of another realm.[128] The descriptions of *Parabel* of both Stockmeyer and Jülicher appear very similar in that *Parabel* is basically a narrative being used for comparing two realms of things. Concerning Stockmeyer's *Allegorische Schilderung* and Jülicher's *Gleichnis*, the former refers to the use of general description for making analogical comparison to the higher area, while the latter compares two sets of propositions.[129] However, the comparison with the higher area in Stockmeyer's *Allegorische Schilderung* is not in the details but it is a general one.[130] On the other hand, the sets of concepts being compared in Jülicher's *Gleichnis* can be between words or between thoughts.[131] Thus, Stockmeyer's *Allegorische Schilderung* and Jülicher's *Gleichnis* are slightly different in the sense of how details are handled in their comparison process. In other words, the three parable categories of Stockmeyer and of Jülicher bear both similarities and differences. In fact, Jülicher has used the three terms, *Gleichnisse*, *Parabeln*, and *Beispielerzählungen* (example stories), in his parable categorization since his first edition.[132] He also maintains the basic definitions of these three terms in the revised edition while providing more elaboration for example stories.[133] The similarities between the categories of Stockmeyer and Jülicher could be the result of Stockmeyer modifying the categories of Jülicher to develop his own.

---

127. Stockmeyer, *Exegetische und praktische Erklärung*, 3.

128. Jülicher, *Die Gleichnisreden Jesu*, rev. and combined ed., 1:93, 98, 101.

129. Stockmeyer, *Exegetische und praktische Erklärung*, 3; Jülicher, *Die Gleichnisreden Jesu*, 1:69.

130. Stockmeyer, *Exegetische und praktische Erklärung*, 3.

131. Jülicher, *Die Gleichnisreden Jesu*, rev. and combined ed., 1:70.

132. Jülicher, *Die Gleichnisreden Jesu*, 1st ed., 72, 98–99, 117.

133. Jülicher, *Die Gleichnisreden Jesu*, rev. ed., 69, 93–94, 112.

Precursors of Jülicher's Parable Categorization

However, Stockmeyer does not refer to the first edition of Jülicher at all. Indeed, Stockmeyer uses very different words in his categories such as *Allegorische Schilderung* (analogized description) and *Hypotypose* as compared to Jülicher's *Gleichnis* and *Beispielerzählung* (example story). Thus, it is uncertain if Stockmeyer builds his theory upon Jülicher. As the categorization of Jülicher is earlier than Stockmeyer, the similarity between the models of Jülicher and Stockmeyer may be the result of a written work that has used the theory of Jülicher, which Stockmeyer depends upon. It is also possible that both Jülicher and Stockmeyer pick up discussion that has been circulated among academics for a while. Another possibility is a common source that is earlier than Jülicher which is used by both Jülicher and Stockmeyer for developing their categories. In fact, as mentioned in the sections about the categories of Weiss and Goebel, the categories of Jülicher have some similarities with their models. However, instead of citing from Weiss and Goebel, Jülicher refers to Aristotle in the discussion about *Gleichnisse* and *Parabeln*.[134] The silence of Stockmeyer about the source of his parable categories makes it hard to understand the similarity with Jülicher's theory.

Second, as Jülicher has written his parable categories before Stockmeyer, why does he cite from Stockmeyer on the term, *Hypotypose*, in the revised edition? Although the example story of Jülicher is not completely similar to the *Hypotypose* of Stockmeyer, they both affirm their categories as examples. Similarly, Goebel calls typical *Parabel* as direct example.[135] Weiss regards this group of parable as more than examples. However, the historical example of Aristotle under logical proof is related to something that has really happened.[136] Few scholars would call the four example stories as just examples prior to Jülicher. It may be that Jülicher cites from Stockmeyer in order to support his definition for "example stories" in the revised edition even though Stockmeyer's work is later than Jülicher's first edition.

Summary

In general, the term *Parabeln* is used in the parable categorizations of all these scholars to refer to narratives for representing truth, wisdom, or

---

134. Jülicher, *Die Gleichnisreden Jesu*, rev. and combined ed., 1:69–70, 94.

135. Goebel, *Die Parabeln Jesu*, 1:7.

136. Weiss, "Ueber das Bildliche," 327. Weiss, *Das Leben Jesu*, 1:513; 2:64–65, 106, 174. Aristotle *Rhet.* 2.20.2–3.

Part II: On Example Stories

proposition relating to another realm. The comparison in *Parabeln* is explicit between two realms, the lower and the higher, no matter whether such a referential relationship is symbolic, emblematic, or analogical. However, regarding the several example-like parables, terms and definitions vary significantly among these scholars. Table 5 is a summary of the relationship between parables and examples in the above parable categorizations. The examples in Weiss's example-like parables, Goebel's typical *Parabeln*, and Jülicher's example stories form a branch of *Parabeln* carrying the features of parable and story. Example stories can only be considered as a branch of inductive examples placed next to *Parabeln* when Jülicher provides a clear distinction between *Parabeln* and example stories. On the other hand, Stockmeyer's *Hypotypose* is just an example with no parabolic or comparative feature. Thus, the example of *Hypotypose* is a separate category from *Parabeln*.

	Parables			Not Parables
	Explicit Comparison	Narrative		Examples
Aristotle	παραβολή	Fables		Historical Examples
Weiss	*Gleichnisse*	*Parabeln*	Example-like Parables	
Van Koetsveld		Kingdom of Heaven	Gospel of the Kingdom	
Goebel		Symbolic *Parabeln*	Typical *Parabeln*	
Jülicher	*Gleichnisse*	*Parabeln*	Example Stories	
Stockmeyer	*Allegorische Schilderung*	*Parabel*		*Hypotypose*

Table 5. Relationship between Parables and Examples in Parable Categorization

In comparison with the παράδειγμα (example) of Aristotle under logical proof, these scholars as well as Stockmeyer never consider their example-like parables in their categorizations to be examples from historical events. Indeed, Aristotle himself places historical examples in a different category from παραβολή and fables. If the background for the categorizations of these scholars except Stockmeyer is Aristotle's system for making logical proof, they are referring to a kind of example-like parable found inside instead of outside of narrative parables. However, the whole system of Aristotle is indeed example (παράδειγμα). Thus, if any of these scholars is using the model of Aristotle to lay out a parable categorization, no matter what a category is called, it is still considered as an example for proving something. That is, *Gleichnisse*, *Parabeln*, or example stories are all branches under examples. Thus, making any category using the terms "examples" or "example stories" does not help to distinguish them from other categories. The problem is that using "example" as a category is too general.

Although Goebel and Stockmeyer make example-like parables into a category, they both have problems in their theories. Goebel uses circular reasoning to his definition by considering typical *Parabeln* as application of the truth behind them through direct examples while treating them as comparison with the truth. Stockmeyer also makes contradiction in his own argument by disregarding *Hypotypose* as having comparative features while indeed he finds it. Comparison does exist in *Hypotypose*, but it is not the comparison with the higher area. The result of making "example" a category is never satisfactory.

6

Evaluation of the Categorization of Jülicher

AFTER REVIEWING THE PARABLE categorizations from several precursors of example stories, it is stunning to see how similar they are to each other as well as how different they arrange their categories. They are trying to distinguish one group of narrative parables from the other owing to their example-like characteristic. While Bernhard Weiss has never specified these parables as a category of "example," other scholars single them out as a separate category owing to the lack of explicit comparison with the heavenly realm. However, the issue with these example-like parables is not whether they are example or not, but how to interpret them when hints are not obvious. Alternatively, why should the comparison between lower and higher areas be the only way to categorize parables? If example-like parables are called examples simply because they do not show obvious comparison between the earthly and the heavenly realms but they make referents through their stories, they are truly more than examples. Weiss is correct on that. The real problem occurs in the approaches to look for comparison in these example-like parables. Although the theory of parable categorization of Jülicher is relatively comprehensive among these scholars, his model contains many problems as well. The following is a critical evaluation of the conceptual idea of Jülicher's parable categorization. From the problems in defining example stories to the issues in the categorization, the critique will go through systematically.

Evaluation of the Categorization of Jülicher
Critique of the Parable Categorization of Jülicher

"Same"

The basic idea about *Beispielerzählung* (example story) is that it is a story running from the same area as the proposition in order to secure it.[1] The kind of sameness that Jülicher refers to is really that both the story and the proposition to be affirmed are in the religious-moral area.[2] That is, the "same" area is really that both the story and the proposition come from the higher area. He points out that example stories do not run from one area into another area like how a parable is defined, which is the assumption that Jülicher uses to set the major distinction between example story and the other two categories, *Gleichnis* and *Parabeln*.[3] While *Gleichnisse* and *Parabeln* make comparison between the earthly and the heavenly areas, example stories have already moved to the higher area.[4] In other words, the kind of explicit comparison between the lower and the higher areas is not found in an example story. There are some problems with the whole concept of the definition of example stories.

Comparison Can Occur in the Same Area

Jülicher limits comparison in parables to just one type, namely between earthly and heavenly areas. When example stories are presented as coming from the same area as their propositions, he cannot find the particular kind of comparison that he prefers. As a result, he considers example stories as just examples. The reality is that comparison can occur as simply as between one thing and another in parables. Restricting comparison to something between earthly and heavenly realms only is much too narrow and is never the definition of a parable. Whether a story and its proposition to be presented are both from earthly things, or both from heavenly things, such a relationship is already making one thing as a referent of another thing. Consequently, if an example story is used to refer to a proposition, it is already a kind of comparison regardless of whether or not the story and its proposition come from the same area. Like the Good Samaritan, the whole

---

1. Jülicher, *Die Gleichnisreden Jesu*, rev. and combined ed., 1:112.
2. Ibid.
3. Ibid.
4. Ibid.

story points back to the question that the lawyer asked Jesus, "Who is my neighbor?" (Luke 10:29, 36). The proposition is found in the lawyer's own answer to Jesus, "The one who showed mercy" (Luke 10:37). Both the story of the Good Samaritan and the proposition about "neighbor" are from the religious-moral area or higher area. Even though they are from the "same" area, the story does make the proposition as the referent. What is missing is that the proposition has not been stated completely. As a result, hearers need to infer from the story that "a neighbor is one who shows mercy to another." The comparative feature does occur in the Good Samaritan though it is an implicit relationship. Therefore, the word "same" places an unrealistic restriction upon earthly and heavenly realms of comparison in parables, which misleads others as if the stories had not been compared with any referent.

Coming from the Same Area Does Not Equal to Identical

The word "same" creates confusion as if example stories were identical with their propositions as well. Obviously, example stories and their propositions are not identical. No matter whether Jülicher calls it as higher area or religious-moral area, the "same" area can be a huge area covering plenty of topics, concepts, things, and events. For example, the same higher area can include such things as the status of the kingdom of God, the coming of Christ, Christian character, and the work of God. Under the same area, a comparison can occur anytime as long as a relationship of one thing with its referent is established. Thus, even when a story and its proposition are coming from the same area, it does not mean that comparison cannot exist in a parable. Although an example story gives a description that is very close to the proposition being presented, the description and the proposition are nevertheless two things in a speech. Alternatively, a story is only a part of a proposition at most. Like the Good Samaritan, the story describes something about the proposition concerning who one's neighbor is. However, the reverse can be quite different. That is, the same proposition "a neighbor is one who shows mercy to another" can be represented by many stories instead of just the Good Samaritan. No matter how close an example story is to its proposition from the same area, it can rarely be the same as the proposition.

Evaluation of the Categorization of Jülicher

Comparison within the Same Area Is Not a Reason to Call a Story an Example

Jülicher treats example stories as examples with no need to look for their explanations.[5] What drives Jülicher to the conclusion that these example stories are examples is the consideration that these stories are from the same area as their propositions.[6] Why is it that when an example story and its proposition are from the same area, the story should be considered as an example? Indeed, parables such as those found in *Parabeln* that come from different areas with their propositions can still be considered as examples. To elaborate further, in the Unjust Judge, an earthly story is used to illustrate a heavenly principle about prayer (Luke 18:1–8). The widow finally moved the unjust judge to grant her legal protection (Luke 18:4–5). Indeed, Jesus states clearly in the beginning that the story is used to illustrate that "they should always pray and not give up" (Luke 18:1). Therefore, whether it is an example story making a proposition from the same area or a parable that makes comparison between the lower and the higher areas, both of them can be examples. Not only does the term "example" fail to distinguish example stories from parables that make explicit comparison between earthly and heavenly realms, but also there is no valid reason to label example stories as examples simply because these stories are from the same area as their propositions. In fact, when wording such as "same" or "different" is used, Jülicher is referring specifically to whether there is a comparison between earthly and heavenly realms in a parable, as mentioned above. Anything can be an example if it illustrates another thing regardless of whether or not the two things come from the same area. As example stories come from the "same" area as their propositions having no explicit comparison between the lower and the higher areas, they should be called "non-explicit comparison between the higher and the lower areas" parables instead of being considered as "examples." That is, even though both the stories and the propositions come from the same area, it will not be a reason to call these parables as examples. The issue is simply different styles of comparison.

---

5. Ibid., 1:112, 114.
6. Ibid., 1:112.

Part II: On Example Stories

Different in Style of Comparison

The term "example stories" misleads hearers to call these parables as examples when it is indeed a problem of defining comparison. Jülicher suggests in the first edition that comparative law is meaningless in example stories because the bottom-line of ὅμοιος (like) is "actually" abandoned.[7] He also recommends that as the narrator does not make any comparison, the hearer should similarly make no comparison.[8] Thus, he originally proposes putting example stories out of the orbit of *Mashal*.[9] That is, he does not consider example stories to have any comparative feature nor does he treat them as parables initially. However, he changes his position in the revised edition. Instead of saying the bottom line of ὅμοιος (like) is "actually" abandoned in example stories, he amends it as the bottom line of ὅμοιος (like) is "almost" abandoned.[10] That is, he finally admits that there are some comparative features in example stories. Another change Jülicher makes is that instead of saying neither the narrator nor the hearer should practice comparison in example stories, he alters it to "hearers should practice" comparison between oneself with the behavioral principles of the characters in the stories.[11] When Jülicher equates the comparison that the hearers make with the characters in the example stories with the comparison of the parables, he returns these stories to the category of *Mashal* but insisting that the narrator does not intend to make comparison.[12] Thus, the major points that he revises are that example stories carry comparative features and they are parables.

Comparison by Reader's Approach Cannot Be Counted as Author's Intended

However, the comparison that Jülicher sees in example stories is purely a reader's approach instead of author's approach as he states it clearly that the author has not made comparison.[13] What he considers as "comparison"

---

7. Jülicher, *Die Gleichnisreden Jesu*, 1st ed., 117.
8. Ibid., 118.
9. Ibid.
10. Jülicher, *Die Gleichnisreden Jesu*, rev. ed., 113.
11. Ibid.
12. Ibid.
13. Jülicher, *Die Gleichnisreden Jesu*, rev. ed., 113. Osborne, *The Hermeneutical Spiral*,

in example stories is really that the hearers compare themselves with the example stories. However, Jülicher is misleading about what he counts as comparison. While he emphasizes that the narrator has no intention to do comparison, he counts the comparison that is made by the hearers between themselves with the parables as the comparison of example stories. By doing so, Jülicher can finally give a reason to return example stories back to be parables. The real problem, however, is that Jülicher has not yet found the intended comparison of the author in example stories.

Comparison Framework in Some Narrative Parables Is Implicit instead of Explicit

Jülicher reads the explicit comparison that is made between earthly and heavenly areas as in *Parabeln* into example stories. As a result, Jülicher does not find any comparison in the example stories that is from the author. He replaces it with a reader's approach comparison as mentioned above. However, are explicit comparison and reader's approach comparison the comparison that is found in example stories? Obviously, they are not. In fact, a comparison that is coming from reader's approach is not the same as the comparison designed by the author of the stories. Although example stories do not show explicit comparison between the higher and the lower areas, they can still have comparison or referent. In fact, in *Parabeln*, Jülicher uses the stories as a whole for making comparison instead of looking for the correspondence of the details.[14] If this is the basis of comparison in *Parabeln*, the narrative nature of example stories should not be too far away from it. Indeed, the very definition of example stories is using these stories to assert and secure some propositions.[15] Thus, both *Parabeln* and example stories are using the stories as a whole to make comparison.

To *Parabeln*, the comparison is made explicitly between earthly and heavenly areas. Nevertheless, what about the comparison that is used in example stories? Although Jülicher describes example stories as narratives

---

377. "Reader's approach" or Reader-response criticism puts emphasis over interpreters instead of the text for creating meaning. Yet the theories relate to reader-response are very diverse. Thiselton, *New Horizons in Hermeneutics*, 60–61, 538. Fish, *Is There a Text in This Class*, 12–13. While minimizing the objective meaning in the texts, Fish who is a major advocate of Reader-response argues that interpretative strategies instead of the texts shape the meaning of the texts.

14. Jülicher, *Die Gleichnisreden Jesu*, rev. and combined ed., 1:95.

15. Ibid., 1:112.

that are readily moving to the higher area, the difference between *Parabeln* and example stories is really not about whether there is a comparison between higher or lower areas. As both types of narrative parables make referents, the real difference between *Parabeln* and example stories is whether or not the stories express their propositions explicitly. Using the formula of Kubczak, "x is like y with regard to z," for illustration, x is absent in an implicit metaphor or metaphorical implication.[16] That is, when the subject is absent or lacks description, it is an implicit expression. Just like some of the example stories, the narratives make referents to their propositions. However, the stories are present but the propositions are not fully stated or even missing. Thus, this is an implicit comparison.

We can take the Good Samaritan as an example. A man being robbed and badly injured was not rescued by a priest or a Levite, but he was saved by someone unlikely, a Samaritan (Luke 10:29–35). After the story is told, the proposition concerning who one's neighbor is has not been stated directly (Luke 10:29, 36). Instead, it requires implication from the story. That is, neighbor is the one who shows mercy to other (Luke 10:37). Since the subject matter can still be traced although it is not fully expressed, the implicitness in the Good Samaritan is only partial. However, the comparison in the Rich Man and Lazarus is completely implicit. In this story, Lazarus who lived miserably while alive became comforted in the bosom of Abraham after death (Luke 16:19–22). On the contrary, the rich man who lived in luxury while on earth became in great torment in Hades after death (Luke 16:23–26). Upon realizing that he could not ask to have Lazarus sent to his place to relieve his torment, the rich man requested to send someone from death to remind his living brothers to repent (Luke 16:27–30). In response, Abraham says that if his brothers do not listen to Moses and the Prophets, they will not listen even someone is raised from the dead (Luke 16:31). The theme of the story is not very clear. However, the irreversible destiny of the rich man after death and his desire for his living brothers to repent may suggest that the proposition of the story could be about "returning to God and his teaching while one is still living." This is a typical implicit comparison, as the subject matter is almost absent. Obviously when some of these example stories are placed in a different comparative system looking for implicit expression, there is no way that using a system of explicit comparison can help to locate the propositions in the parables. At best, these narrative parables will only be treated as examples.

16. Kubczak, *Die Metapher*, 69.

Evaluation of the Categorization of Jülicher

Different in the System for Categorization

Jülicher considers example stories as examples because he finds the stories and their propositions running from the same area instead of comparing between earthly and heavenly areas for asserting propositions.[17] As mentioned previously, not only is it problematic reasoning to call example stories as examples in this way, but also the idea to call them examples indeed builds around an unrealistic assumption of explicit comparison that cannot help to explain the implicit comparison in example stories. If indeed "example" is not the distinctive feature to help in differentiating between example stories and the other two categories, *Parabeln* and *Gleichnisse*, the categorization of Jülicher may need to be regrouped or be replaced by a different categorization.

Example Stories Are More Than Examples

Are example stories really examples? The answer is both "yes" and "no." Example stories are not just examples but they are more than that. Before Jülicher, Weiss finds the difficulty in interpreting these four parables. He observes that these parables borrow materials from closely related areas making them like examples but he never names them as a particular group.[18] In the later work of Weiss, he emphasizes that these four parables are not merely examples, for he finds their interpretative hints and general principles.[19] In his illustration about the Rich Man and Poor Lazarus, Weiss suggests that if reversal of position after death were the teaching of the parable, it would be just an illustrative narrative about the rich man going to the place of torment.[20] He points out that even if irrevocable change occurs when death separates one from temporal possession, this truth is only a preparation for the closing of the story.[21] He suggests that the real theme of the narrative is that "if they do not listen to Moses and the Prophets, neither will they be persuaded by other means (Luke 16:27–31)."[22] In other words, the way in which Weiss sees example stories to be more than just

---

17. Jülicher, *Die Gleichnisreden Jesu*, rev. and combined ed., 1:112.
18. Weiss, "Ueber das Bildliche," 327.
19. Weiss, *Das Leben Jesu*, 1:512–13; 2:64–65, 106, 174.
20. Ibid., 2:62–63.
21. Ibid., 2:63–64.
22. Ibid., 2:64.

examples is that they are not straightforward illustration but they are presenting some truths or themes behind the stories. That is, if example stories are treated as examples only without going further to explore carefully the intended propositions of the narrator, the stories can be completely misunderstood as something very general. It is still correct to call example stories as examples, but it will not help to describe specifically the features of these parable stories. Whether they are examples or more than examples, the real issue that distinguishes the two is that the propositions or themes in example stories are not expressed directly or explicitly. When their subject matters are intentionally left out by the author, people can see only their pictorial description like any example. Thus, calling these parables as examples will not be enough. In fact, the reason that Jülicher calls them as example stories is really because they do not show explicit comparison between earthly and heavenly areas.[23] Therefore, the problem is always around whether the story is expressed explicitly or implicitly. By saying that example stories are more than examples, the underlying issue behind is really their implicitness in expressing their propositions.

"Example" Is Not a Good Description for Example Stories

Moreover, not only are example stories examples, but also *Parabeln* and *Gleichnisse* are examples. Wolfgang Harnisch suggests that in spite of the difference among *Gleichnisse*, *Parabeln*, and example stories of Jülicher, they share the common feature of paradigmatic function, in which "exegetically all parables of Jesus are basically to be treated as example stories."[24] In fact, Jülicher uses παραβολή (comparison) and fables of Aristotle to explain *Gleichnisse* and *Parabeln*.[25] They both belong to invented παράδειγμα (example) under Aristotle's logical proof of induction.[26] Thus, the two categories of Jülicher are types of examples already. Yet Jülicher also defines example stories as examples or *Hypotyposen*, a term he cites from Stockmeyer.[27] In other words, whether or not he places example stories under παράδειγμα (example) of Aristotle, *Gleichnisse*, *Parabeln*, and example stories are similar kinds of examples. As they are all examples, calling example

23. Jülicher, *Die Gleichnisreden Jesu*, rev. and combined ed., 1:112.
24. Harnisch, "Language of the Possible," 46.
25. Jülicher, *Die Gleichnisreden Jesu*, rev. and combined ed., 1:69, 94.
26. Aristotle *Rhet.* 2.20.1–3.
27. Jülicher, *Die Gleichnisreden Jesu*, rev. and combined ed., 1:112.

stories as examples will not distinguish them from the other two parable categories of Jülicher. With this in view, it creates a problem when the term "example stories" is used.

Jülicher's Grouping of the Categories Is Not Homogeneous

If the term "example stories" does not help to distinguish this category with *Gleichnisse* and *Parabeln*, will replacing it with a new name solve the problem? Assuming that the three categories of Jülicher are homogeneous, giving a different name to these four parables in place of "example stories" may help. However, there are some considerations. First, other parables can be grouped together with the four example stories owing to similar style of implicit comparison or inadequate hints for understanding their subject matters. For example, Weiss considers the Lost Son together with the Rich Man and Poor Lazarus as difficult parables to look for interpretative hints.[28] Although van Koetsveld has a different categorization for grouping parables, he adds two more parables, the Lost Son and the Judge and Widow, along the four parables that are example-like or lack of symbolic reference to the kingdom of heaven.[29] That is, there can be more parables instead of just four that appear like examples but indeed implicitness is used for expressing their subject matters. In the Lost Son, the proposition is not clearly stated. However, the son in the story said twice both to his heart and to his father, "Father, I have sinned against heaven and in your sight; I am no longer worthy to be called your son" (Luke 15:18–19, 21). The father also spoke repeatedly with great joy to both his servants and his older son in slightly different wordings, "For this son of mine was dead and is alive, he was lost and is found" (Luke 15:24, 32). It may imply that the subject matter of this story is about the joy and aliveness in heaven upon the repentance of a sinner as in the Lost Sheep and the Lost Coin (Luke 15:7, 10). Concerning the Unjust Judge, the proposition is stated in the beginning, "they should always pray and not lose heart" (Luke 18:1). If the categorization of Jülicher is used, the two parables will not be placed under example stories as they show two realms, earthly and heavenly. However, even putting them under *Parabeln*, the proposition of the Unjust Judge is obvious while the subject matter of the Lost Son is not explicit. If the whole issue about example stories is really that the subject matters under comparison are not explicitly

---

28. Weiss, "Ueber das Bildliche," 324.
29. Van Koetsveld, *De Gelijkenissen van den Zaligmaker*, 1:xxxii, xxxiv.

PART II: ON EXAMPLE STORIES

shown instead of they do not make comparison clearly between heaven and earth, there can be more parables which appear like example stories within *Parabeln*. That is, distinguishing parables just based upon having a comparison between earthly and heavenly areas will not help to establish a homogeneous group for *Parabeln*.

Another problem is that the implicitness of the proposition in example stories varies in expression. While the proposition of the Good Samaritan can still be implied from the context (Luke 10:29, 36–37), the subject matter is not very clear in the Rich Man and Lazarus. In contrast, the referents of the other two example stories are relatively easier to locate than the Rich Man and Lazarus. Like the Rich Fool, the subject matter is about the answer of Jesus to someone who asked for help in dividing inheritance with his brother (Luke 12:13–14). In the story, a certain rich man planned to build a bigger storage for his produce. However, God came to remind him that his life was about to be taken away that night (Luke 12:15–20). The proposition is stated in verse 21, "In this way a man who stores up treasure for himself is not rich toward God." Similarly, the proposition in the Pharisee and Tax Collector is clearly stated. The story is about a Pharisee who boasted in prayer how righteous he was and how unrighteous the others were. On the contrary, the tax collector loudly confessed to be a sinner and he asked for the mercy of God (Luke 18:9–13). The proposition is found at the end of the story, "For everyone who exalts oneself will be humbled, but one who humbles himself will be exalted. (Luke 18:14)." Although the propositions in the parables of Rich Fool and the Pharisee and Tax Collector are indirect, they are more like the style of the Good Samaritan in that they are easier to be found than the Rich Man and Lazarus. In other words, even within the same group of example stories, their propositions express in a spectrum regarding their implicitness. If the comparison between heavenly and earthly realms do not provide a good framework for distinguishing *Parabeln* from example stories, and the parables in both categories are not homogeneous, replacing "example stories" with a different name will not help to solve the problem.

In fact, some parables in *Parabeln* and *Gleichnisse* can be regrouped. While *Parabeln* contain mainly a story style of parables that compare between earthly and heavenly areas, Jülicher puts the Building on Rock or Sand (Matt 7:24–27; Luke 6:47–49) awkwardly under it.[30] It is indeed better to place it under *Gleichnisse* as the parables in this group are more straight-

---

30. Jülicher, *Die Gleichnisreden Jesu*, rev. and combined ed., 2:viii.

forward and explicit in making comparison between two sets of referential relationships. Similarly, Jülicher places the Bridegroom under *Gleichnisse* (Luke 5:33–35; Mark 2:18–20; Matt 9:14).[31] Indeed, the implied heavenly content and the earthly event of the parable match better with those parables under *Parabeln*. It suggests that some parables within *Gleichnisse* and *Parabeln* are not homogeneous. If the parables under the three categories of Jülicher are not grouping well, and the term "example stories" does not help to distinguish this group from the other two categories, regrouping all parables of Jesus under a different categorization is necessary.

Structural Problems Exist in the Categorization of Jülicher

Adding to all the problems above, the parable categorization of Jülicher also has some structural issues. The parable model of Jülicher is based upon the artificial logical proof of Aristotle with the use of inductive examples (παράδειγμα).[32] Although there are two types of examples, invented and historical, Jülicher only uses the former. He associates his *Gleichnisse* with Aristotle's παραβολή (comparison) and *Parabeln* with λόγοι (fables).[33] Rather, he has never considered example stories to be examples for enriching historical knowledge.[34] Thus, the framework of Jülicher's parable categorization is developed mainly from παραβολή (comparison) and λόγοι (fables) of Aristotle's invented examples. When he sees that some parables neither fit well in *Gleichnisse* nor *Parabeln*, he calls these parables example stories.[35] However, he still considers example stories to be narrative parables even though he does not indicate their relationship with *Parabeln*. This raises some questions. Should example stories be another branch under *Parabeln*? Alternatively, would it be better to place example stories under invented examples to be next to *Parabeln*? There are two concerns about the modification of Jülicher as well. Is it legitimate to expand on the model of Aristotle for the categorization of the parables of Jesus? Is such a model sufficient to facilitate the categorization of the parables of Jesus? This will be discussed below.

31. Ibid., 2:vii.
32. Aristotle *Rhet.* 2.20.1.
33. Jülicher, *Die Gleichnisreden Jesu*, rev. and combined ed., 1:69, 94, 98. Aristotle *Rhet.* 2.20.3.
34. Jülicher, *Die Gleichnisreden Jesu*, rev. and combined ed., 1:112.
35. Ibid., 1:112.

Part II: On Example Stories

Inductive Examples of Aristotle May Not Be the Best System for the Categorization of the Parables of Jesus

Whether or not it is justifiable to expand on the model of Aristotle for the parables of Jesus, it is first necessary to understand the nature of Aristotle's system. Aristotle defines rhetoric as looking for possible ways of persuasion.[36] They can be non-artificial or artificial proof.[37] A kind of artificial proof for persuasion uses the speech itself to demonstrate certain truth.[38] This kind of logical persuasion is done inductively using examples or deductively through syllogism.[39] Aristotle explains dialectic induction in the form of rhetorical example as using a particular case to prove a general principle.[40] Indeed, Jülicher defines example stories similarly in which specific cases are used to demonstrate general principles.[41] Though Jülicher does not associate example stories with the rhetoric of Aristotle, they are alike in using inductive proof for persuasion.

Aristotle identifies three kinds of rhetoric, which are συμβουλῆς (deliberative), δίκης (forensic), and ἐπιδεικτικοῦ (epideictic).[42] Among them, he suggests that παράδειγμα (example) is more common in deliberative speech, which examines the past for deciding the future, while ἐνθύμηματα (enthymemes) is more suitable for forensic rhetoric, which investigates causes and demonstrates proof from the past.[43] However, the nature of deliberative speech is possibility instead of an event that is, will be, or cannot possibly come to pass.[44] That is, deliberative speech is about the possibility of something in the future rather than certainty. In addition, Aristotle points out that narrative (διήγησις) is rare in deliberative speech.[45] His explanation is that narrative is usually something in the past instead of something that is about to occur.[46] He even suggests that if the past of a

---

36. Aristotle *Rhet.* 1.2.1.
37. Aristotle *Rhet.* 1.2.2.
38. Aristotle *Rhet.* 1.2.6–7.
39. Aristotle *Rhet.* 1.2.8.
40. Aristotle *Rhet.* 1.2.9.
41. Jülicher, *Die Gleichnisreden Jesu*, rev. and combined ed., 1:114.
42. Aristotle *Rhet.* 1.3.3.
43. Aristotle *Rhet.* 1.9.40, 3.17.5.
44. Aristotle *Rhet.* 1.4.1–2.
45. Aristotle *Rhet.* 3.16.11.
46. Aristotle *Rhet.* 3.16.11.

Evaluation of the Categorization of Jülicher

narrative is used as advice for the future, it will no longer be deliberative but more of praise and blame kind of speech.[47] In fact, narrative can be found not only in epideictic rhetoric but also in forensic oration.[48] Since inductive examples (παράδειγμα) are more commonly found in deliberative speech and narrative is rare in deliberative rhetoric, does it mean that narrative is also rare in inductive examples? However, among the kinds of examples (παραδείγμα) for inductive proof, Aristotle has historical examples and fables of invented examples.[49] Historical examples are events that have actually occurred though they are not necessarily in narrative form. Fables can be narratives but Aristotle does not associate them in this way. Does it mean it is possible to have narrative in inductive examples but not in deliberative rhetoric? There are two possible explanations about the discrepancy between inductive examples (παράδειγμα) and deliberative speech concerning narratives. One of them is that inductive example and deliberative speech are not in absolute equivalence. That is, deliberative speech only partly overlaps with inductive examples leaving room for narrative to be used. However, aside from deliberative speech, Aristotle only uses forensic and epideictic for rhetorical usage. While it is more common to use syllogism in forensic rhetoric for accusation or defense with deductive proof, and it is more suitable to use amplification in epideictic rhetoric either for praise or blame, what is this kind of narrative in inductive examples?[50] Should they be simply called non-deliberative? Alternatively, if it is about the difference of time such that narrative is always about the past while deliberative is about the future, it should not be a problem to list a narrative that is produced by invention under inductive example similar to the way a fable is handled. Indeed, if the requirement of inductive example is really about using a specific case to prove a general principle, it can be anything including the invention of narrative. In fact, one group of inductive examples is produced by invention such as comparison (παραβολή) and fables.[51] It may be the approach of Jülicher as well to consider some parables of Jesus as invented narratives. By associating *Parabeln* or narrative parables with the fable of Aristotle, Jülicher makes a way for narratives

---

47. Aristotle *Rhet.* 3.16.11.
48. Aristotle *Rhet.* 3.16.1, 6.
49. Aristotle *Rhet.* 2.20.2–3.
50. Aristotle *Rhet.* 1.10.1, 1.9.1, 40.
51. Aristotle *Rhet.* 2.20.2.

to be a part of Aristotle's inductive examples although Aristotle never includes this idea in any of his discussion.

On the other hand, if narrative is not common to deliberative speech, but is found in forensic or epideictic rhetoric, does it mean that narrative needs to be excluded from Aristotle's system of inductive examples? That is, narrative is really not suitable to be used in inductive examples. This may help to ease any possible inconsistency between deliberative speech and inductive examples concerning narrative. Aristotle has never associated anything in inductive example with narrative. Rather, Jülicher draws the connection between narrative parables and the fables of Aristotle in the discussion of *Parabeln*.[52] Indeed, Jülicher also considers example stories as narrative parables.[53] It is a continuing problem of how to lay out *Parabeln* and example stories of Jülicher under Aristotle's system of inductive examples. *Parabeln* can still be associated with fables. However, it is a bit uncertain where to place example stories under inductive examples. Although example stories can either be put under or next to *Parabeln*, a clear distinction between *Parabeln* and example stories is necessary in order to make this decision. Unfortunately, the parable categories of Jülicher are not homogeneous in categorization, which makes it hard to decide if a branch of example stories that are also narrative parables can be included in the system of Aristotle for inductive proof. Indeed, example stories become such an awkward branch to fit into the inductive examples of Aristotle that Jülicher needs to cite from Stockmeyer for support in his revised edition. As stated previously, Stockmeyer regards *Hypotypose* as purely an example instead of a parable.[54] Not only is it different from what Jesus has called some of these parables (Luke 12:16, 18:9), but Jülicher also affirms example stories as parables in the revised edition.[55] Although Stockmeyer is added as support, it is still difficult to secure a category for example stories in the categorization of the parables of Jesus under the inductive examples of Aristotle.

In fact, it is also challenging to use *Parabeln* of Jülicher or fables of Aristotle to categorize all narrative parables of Jesus owing to their complexity in comparison. After all, the major focus of Aristotle's system of inductive proof is persuasion instead of telling the differences in the narratives.

52. Jülicher, *Die Gleichnisreden Jesu*, rev. and combined ed., 1:94.
53. Ibid., 1:119.
54. Ibid., 1:112. Stockmeyer, *Exegetische und praktische Erklärung*, 2.
55. Jülicher, *Die Gleichnisreden Jesu*, rev. and combined ed., 1:113.

Evaluation of the Categorization of Jülicher

Thus, Jülicher may not be wrong to arrange some narrative parables under inductive examples and to call them *Parabeln*. However, the persuasion of Aristotle for inductive proof through examples may not be the best system to distinguish the differences in the narrative of the parables of Jesus with various kinds of comparisons. Although it is nice to build a parable categorization on Aristotle's inductive examples, it demands quite a bit of stretch of Aristotle's system by adding in narratives that are featuring with different kinds of comparisons. It is expecting too much from a logical system that is designed for persuasion.

Aristotle's Inductive Examples Are Not Designed for Distinguishing the Complexity of Comparisons

The major structural problem that Jülicher encounters in grouping the parables of Jesus is less about inserting narrative into Aristotle's system for persuasion and more about using Aristotle's inductive examples in categorizing the complexity of comparisons in the parables of Jesus. What Jülicher looks for as comparison is an explicit relationship between heavenly and earthly areas. As he finds some parables lacking of this particular kind of comparison and they rather have stories and propositions coming from the "same" area, Jülicher considers these parables as example stories.[56] Unfortunately, he reads explicit comparison into the implicit comparison of example stories. As a result, what he sees as no comparison but just examples in example stories is indeed a different kind of comparison. It is doubtful if the inductive examples of Aristotle for persuasion can help to distinguish the difference in various types of comparisons in the parables of Jesus for the purpose of categorization.

Apart from that, the grouping of the categories of Jülicher is not distinctive. Some parables in *Parabeln* are indeed partially implicit in making comparison such as the Lost Son and the Unjust Judge. However, they are grouped under *Parabeln* instead of example stories because of their earthly-heavenly comparison. The implicitness of these two parables varies too. The subject matter of the Unjust Judge appears more obvious than the Lost Son (Luke 18:1; 15:24, 32). That is, within the same category of *Parabeln*, not only does different kind of comparison exist but also mixed forms of explicitness and implicitness occur in comparison. *Parabeln* is not as homogeneous as it appears to be a unique category. In fact, within the

---

56. Jülicher, *Die Gleichnisreden Jesu*, rev. and combined ed., 1:112.

category of example stories, the implicitness of the subject matter of the Rich Man and Lazarus is more difficult to be found than those in the Good Samaritan, the Rich Fool, and the Pharisee and Tax Collector. Thus, putting the parables of Jesus under the framework of explicit comparison between the higher and the lower areas may not be sufficient in expressing the variety of implicitness in some parables nor is it helpful in making each parable category distinctive.

In this context, the effort of Jülicher in making the inductive examples of Aristotle as the backdrop to fit into his own categorization for the parables of Jesus becomes more awkward. The inductive examples of Aristotle are only a kind of persuasion. It does not help to explain the complexity from explicit comparison to implicit comparison in the parables of Jesus. Indeed, Jülicher associates his *Gleichnisse* with Aristotle's παραβολή (comparison) and *Parabeln* with λόγοι (fables).[57] Using the framework of Aristotle for inductive examples in developing a categorization for the parables of Jesus may at most address the explicit comparison of the parables of Jesus. However, further variety and complexity of comparison in the parables of Jesus such as various degrees of implicit comparison may lead to their falling off from the framework of Aristotle on inductive examples. The system of Aristotle for persuasion does not seem to have a place for parables with implicit comparison or parables that are between explicit comparison and implicit comparison. As a model for persuasion, the inductive examples of Aristotle are sufficient. However, if the focus is about grouping the variety of comparisons in parables, the inductive proof of Aristotle is really not designed for such matters. Therefore, it is not surprising at all that we encounter difficulty in locating example stories on Aristotle's system of inductive proof. Using the model of Aristotle that is not designed for expressing various types of comparisons but persuasions only may not seem to help in the categorization of the parables of Jesus.

No matter it is the definition of example stories, identification of comparison style, or system of categorization, the problems that are found in Jülicher's parable theory suggest that his categorization is better discarded than continuously used.

---

57. Jülicher, *Die Gleichnisreden Jesu*, rev. and combined ed., 1:69, 94, 98. Aristotle *Rhet.* 2.20.3.

Evaluation of the Categorization of Jülicher

Rhetorical Discussion around Biblical Times

If the system of Aristotle on inductive proof with invented examples for persuasion does not help to explain the complexity of the parables of Jesus very well, are there other systems that can facilitate a better categorization of parables? Although the parables of Jesus can be persuasive, his parables are more on the development of the narrative and how the stories are geared toward their subject matters expressed in various levels of implicitness, which should be termed as allegorical features. Indeed, the complexity of implicit comparison makes some biblical parables very difficult to fit into the inductive examples of Aristotle for categorization. The following will be an exploration of rhetorical discussion before and during biblical times. Attention will be given to a more structural and systematic approach to rhetoric that helps in addressing the allegorical features in public speech such as narrative parables.

The Rhetoric of Greco-Roman Period

According to Quintilian, Empedocles was the earliest to write about rhetoric.[58] Corax, Empedocles' student, and Tisias, Corax's student, produce some written works in this area.[59] Gorgias, another student of Empedocles, has a discussion with Socrates about the definition of rhetoric.[60] In response to Socrates, Gorgias gives a further refinement of rhetoric.[61] Gorgias considers rhetoric as power to persuade with speech.[62] The whole function of rhetoric is designed to persuade.[63] However, other arts such as teaching of any kind can be persuasive too.[64] Thus, Socrates suggests that rhetoric is not the only way to persuade.[65] However, the rhetoric that Gorgias and Socrates refer to is mainly about using persuasion to make others believe such as

---

58. Quintilian *Inst.* 3.1.8.

59. Quintilian *Inst.* 3.1.8. IJsseling, *Rhetoric and Philosophy in Conflict*, 26. According to IJsseling, Corax sets five parts in a speech: introduction (*exordium*), narration (*narratio*), argumentation with positive proof (*probatio*) or refutation (*refutatio*), digression (*digressio*), and conclusion (*peroratio*).

60. Quintilian *Inst.* 3.1.8. Plato *Gorg.* 453A.

61. Plato *Gorg.* 454B-C.

62. Plato *Gorg.* 452E. Quintilian *Inst.* 2.15.10.

63. Plato *Gorg.* 453A.

64. Plato *Gorg.* 453D.

65. Plato *Gorg.* 454A.

in a lawsuit instead of giving instruction on right and wrong.[66] Indeed, Quintilian points out that Socrates limits Gorgias' discussion on rhetoric to persuasion only, but not teaching.[67] Based on the context of discussion by Socrates and Gorgias, teaching through parables like those of Jesus may not be explained very well under their definition of rhetoric. The reason is that their focus of rhetoric is really about legal situations without the need of giving additional knowledge for convincing anyone in the process of persuasion.

Quintilian suggests that there are indeed many ways to define rhetoric. He finds that the two main areas of difference in the definitions of rhetoric are the virtue of the orator and the wordings in definition.[68] Setting aside the virtue of the speaker, rhetoric can be generally defined as "the power of persuading."[69] Gorgias and his student, Isocrates, hold this view.[70] Along this line, Cicero emphasizes the manner to carry out persuasion.[71] Theodectes, on the other hand, looks toward guiding others to the desired conclusion of a speaker.[72] Some want to achieve the results of persuasion, while others like Aristotle focus on the elements to make persuasion.[73] Some consider rhetoric as a science, while others treat it as an art.[74]

Others put the virtue of the speaker and persuasion together in rhetoric. Socrates and Plato prefer a person who is well known for carrying out justice to be an orator.[75] They suggest that if an orator cannot distinguish what is good from what is evil, the speech of such a person will not be effective.[76] Quintilian puts "being a good man" as the first criterion of a perfect orator.[77] Quoting from Xenocrates, Quintilian considers the best definition for rhetoric as "the science of speaking well."[78] The view of Quin-

---

66. Plato *Gorg.* 454B, 454E-455A.
67. Quintilian, *Inst.* 2.15.18.
68. Quintilian *Inst.* 2.15.1.
69. Quintilian *Inst.* 2.15.3.
70. Quintilian *Inst.* 2.15.3–5.
71. Quintilian *Inst.* 2.15.5–6
72. Quintilian *Inst.* 2.15.10.
73. Quintilian *Inst.* 2.15.12–13.
74. Quintilian *Inst.* 2.15. 19–22.
75. Plato *Gorg.* 460C, 508C.
76. Plato *Phaedr.* 260C.
77. Quintilian *Inst.* 2.15.33.
78. Quintilian *Inst.* 2.15.34, 34n41.

Evaluation of the Categorization of Jülicher

tilian is that rhetoric involves both the "virtues of speech" and the virtue of the orator.[79] In other words, rhetoric consists of a variety of public speeches for making persuasion. Preferably, these are speeches that contain good moral content and they are spoken by a virtuous person. In this sense, Jesus and his teaching with parables shares a lot of commonality with rhetorical speeches. Though rhetoric is usually found in forensic, deliberative, and epideictic speeches, Quintilian suggests that the types of rhetoric are countless.[80] However, Quintilian sees that all other rhetorical speeches in some way share common features with forensic, deliberative, and epideictic speeches such as narrative, instruction, and some others.[81] Thus, it should not be surprising that the style of parable teaching of Jesus shares some common features with deliberative rhetoric like the inductive example of Aristotle for proof by explicit comparison and fable. However, it is also difficult to fit the narrative parables of Jesus into the same system, particularly those parables that are storytelling and allegorically implicit in expression. That is, rhetoric like those in forensic, deliberative, and epideictic will not be found in the parables of Jesus or other types of rhetoric.[82] Nevertheless, the common features that these three share with other types of rhetoric are useful in giving more understanding to other rhetorical styles that have not been mentioned.

Cicero uses a whole book to explain the principles of style in rhetoric.[83] Like the invention of persuasion in legal cases, Cicero notices the complexity of narration. He discusses the embellishment of narratives under the rules of style.[84] The rhetoric of the style of public teaching of Jesus using parables obviously will not be anything less complicated than the narration of court cases. Style is defined as adaptation of words and sentences, which is one of the five parts in oration.[85] Under qualities of rhetorical style, Cicero further distinguishes between figures of diction and figures of thought.[86]

---

79. Quintilian *Inst.* 2.15.34.

80. Aristotle *Rhet.* 1.3.3; Quintilian *Inst.* 3.4.1–3.

81. Quintilian *Inst.* 3.4.11, 15–16.

82. Cicero *Inv.* 1.14.19. Cicero has six parts in the invention of rhetoric: exordium, narrative, partition, confirmation, refutation, digression, peroration, and peroration.

83. Cicero *Rhet. Her.* 4.7.10.

84. Cicero *Inv.* 1.19.27.

85. Cicero *Rhet. Her.* 1.2.3. The five parts for oration are invention, arrangement, style, memory, and delivery. Cicero *Inv.* 1.7.9. Cicero suggests that Aristotle agrees with these five parts for rhetoric.

86. Cicero *Rhet. Her.* 4.12.18–13.19. Figures of diction refer to the embellishment of

Part II: On Example Stories

Among so many rhetorical styles, the principle on allegory is the most helpful in understanding the implicit expression in the parables of Jesus, as discussed in the first two chapters. Cicero identifies ten figures of diction, which are similarly departing from the words into other meanings.[87] That is, they all show a gesture of transferring from the original meaning of the words in the speech to another meaning. Indeed, Cicero considers these ten figures of diction belonging to one class.[88] Allegory is one of these ten figures of diction. Cicero subdivides allegory into three types: *similitudinem* (comparison), *argumentum* (argument), and *contrarium* (contrast).[89] Although Cicero gives a very systematic explanation about the principles of style in rhetoric, Quintilian exceeds him by providing a more comprehensive description.

Quintilian also uses the five parts of rhetoric as Cicero did for the structure of his book on teaching others to do oration.[90] He utilizes three books to explain the styles in rhetoric.[91] Quintilian prefers ornament to the other three virtues for a speech namely speaking correctly, speaking clearly, and appropriateness.[92] He sees that ornament with elegance in a speech is a powerful and sharpened weapon, not just to convince the professional critics but also the public.[93] He explains that while ornament in a speech gives audience a sense of pleasure, it draws their attention away with an unexpected strike.[94] Instead of being just about beauty and elegance, ornament needs to be useful.[95] However, he points out that the same kind of ornament may not be useful to each type of rhetoric.[96] In other words, each kind of rhetoric has its specific ornament. It is less about making decoration and more about powerfully attracting the audience into the speech.

---

the language, while figures of thought look for distinction from the idea.

87. Cicero *Rhet. Her.* 4.31.42–4.34.46. The ten figures of diction that Cicero groups together are onomatopeia, antonomasia, metonymy, periphrasis, hyperbaton, hyperbole, synecdoche, catachresis, metaphor, and allegory.

88. Cicero *Rhet. Her.* 4.31.42.

89. Cicero *Rhet. Her.* 4.34.46.

90. Quintilian *Inst.* 3.3.1–3. Cicero *Rhet. Her.* 1.2.3. From 1.1–3.5, Quintilian gives detailed guidance on how to train someone to be an orator beginning from childhood.

91. Quintilian *Inst.* 8–10

92. Quintilian *Inst.* 8.3.1; 11:1.

93. Quintilian *Inst.* 8.3.2.

94. Quintilian *Inst.* 8.3.5.

95. Quintilian *Inst.* 8.3.7, 11.

96. Quintilian *Inst.* 8.3.11.

Evaluation of the Categorization of Jülicher

The style of speech in the parables of Jesus is somewhat similar. Like the Rich Fool, someone came to Jesus for help in dividing inheritance with his brother (Luke 12:13). Not only was the initial response of Jesus refusal, but also he built a parable story at the scene about a certain rich fool (Luke 12:14). At the end of the parable, God told the rich fool that his soul would be required from him that night (Luke 12:20). Jesus continued, "In this way is the one who stores up treasure for himself and is not rich toward God" (Luke 12:21). Instead of something that the listeners of Jesus like to hear, his story drew them in while giving them a punch at the end.

Under the systematic categorization of rhetoric of Quintilian, he further divides the virtue of ornament by single words, groups of words, magnifying and minifying, the expression of sentiment, and tropes and figures.[97] Instead of grouping tropes under figures like Cicero, Quintilian separates the two.[98] He defines a trope as transference of meaning from what the expression of a language originally meant for a good purpose.[99] Instead of restricting it to the substitution of one word for another, a trope indeed can help in expression of meaning and ornament.[100] The corresponding relationship can occur between contexts from one that is usual to one that may not be normally used.[101] Among the tropes he mentions, Quintilian finds that allegory and hyperbole place emphasis on both the words and the things.[102] In other words, instead of just substitution of words, the things or contexts being transferred from one to another are also very important in allegory and hyperbole. He describes several types of allegory and irony,[103] which can be arranged on a gradient from explicit to implicit in expression in transference. The gradient is credited to Quintilian in chapter 1.

Jewish Rhetoric Period

Concerning the use of parables for public teaching among the Jews, it is easier to find parables being used. However, written instruction for such use is not so clear. Parables are found as early as OT. Most of them are

---

97. Quintilian *Inst.* 8.3.15, 8.5.1, 8.6.1; 9.1.1.
98. Quintilian *Inst.* 9.1.7, 11, 16.
99. Quintilian *Inst.* 8.6.1; 9.1.4.
100. Quintilian *Inst.* 8.6.3.
101. Quintilian *Inst.* 9.1.4.
102. Quintilian *Inst.* 9.1.5; 8.6.2–76.
103. Quintilian *Inst.* 8.6.44–59.

PART II: ON EXAMPLE STORIES

used as proverbs (1 Sam 24:13; Ps 49:4; Prov 1:6; Jer 24:9; Ezek 12:22; Mic 2:4; Hab 2:6), with the exception that in Numbers, parables are referred to as oracles (Num 23:7–10, 18–24). On several occasions, parables are used as allegorical stories with explanation provided (Ezek 17; 24:1–14). The speech of Nathan to David is a typical parable although the word "parable" is not found in the story. Using a story of how a rich man coveted and took away the lamb of a poor man, Nathan has successfully baited David into a mindset of bringing justice (2 Sam 12:1–6). However, at the end, he pointed the story back to David on the sin that he committed in secret (2 Sam 12:7). The story is transferred to the context of what the Lord wanted to tell David through Nathan (2 Sam 12:8–14). The parable story is an allegory with explanation.

Within the Second Temple period, parables are mostly used as proverbs or bywords (Tob 3:4; Sir 1:25, 13:26; Wis 5:4). There are several long sections of parables found in 1 Enoch 37–71. Even though they are called parables, these writings are addressed as "visions" that were produced by an unknown author written about future judgment.[104] However, these materials are better considered as a collection of thoughts instead of actual visions. As Nickelsburg points out, some sections in the parables of 1 Enoch are interpretation of Daniel 7, while other sections are interpolations of the first book of 1 Enoch.[105]

Although the use of parables can be found from Jewish to Greco-Romans literature, the writings of Cicero and Quintilian apparently give a more comprehensive description about matters of oration. Instead of just a public saying, rhetoric demands the good virtue of the speaker as well as the speech content. The teachings of Jesus obviously meet the requirement of rhetoric. Indeed, there are numerous types of rhetoric and each type carries a unique style. The problem in the past has been that the parables of Jesus

---

104. 1 *En.* 37.1–4; 38; 68.1. According to the author of 1 *En.* 37–71, he received these parables from his grandfather. However, "vision" in 1 *En* 83–90 is an allegorization of Jewish history from the flood to Maccabean period. As information about the time lap between 1 *En* 37–71 and 1 *En* 83–90 is lacking and the identity of their authors are uncertain, it is better treating these materials with carefulness. At best, they are some thoughts or wishes of people during that period. However, they do not have the equivalence of prophecy as Scriptures do though they are termed as "visions" or claimed to be from the Lord of the spirits.

105. Nickelsburg and VanderKam, 1 *Enoch* 2, 13. Nickelsburg points out the similarities between 1 *En.* 46–47 and Dan 7. In 1 *En.* 46, Enoch sees the Son of Man ready to judge the kings and the mighty. 1 *En.* 47 is also like a combination of the angelic prayer from 1 *En.* 9 and the heavenly court scene from Dan 7.

are associated too quickly with Aristotle's system of inductive proof. Such an approach on categorization only brings confusion when it comes to the varieties of styles in narrative and allegory in the parable speech of Jesus. Thus, it is more appropriate to categorize his parables by using the styles in his speech rather than simply fitting them into any known system. The ornament that is most featured in the parables of Jesus is allegory. By using transference of contexts in allegory explicitly and implicitly, Jesus makes his narrative stories alive. This is why his parables are better categorized with a spectrum of allegory as set forth in chapter 3.

Conclusion

After an in-depth critique of Jülicher's categorization, it shows a better picture of the problems in his parable theory. A major blow to his theory is found in his confusing concept of "sameness" in the definition of example stories. While he looks intensely for explicit comparison between earthly and heavenly realms in a parable, he neglects that referential relationship can occur between contexts of a story and a subject matter regardless of whether they are both from the "same" area. The comparison or better transference indeed occurs in example stories implicitly. Transference from the same area is not equivalent to identical, nor a reason to categorize a story as an example.

The hidden issue is less about whether these stories are examples or not, and more about how they express a different style of comparison. By reading explicit comparison between heavenly and earthly realms into implicit comparison, Jülicher misidentifies these parables as examples with no comparative feature. From the consideration of example stories as having no comparison to the acceptance that they contain some, he moves example stories back to be parables. However, the comparison he sees in example stories is a reader's approach instead of author's intended. By allowing the audience to read their own comparison into the parables while insisting that the author does not make comparison, Jülicher creates a huge confusion on what he considers as comparison. Obviously, comparison by reader's approach cannot be counted as the comparison from the author. The actual problem is that Jülicher has not found the comparison made by the author. If a narrative parable is allegorically implicit about its proposition, the story becomes just an example to Jülicher. Calling a group of narrative parables as "example stories" out of the misunderstanding of their implicit style of allegorical transference toward their subject matters is improper. A better option would be to rename or dissolve the category, example stories, for regrouping.

In reality, the term "example stories" does not correctly describe this group at all, nor does it help to distinguish it from the other two categories, *Gleichinisse* and *Parabeln*, owing to their example nature under Aristotle's inductive system. When implicitness is in view, Jülicher's three parable categories appear shortage of homogeneousness. Implicitness in expressing the subject matters in parable stories does affect the grouping of the categories of Jülicher. If implicit transference is the real concern that causes difficulty in categorization, instead of renaming "example stories" to continue with the fracturing system of Jülicher, it is better to regroup all parables of Jesus with a new categorization. After all, Aristotle's system that is mainly for logical persuasion cannot help to distinguish the complexity of comparisons and narrative in the parables of Jesus. The inductive examples of Aristotle may not be the best system for the categorization of the parables of Jesus. In view of all these, the parable categorization of Jülicher is better discarded. Regrouping the parables of Jesus under a new categorization becomes necessary.

Therefore, it is preferable to focus on Jesus's style of rhetoric for setting up a new parable categorization. The use of allegory as ornament in his parable teaching marks the distinctive feature of his speech. While his parable speech attracts the audience into a story, it punches them right at the spot. Arranging his parables with gradation of allegory, which I name as Allegorical Spectrum of the Parables of Jesus, thus gives a better platform for the expression of transference style of each parable.

7

Interpreting Allegory in Parables

With the finding of allegory in the parables of Jesus expressed in gradation of implicitness together with the problems that are found in Jülicher's parable categories, especially example stories, the insufficiency of the parable categorization of Jülicher is shown prominently. I want to use the new allegorical model developed in chapter 3, Allegorical Spectrum of the Parables of Jesus, to demonstrate how to interpret allegory in parables. I will first explore hermeneutic guidelines in the current chapter for understanding allegorical features in parables. Afterward, I will demonstrate with two parables in the next chapter. The primary purpose is to show allegorical transference instead of providing full scale interpretation of the parables.

Hermeneutic Guidelines

The basic concern in handling allegory accurately in parables is no different from interpreting other passages. The priority is reading the whole parable carefully. Klyne Snodgrass suggests that inserting personal opinion or theological concern to the "form or meaning" of a text is not allowed.[1] Although there are allegorical features in many parables as illustrated in chapter 3, this does not give permission to treat every part of a passage as a metaphor or an allegory. Snodgrass recommends that "knowing when to stop interpreting" and paying attention to the "significance" of the correspondence are important.[2] The temptation of interpreters is either reading too many metaphorical referents into a passage or reading too little as if

---

1. Snodgrass, *Stories with Intent*, 25.
2. Ibid., 27–28.

every parable only had a very condensed single point. A parable indeed can have more than one point or theme.³ If an allegory is explained in a parable, interpretation is easy. When the explanation of an allegory in a parable is implicit, this is the real work of interpretation. Therefore, getting the right balance regarding allegorical content in a parable is essential so that the teaching points or themes according to the author's intention will not be missed nor any foreign idea may be added into the passage.

The following guidelines are not comprehensive but they are the essentials in handling allegory in a parable. Being a trope, allegory is the transference of one thing or a context in words to another thing or another context in meaning without limiting this to the substitution of words.⁴ In an allegory, image giver refers to the image giving field, which can be a character, an action, or the story as a whole.⁵ On the other hand, image receiver refers to the image receiving field in an allegory, which can be a theme, a subject matter, or abstract element such as thought or feeling.⁶ What we look for in interpreting allegory in a parable is truly about the transference of contexts between image giver and image receiver.

Context

Reading a Parable as a Whole

The first place to look into a parable, however, is never its allegorical correspondence. Snodgrass suggests that it is rather to read a parable as a whole.⁷ He points out that being overly concerned about looking for correspondences in a parable will result in missing "the force" of it.⁸ E. J. Tinsley puts it this way, "Where the details or characters really are separate from

---

3. Ibid., 29, 26. Snodgrass suggests that the limit on one point for each parable does not work. Blomberg, *Interpreting the Parables*, 165. Blomberg points out that each parable has only one point is misleading. Ryken, *How to Read the Bible as Literature*, 149. Ryken proposes that the one-point rule of each parable is extremely arbitrary.

4. Quintilian *Inst.* 8.6.1–3, 44; 9.1.4.

5. Weinrich, *Sprache in Texten*, 284. Hough, "The Allegorical Circle," 203. Lewis, *The Allegory of Love*, 44–45. Ryken, *How to Read the Bible as Literature*, 147.

6. Weinrich, *Sprache in Texten*, 284. Hough, "The Allegorical Circle," 203. Lewis, *The Allegory of Love*, 44–45.

7. Snodgrass, *Stories with Intent*, 26.

8. Ibid., 27.

the main plot is an allegory that has broken down."[9] In other words, good allegory is difficult to be located owing to its cohesiveness with the drama. Moreover, instead of fragmenting a parable for allegorical referents, a parable should be read as a whole during the interpretation process.

If a parable should be read as a whole, what should be the focus and how should the details in it be handled? In the Good Samaritan, even though the parable starts at verse 30, the discussion begins at verse 25. A lawyer wanted to test Jesus about how to inherit eternal life (Luke 10:25). Jesus asked him what the Torah said and how he interpreted the passage (Luke 10:26). The lawyer replied with Deut 6:5 and Lev 19:18 concerning loving God and neighbor (Luke 10:27). As the lawyer wanted to justify himself, he asked Jesus who his neighbor was (Luke 10:29). So Jesus used the Good Samaritan to teach a lesson (Luke 10:30–37). At the end, Jesus asked the lawyer which person was a neighbor to the man who was robbed (Luke 10:36). The lawyer replied, "The one who showed mercy to him" (Luke 10:37). The interpretative hint is located implicitly at the end of the story echoing with the question that the lawyer asks Jesus in verse 29. However, if the question "who is my neighbor" at verse 29 is missed, the context of the theme or explanation at the end will not be easily understood.

Handling the Details Properly

Some parables are longer than others and in story-style. Leland Ryken recommends reading them according to their characteristics as stories namely their setting, their characters, and their plots from conflict to solution.[10] The physical setting in the Good Samaritan is about a man going down from Jerusalem to Jericho (Luke 10:30). Questions may arise such as why the text said going down? Geographically, Jerusalem was on Temple Mount while Jericho was at the exit of a wadi during NT times.[11] This explains why the text says that he went down. Or, which route did the man take?[12] While a lot of information can be discovered in this way, it contributes only slightly to the understanding of the context. However, it makes no difference to the meaning of the story, namely who one's neighbor is (Luke 10:29,

---

9. Tinsley, "Parable, Allegory and Mysticism," 177–78.
10. Ryken, *How to Read the Bible as Literature*, 139, 35.
11. Lancaster and Monson, *Regional Study Guide*, 80–81.
12. Ibid., 81. There is a route located between Jerusalem and Jericho called Ascent of Adummim. Could this route be used by the man who was robbed on the way to Jericho?

36–37). Craig L. Blomberg suggests that not "every detail in the parables must stand for something" as they just help to develop the stories.[13] Snodgrass proposes that the details may not be referential but they communicate "significance."[14] Blomberg and Snodgrass are indeed speaking similarly in that details of a parable should not be missed in the interpretation process. However, neither should details be over interpreted into allegories. Therefore, while reading a parable as a whole, the details in it should be addressed properly during interpretation.

Instead of treating each detail separately for its correspondence, it is better to screen for those that can help in understanding the development of a story. In the Pharisee and Tax Collector, several significances or sub-points can be found in the contrast of the characters. A Pharisee prayed to himself by telling God how upright he was in comparison with other sinners (Luke 18:11). A tax collector, on the other hand, admitted that he was a sinner and asked God for mercy (Luke 18:13). The Pharisee stood in the temple to pray while the tax collector stood at some distance unwilling to lift up his eyes to heaven (Luke 18:10–11, 13). The theme of the parable is stated in the beginning and at the end. The parable speaks to those who are self-righteous and look down on others. Its theme is "everyone who exalts himself will be humbled, but the one who humbles himself will be exalted" (Luke 18:9, 14). The details such as the points of contrast are not the theme but they are sub-points in developing the main theme in this story.

Surrounding Context

A parable does not always occur suddenly in a passage. Usually, the surrounding context explains why a parable is spoken.[15] Particularly, the preceding context gives readers the setting concerning where the teaching of Jesus or conversation with his audience begins. Surrounding context is a great help in understanding a simple parable such as the proverbial statement "Physician, heal yourself" in Luke 4:23. The narrative of this statement actually begins at verse 16. Jesus went to his home town and read Isaiah 61:1–2 in the synagogue (Luke 4:16–20). When every eye looked at him, he declared himself to be the Anointed One bringing the fulfillment of this passage (Luke 4:21). Although they spoke well of him, they looked down

---

13. Blomberg, *Interpreting the Parables*, 68.
14. Snodgrass, *Stories with Intent*, 27.
15. Ryken, *How to Read the Bible as Literature*, 148.

Interpreting Allegory in Parables

on him to be the son of Joseph (Luke 4:22). Using their parable "Physician, heal yourself" which they quoted to him to ask for his healing work in his hometown as what he did in Capernaum, Jesus responded that no prophet would be welcomed in his hometown (Luke 4:23–24). Then, he used the events of Elijah being sent to a widow in Sidon and Elisha's healing of a Syrian leper to illustrate to his audience the severity of his rejection by his own people (Luke 4:25–27). That is, miraculous works would be more beneficial to gentiles than to his people who asked for such things but disbelieved. After listening to this, his audience immediately got mad and attempted to throw him down the cliff (Luke 4:28–30). Thus, even with a simple statement style of parable, reading the parable as a whole should be extended to the whole narrative or the surrounding context of a parable.

Hints of Allegory

While interpretation of a parable begins with the context, it is also continued with the context. As mentioned above, it is difficult to locate a good allegory in a parable. However, how should allegory be interpreted in a parable? To say that one should not look for allegory everywhere is indeed not to predetermine any image giver, such as a character or an action, is an allegory when the text has no indication of it. However, allegories do exist in parables and they are expressed either explicitly or implicitly, or both. How to grasp the author's intended allegorical transference accurately between the contexts of image giver and image receiver in a parable is the real concern in interpretation.

Fusion

Explicit Allegory

Fusion is a term modified from the allegorical circle of Graham Hough, which refers to the implicit relationship between image (image giver) and theme (image receiver).[16] In the case of explicit allegory, image giver and image receiver are not fused. In fact, the image receiver or "allegorical significance" is explicitly indicated in the context.[17] That is, explanation (im-

---

16. Hough, "The Allegorical Circle," 204–5. Tinsley, "Parable, Allegory and Mysticism," 176.

17. Eggen, *Gleichnis, Allegorie, Metapher*, 300. Kurz, *Metapher, Allegorie, Symbol*, 43.

age receiver) of the image giver can be clearly found in a parable. If simile or similitude is used, the relationship between image giver and image receiver is an obvious comparison.[18] Simile or similitude in explicit allegory is usually indicated with words such as ὡς (as), καθώς or ὥσπερ (just as), ὅμοιος (like), or ὁμοιόω (is compared to). In the Leaven, the context of subject matter (image receiver) namely the kingdom of God (Luke 13:20) is compared to the context of image giver regarding the extensiveness of the activity of leaven in three measures of flour (Luke 13:21). If a metaphor is used, the image giver directly refers to the image receiver. At times, the image receiver of the image giver is clearly explained in the context. In the parable of Defilement, the context of the image giver deals with what really defiles a person comes from inside instead of entering from outside (Mark 7:15). Jesus was speaking in response to the challenge of Pharisees and scribes concerning his disciples who violated the tradition by eating bread with impure hands (Mark 7:5). The context of image receiver of the parable is explained right afterward (Mark 7:17). Things from outside cannot get into one's heart but it goes into the stomach and is then eliminated (Mark 7:18–19). Rather, things from inside, such as evil thoughts, fornications, thefts, murders, adulteries, coveting, wickedness, deceits, debauchery, envy, slander, pride, and foolishness are what really defile a person (Mark 7:20–23). In other words, cleanness is inner matter. Additionally, image receiver in explicit allegory can also be expressed with teaching points. In the Wheat and Weeds, there are several pairs of allegorical transferences. One of the image givers is the one who sows the good seed and its corresponding image receiver is the Son of Man (Matt 13:37). The field (image giver) is the world (image receiver) (Matt 13:38). "The good seed" (image giver) are the sons of the kingdom (image receivers), while the tares (image givers) are the sons of the evil one (image receivers) (Matt 13:38). The enemy (image giver) is the devil (image receiver), while the reapers (image givers) are the angels (image receivers) sent by the Son of Man at the end times to get rid of all those who are lawless (Matt 13:39–42). In general, in explicit allegory, an image receiver of the image giver in a parable is clearly indicated in the context.

Kubczak, *Die Metapher*, 69. In case of explicit metaphor, x and y are both present in the formula "x is like y to z."

18. Quintilian *Inst.* 8.6.9. While one thing "is compared with" another in a simile or a similitude, one thing "is" another in a metaphor.

Interpreting Allegory in Parables

Implicit Allegory

In contrast to explicit allegory, image giver and image receiver are either partially or completely fused in implicit allegory. Image (image giver) and theme (image receiver) form such a tight unit in implicit allegory that they will not be easily detached from the plot of a story.[19] In other words, when image giver and image receiver are fused, the image giver tries to make a good story while the image receiver (theme or explanation) remains unclear or silent as to form a tight unit with the image giver in the story. When the image giver is given while image receiver is not obvious, the context of a parable remains as the primary source for identifying the image receiver.[20] Carefulness in looking for hints from the context for explaining the image receiver of the image giver is necessary. Sometimes, hints can be found at the end of a parable.[21] In the Wedding Feast, the theme (image receiver) is found in the ending statement, "For many are called, but few are chosen" (Matt 22:14). Hints can also be located in the beginning of the stories. In the Unjust Judge, the image receiver or theme is found in the beginning of the parable that people should pray at all times and not lose heart (Luke 18:1). Moreover, hints for the image receiver or theme can be found in an answer to a question as in the Good Samaritan (Luke 10:29, 36–37). At times, hints occur in repeating phrases. In the Prodigal Son, the image receiver or theme is located both at Luke 15:24 and 32 in slightly different wordings, "This son of mine was dead and he is alive, and he was lost and he is found." However, the image receiver is not stated completely in this parable. Some supporting hints related to the Prodigal Son can be found in the preceding two parables, the Lost Sheep and the Lost Coin. It is a great joy to the father when a son truly repents from sin as opposed to a son who does not need repentance (Luke 15:31–32, 7, 10). Hints can also be found in the responses of Jesus to some situations presented in the scenes. In the Rich Fool, someone came to Jesus asking him to help in dividing inheritance with his brother (Luke 12:13). In response to this request, Jesus spoke a parable (Luke 12:14). The whole parable of a rich fool is the image giver (Luke 12:16–20). The theme (image receiver) is found in the beginning and at the end of the parable (Luke 12:15, 21). Life does not consist in how much one has because one can still be poor to God by storing up

---

19. Tinsley, "Parable, Allegory and Mysticism," 176–78.
20. Eggen, *Gleichnis, Allegorie, Metapher*, 300.
21. Weiss, "Ueber das Bildliche," 324–25.

PART II: ON EXAMPLE STORIES

possession. At times, no hint regarding the image receiver can be located in a parable such as the Barren Fig Tree (Luke 13:6–9). Therefore, in interpreting implicit allegory, hints from the context can help in identifying an image receiver that is stated either indirectly or incompletely, or that may even be missed in the explanation.

Drama

A good allegory is indeed a good drama in that image giver and image receiver are in dramatic coherence so that the story will not be broken down by metaphorical referents.[22] In other words, a story from a good allegory is fluent instead of being fragmented by the explanation of metaphors. Like the Seed, the image receivers or themes are explicitly explained with farming conditions after a seed is sowed (image givers) (Luke 8:11–15). However, the parable looks more like teaching points instead of a good story. On the contrary, some parables are good stories such as the Rich Man and Lazarus (Luke 16:19–31), the Big Feast (Luke 14:12–24), and the Barren Fig Tree (Luke 13:6–9). The image givers run so fluently in these parables that their image receivers or themes cannot be easily identified.

The tendency of interpreters is to over interpret a good allegory in a parable into many allegories instead of reading the story according to its flow. In the Wicked Tenants, the story as a whole is an image giver but the theme (image receiver) is indirect. Without the hints in the middle and at the end concerning the reaction of the scribes and chief priests (Luke 20:16, 19), the image receiver could turn out to be various things from Christology to Soteriology. However, the story needs to be read carefully. Before Jesus told the Wicked Tenants, he was confronted and was challenged by the scribes and the elders in the temple concerning his authority to teach (Luke 20:1–8). Therefore, the Wicked Tenants was spoken to the religious leaders as a consequence of their escalation in rejecting God. Thus, the primary protagonists are the wicked tenants in the story. However, with the quotation from Psalm 118:22, the second half of the story turns to the rejected stone (Luke 20:17–18). If the wicked tenants are the religious leaders, the son and the stone being rejected are implicitly referring to Jesus himself in the context. However, which one of them, or perhaps even both, should be considered as an image giver or image givers in the parable? Blomberg states it this way, "In any lengthy allegory a sizable majority of the details

---

22. Tinsley, "Parable, Allegory and Mysticism," 178.

do not have double meanings; only a few key elements do."[23] Thus, not everything in a parable needs to refer to something nor be considered as an allegory.

Understanding the flow of a story in a parable is necessary as this is what a good allegory means. Paying attention to things in a story such as settings, characters, and the plot, can help in grasping a story tightly.[24] Blomberg suggests that the main characters are associated with its main points or themes.[25] However, Snodgrass disagrees with "one point per main character" and he recommends letting the context to present as many points as it has.[26] If a parable story is built around an important character or two, Blomberg and Snodgrass have no contradiction with each other regarding the proportional relationship between the number of characters and the points in a parable. In the Wicked Tenants, a major theme or image receiver is built around the wicked tenants (image givers) concerning the rejection of God by the religious leaders (Luke 20:10–15). A sub-theme or image receiver is implicitly located at the end in that Jesus himself is the rejected stone, which will become the chief corner stone (image giver) causing the fall of the religious leaders (Luke 20:17–18).

However, if a parable does not have any specific hint or description about a character, its theme or image receiver may not be dependent on the character. As in the Lost Coin, nothing was told about the woman who had ten coins but looked for the one coin she lost. The image giver is rather her actions from searching for a lost coin desperately to the joy of finding it (Luke 15:8–9). The image receiver or theme is stated at the end that the angels of God will express the same kind of joy when one sinner repents (Luke 15:10). Nothing significant about the woman is told in this parable. A similar example is found in the Leaven. The brief parable has nothing to say about the woman except what she has done with the flour (Luke 13:20–21). The theme of the parable states explicitly in verse 20. The effect of a little bit of leaven on three measures of flour is compared with the extensive

---

23. Blomberg, *Interpreting the Parables*, 52.

24. Ryken, *How to Read the Bible as Literature*, 35–38, 40–41, 43, 52–54. According to Ryken, the actions, responses, or sayings can help in understanding the characters in a story. This also includes the direct descriptions from the narrator. Conflict, contrast, and changes in the events of a plot as well as among characters are also important things in a story.

25. Blomberg, *Interpreting the Parables*, 166.

26. Snodgrass, *Stories with Intent*, 28.

outcome of the kingdom of God.²⁷ Basically, the woman can be replaced by anyone. Even if the Leaven does not have any character, the parable will be unaffected. Thus, using characters to look for themes or image receivers that are implicit may not work in some parables.

In general, observation for story or drama elements such as characters and plot in a narrative will help to identify interpretative hints. However, which image receiver (theme) is referred to by the image giver in a good and implicitly expressed allegory in a parable should be decided by how a story is told in the context.

Dominant Image

A lot of parables indeed contain several images. Which should be considered as the image giver or image givers that can lead to the theme or themes (image receivers)? Not only is the image receiver not easily found when it is cohesive with the image giver in a good allegory, but also such an allegory connects with the details to become "the motor force of the whole."²⁸ That is, a way to determine the dominant image for allegorical transference in a parable is by observing which image giver is the backbone of the whole story. Such an image giver connects with most of the details and leads through the entire parable story. In the Seed, which image is the dominant image, the seed or the sower? The sower is only mentioned in verse 5 while the conditions of the seed in the soil are described all through the parable (Luke 8:5–8, 11–15). Thus, the dominant image giver is the seed instead of the sower. However, the story is not a smooth one as it is broken up by the explanation (image receiver) for the image giver. Some image givers use the whole parables to express the theme. As in the Good Samaritan, the image receiver (theme) cannot be fully described by any image giver in the story such as the man being robbed, the priest, the Levite, and the Samaritan. Rather, the contrast in what these characters do to the man in a miserable situation explains what a neighbor truly means. That is, without the differences among the actions of the characters, the concept of "one who shows mercy is a true neighbor" can be very plain. The whole story is an image giver instead of the details in response to the idea of neighbor (Luke 10:29, 36–37). Thus, the dominant image giver can be the whole story or a small

---

27. BDAG, s.v. "σάτον." Three measures (σάτα τρία) are about thirty-five liters.
28. Tinsley, "Parable, Allegory and Mysticism," 178.

Interpreting Allegory in Parables

element in the parable depending on which image leads through the entire parable story.

Synoptic Comparison

If a parable occurs in more than one gospel, it is a great source to look for additional hints for interpreting the allegorical transference. Snodgrass recommends a "comparative analysis of the various accounts."[29] The differences among the synoptic indeed help to show the same event from various angles. It is just like watching the same event of a traffic accident from different news channels. Reporters choose what they think as significant to report to the public, but their reports are hardly the same or in exact wordings. Comparison among the synoptic of a parable is particularly helpful in identifying hints for interpretation. Indeed, if a parable occurs in all three gospels or even just two, rarely will one of them contain allegorical content while the other does not. As in the parable of Thief and Stewardship, both Luke and Matthew have the image giver of the sudden coming of a thief that is implicitly referred to the unexpected timing of the return of the Son of Man, the image receiver (Luke 12:39–48; Matt 24:43–51). The differences among the synoptic concerning the same parable is just a matter of details. Matthew, Mark, and Luke all contain the scene about Jesus being confronted and challenged by religious leaders in the temple right before the Wicked Tenants (Matt 21:23–27; Mark 11:27–33; Luke 20:1–8). However, only Matthew places the parable of Two Sons between the conflict of Jesus with religious leaders and the parable of Wicked Tenants (Matt 21:28–32). Matthew provides more information about the problem of the religious leaders in that they do not do the will of God though they say that they do (Matt 21:30–32). Thus, by examining a parable in each of the synoptic, it gives more understanding to a story from different perspectives.

However, there are parables that look alike but they are actually different. Not only can a parable be reused at different occasions, but also a story can be modified for teaching purposes. Although the Big Feast and the Wedding Feast (Luke 14:12–24; Matt 22:1–14) look similar such as the readiness of a feast and the declined attendance of the original guests, the context and some of the details show that these two parables are probably two different accounts. The setting for the Big Feast is at a house of a Pharisee on a Sabbath (Luke 14:1). Indeed, the Big Feast is arranged earlier

---

29. Snodgrass, *Stories with Intent*, 25.

in time than the Wicked Tenants in Luke. However, the Wedding Feast is located after the Wicked Tenants in Matthew (Matt 21:44—22:1). The Wedding Feast is also more specific in that the feast is arranged by a king and it is a wedding feast for his son (Matt 22:1–2). On the other hand, the Big Feast in Luke 14 is non-specific. The servants are ill-treated by the declined guests in the Wedding Feast (Matt 22:6), but that is not the case of the servant in the Big Feast. The second group of guests is different too. Those in Matthew's parable can be good or evil (Matt 22:10), but the second group of guests in Luke's parable are mostly the poor (Luke 14:21). Thus, it is necessary to carefully make the comparison among the synoptic to avoid considering similar stories as the same event for interpretative hints. However, if a parable does occur in more than one gospel, the differences of the same account enrich the understanding of the parable.

Background

Ryken suggests paying attention to those details that carry meaning in the OT such as God as a vineyard owner or a father who forgives.[30] Snodgrass also recommends that "ideas and metaphors from the OT and Jewish religious life" are helpful sources.[31] He emphasizes that interpretation needs to "breathe the air of the first century."[32] In other words, anything from the OT to the first century that is related to the Jewish people, such as thought and belief, life style, religious practice, cultural setting including Greco-Roman influence, and history can be used to enrich the understanding of the background of a parable. Early materials after first century can be a help too if they reflect the situation of parables in Jesus times. However, it is necessary to beware of the differences in their contexts to avoid reading anachronically their contexts into those parables of Jesus. Like the Prodigal Son, there is a slight similarity with a parable in rabbinic literature concerning a prince returning to his father (*Pesiq. Rab.* 44.9). The prince was complaining in front of his friend about his lack of strength to go back. However, his father sent word to encourage him to come as far as he could and he would meet with him there and return with him on the rest of the journey. This was a rabbinic interpretation of Mal 3:7, "Return to Me, and I will return to you." The explanation provided by rabbinic literature is

---

30. Ryken, *How to Read the Bible as Literature*, 148–49.
31. Snodgrass, *Stories with Intent*, 25.
32. Ibid.

similar to the father in the Prodigal Son (Luke 15:20). While the prodigal son was still very far away, his father saw him and felt compassion for him. Then, he ran, embraced, and kissed him. However, the context of Mal 3:7 was really about the unfaithfulness of Israel and Judah and the Lord's urging them to return to him, while the prodigal son in Luke repented and returned to his father's place. Thus, it is necessary to explore the contexts of the background materials when they are used in interpreting a parable. It is important to make decision regarding at what point the background material is similar to as well as different from the context of the parable.

To summarize, context is the beginning point and the continuation of the interpretation of a parable. Not only should a parable be read as a whole, but also the surrounding context in the narrative needs to be included. A good balance in reading the details is necessary so that the significant points related to the development of the theme or themes of a parable can be determined. Concerning hints for interpretation, image giver and image receiver are clearly indicated in the context of explicit allegory. However, fusion in implicit allegory causes only image giver to be seen while image receiver is either indirectly or incompletely stated, or missing from the context totally. As a good allegory is drama-like, story elements such as characters and plot are helpful in identifying interpretative hints. However, these narrative elements will not necessarily make allegorical transference. How a story is told determines what an image receiver (theme) of an image giver (image) is in a difficult allegory. Although a parable story can have many images, not all of them are image receivers. Only the one that leads through the whole story is the dominant image giver for the image receiver. However, instead of being just a part in a story, a dominant image giver can at times be the whole story. However, a parable does not need to be limited to one theme only. Additionally, synoptic gospels are great places for interpretative hints. If a parable occurs in more than one gospel, the differences of the same parable account provide more information for interpretation. Background materials from the OT to the first century that depict the life of Jewish people can also help in understanding the situation in a parable. However, being sensitive to the similarity and difference between the contexts of background materials and a parable will further facilitate the interpretation process.

8

Application of Allegorical Spectrum

THE FOLLOWING WILL BE an application of the Allegorical Spectrum of the Parables of Jesus. Parables are arranged according to the points on the spectrum from the most allegorical to the least: implicit-drama major (eight points), implicit-complex drama (seven points), implicit-simple drama (six points), implicit medium (five points), implicit-explicit mixed (four points), implicit-short analogy (three points), explanatory-illustrative story (two points), explanatory-point (one point), and explanatory-brief (zero points). Allegorical transference of two of the most allegorical categories, implicit-drama major and implicit-complex drama, will be illustrated with parables.

Rich Man and Lazarus (Luke 16:19–31)

The Rich Man and Lazarus is one of the most difficult and allegorical parables. Neither does the surrounding context help in understanding the transition from the previous speech to the parable, nor is any parallel description available from synoptic for additional interpretative hint. The preceding context of the Rich Man and Lazarus is a collection of various topics, such as a warning against the love of money, the eternity of the word of God, and the issue of divorce (Luke 16:13–18).

The drama of the Rich Man and Lazarus contains two major parts. The first part began with two men. One was really rich while the other was extremely poor (Luke 16:19–21). They both died. Afterward, the poor man was carried by angels to the bosom of Abraham, while the rich man was in torment in Hades (Luke 16:22–23). The first round of dialogue occurred between Abraham and the rich man. The rich man asked Abraham to send Lazarus to him so that Lazarus could help in cooling his tongue (Luke 16:24). However, Abraham declined his request for two reasons. One of the reasons was that the rich man received good things in life but Lazarus got bad things. So after death, Lazarus was comforted while the rich man was in agony (Luke 16:25). The second reason for rejecting the request of the rich man to send Lazarus to him was that they were separated by a chasm that nobody could cross (Luke 16:26). The plot proceeded to the second major part of the story. It was comprised of another round of dialogue between Abraham and the rich man. The rich man changed his request. He asks if Lazarus can be sent to his father's house to give a warning to his five brothers so that they would not go to Hades like himself (Luke 16:27–28). However, Abraham suggested that they listened to Moses and the Prophets (Luke 16:29). The rich man pressed further as he believed a warning given by someone from the dead might convince his brothers to repent (Luke 16:30). However, Abraham replies that if the brothers of the rich man do not listen to Moses and the Prophets, they will be hardly convinced by someone who rises from the dead (Luke 16:31).

Although there are some interesting discussions regarding parallel stories to the Rich Man and Lazarus as background for understanding, those stories are indeed very different. L. W. Grensted associates the bosom of Abraham in Luke with the corner for the righteous in 1 *En* 22, and the great chasm in Luke with the separation between the righteous and the unrighteous at the corners in 1 *En.* 22.[1] However, among the four corners for the dead in 1 *En.* 22, it includes the one for the righteous waiting for the vindication of judgment (1 *En.* 22.2, 9–11). In addition, the voices of children who died can reach out to heaven from one of the dark corners (1 *En.* 22.5–6). It does say that these four corners in 1 *En.* 22 are somewhere but unlikely to be heaven. However, Lazarus in Luke is sent to the bosom of Abraham by angels and he receives comfort immediately instead of waiting for the judgment day for vindication. The bosom of Abraham does not look like any of the corners described in 1 *En.* 22.

The description in 4 *Ezra* 7.36, 80–99 is indeed slightly closer to the current parable. Those who disobey the Law have no place for rest and a pit for torment is ready for them, while the righteous ones are at the place of rest in paradise guarded by angels to wait for the final glory. Indeed, Snodgrass points out that within the literature of Judaism and Greek, the location for

---

1. Grensted, "The Use of Enoch," 334.

receiving punishment and reward can be both in heaven or both in Hades.[2] He also suggests that the use of ᾅδης (Hades) and γέεννα (Gehenna) are not specific enough to discern their differences in NT.[3] However, the story in Luke does not give much information about the condition of a person who has died and this does not seem to be the focus of the story.

Another parallel account is an Egyptian story about the reversal of fortunes after death.[4] Indeed, similar story can be also found in later Jewish material (*y. Sanh.* 6.6) in which the rich who was buried nicely was under torment in hell while the poor who died without receiving a formal burial was in paradise. Although the fates of the rich man and Lazarus in Luke are reversed after death, no burial is mentioned in the passage. Instead of carrying on the point about reversal of fate after death, the story in Luke develops into a different direction. The real question is how many of the details of the parable should receive attention so that the theme or themes (image receivers) of the parable can be concretely grasped.

What is the dominant image giver that is leading through the Rich Man and Lazarus that can help in understanding the theme or themes (image receivers) of the parable? Is it the rich man, Lazarus, Abraham, life after death, the contrast between the rich and the poor after death, or the whole story? Lazarus is completely silent in the story and so this is obviously not the dominant image giver. Abraham only begins to speak at verse 25 and thus this character is not the leading image giver either. If the rich man needs to be the dominant image giver in the story, attention needs to be given to Lazarus as well to see their contrast both when they are alive and after they are dead. If the story does not include Luke 16:27–31, the image receiver or theme may be the reversals of fate after death of the rich and the poor. Thus, the whole parable is the dominant image giver guiding the audience into the theme (image receiver) although the image receiver (theme) is very unclear. When the rich man pressed hard for sending Lazarus to warn his brothers, Abraham told him that they had Moses and the

---

2. Snodgrass, *Stories with Intent*, 431.

3. Ibid.

4. Gressman and Möller, *Vom reichen Mann und armen Lazarus*, 63–68. Bauckham, *The Fate of the Dead*, 97–98. The story is about a father (Setme) and a son (Si-Osiris) who saw the nice burial of a rich man and the neglected burial of a poor man. While the father wanted a life like the rich man, the son who had died and been returned to earth led his father to see what happened with the two men after death. The rich man was punished with a door hinge pinned to his right eye, while the poor man was exalted with nice clothing.

Prophets to listen to (Luke 16:27–29). That is, in normal situations, if the audience during that time obeys the Scriptures in OT, they will not experience miserable punishment after death. However, the rich man believed that sending someone from the dead to his brothers would lead to their repentance (Luke 16:30). That is, the rich man realized his brothers needed to repent. However, Abraham suggested that if his brothers refuse to listen to Moses and the Prophets, even someone who rises from the dead cannot help them (Luke 16:31). In other words, the issue for the audience during the time of Jesus was disobedience of the word of God, and they apparently would not repent. So the image receiver (theme) of the whole parable (dominant image giver) may be: without genuine repentance to God, those who are persistent in disobedience of the word of God will have no one or nothing to help them.

Although Bernhard Weiss describes the Rich Man and Lazarus as a difficult parable for interpretation, he considers that the story is not about the teaching of Moses and the Prophets related to the repentance from worldly living, awaiting a miracle, nor a warning from the dead to the living.[5] The repentance in the OT is inadequate while what people really need is the repentance prepared by the Lord testified by his miracles and resurrection.[6] Thus, the parable is illustrating the continuation of the Law and the Prophets in Messianic times so that the world can repent.[7] Therefore, the theme of the parable is not the reversal of position after death. He sees that if the brothers of the rich man do not listen to Moses or the Prophets, they will not be convinced by any other means such as a warning from the dead.[8] To summarize, Weiss does not consider the theme (image receiver) of Rich Man and Lazarus to be about the repentance of OT or any warning from the dead, but about the need of a genuine repentance that is prepared by the Lord.

Outi Lehtipuu suggests that the parable is not about the afterlife at all.[9] Rather, it is about the reversal of fates and the calling to repentance as in the teaching of Moses and the Prophets.[10] He emphasizes that as such a turnaround of fates is irreversible, the future of a person is tied to how

---

5. Weiss, *Das Leben Jesu*, 2:64–65n1.
6. Ibid.
7. Weiss, *Das Leben Jesu*, 2:65n1.
8. Ibid., 2:64.
9. Lehtipuu, *The Afterlife Imagery*, 4.
10. Ibid., 6, 169, 171, 186, 299.

one currently lives.[11] He points out that verses 25 and 26 are not used for teaching the deceased rich man but for warning those who live like him.[12] He recommends that the parable serves as a reminder of how one should live, and it urges one toward repentance.[13] The kind of repentance that he refers to is "proper behavior," in particular the correct use of possession.[14] However, he points out that after the resurrection of Jesus, obeying the Law and repentance of pious Jews will be insufficient unless they also believe in Christ.[15] Without the elaboration of Lehtipuu on obedience to the Law and repentance in relation to Christ, his themes (image receivers) would stand in contrast to Weiss about the parable.

Richard Bauckham finds two major motifs in the Rich Man and Lazarus. The first is the reversal of fortunes in Luke 16:19–26. In comparison with the well-off living style of the rich man who experiences torment after death, Lazarus is rather uplifted even though he has been poor and miserable in life.[16] The reversal in Luke is similar to folklore in that it reflects the hope for the justice of God in a world in which it is wanting.[17] However, the parable is also different from local stories. The reversal of fortunes in the Egyptian story and Jewish folklore set the focus on the burials of the rich and the poor, which implies that one's future is decided by the good or bad a person has done while living.[18] The second motif that Bauckham sees is the decline of the petition about sending someone from the dead in Luke 16:27–31, which suggests that the concern of the story is really not the future location of the dead.[19] He argues that the second motif indeed points back to the first, which is still about social injustice and inequality of wealth in the current world.[20] Although Bauckham identifies two motifs in the Rich Man and Lazarus, they are basically referring to similar thing. That is, the image receiver (theme) that he sees is not about the future aspect of life

---

11. Ibid., 166.
12. Ibid.
13. Ibid., 299.
14. Ibid., 303.
15. Ibid., 167.
16. Bauckham, *The Fate of the Dead*, 103.
17. Ibid., 117.
18. Ibid., 103, 105.
19. Ibid., 96, 115.
20. Ibid., 118.

after death, but about the hope in God in bringing justice to a world that is full of unfairness regarding possessions.

Snodgrass rejects all ideas associating the parable with teachings about life after death.[21] He sees that the meanings of ᾅδης (Hades) and γέεννα (Gehenna) in NT usage are not fixed.[22] In addition, Luke does not say enough to affirm anything like an intermediate state in spite of his acknowledgement of life after death.[23] He considers the parable as "a warning" to the rich, as in some folklores, about the proper use of earthly possessions.[24] He argues that the parable is centered on the themes (image receivers) of reversal and judgment in that not only will how people live now be judged, but also their life style on earth may result in a severe consequence.[25] Instead of repentance or social injustice, Snodgrass boldly targets the theme on the rich to remind them that their improper use of wealth will have an eternal consequence.

Blomberg warns against over allegorizing or using popular folklore to treat the details of current parable as a real situation about life after death, an intermediate state, or deceased saints in OT.[26] Tracing the characters in the parable, he identifies two major themes (image receivers) and a sub-theme in the story. He suggests that the theme (image receiver) from the rich man (image giver) is the irrevocable judgment of the unrepentant.[27] Another major theme (image receiver) is that rejecting God and his will as revealed through Abraham, Moses and the Prophets (image givers) cause one to be inexcusable from the destiny that follows.[28] The sub-theme is seen in the name of Lazarus concerning those being helped by God will live in his presence after death.[29] Although both Snodgrass and Blomberg see a theme (image receiver) developing from the rich man (image giver), they emphasize different things. Snodgrass sees that the parable speaks specifically to the rich in that their

---

21. Snodgrass, *Stories with Intent*, 430–32.
22. Ibid., 431.
23. Ibid., 432.
24. Ibid.
25. Ibid.
26. Blomberg, *Interpreting the Parables*, 206.
27. Ibid.
28. Ibid.
29. Ibid., 205–6. GELNT, 'Λάζαρος.' The word Λάζαρος (Lazarus) comes from a Hebrew word לְעָזָר, which is similar to אֱלְעָזָר BDB, "אֶלְעָזָר," the word means "God has helped."

improper use of wealth on earth owing to their life style will lead to eternal judgment in the future. Blomberg rather observes that the unrepentance of the rich leads to irreversible judgment in the future.

To summarize, opinions regarding the themes (image receivers) of the Rich Man and Lazarus vary. Some emphasize the issue of repentance with respect to disobedience of the word of God found in the OT. Others focus on the reversal of fates in that how a person lives currently will lead to an irreversible consequence in eternity. Some see that the heart problem is injustice and unfairness in the world. Others concern about the improper use of wealth leading to eternal punishment. None considers this parable as dealing with life after death.

If a decision needs to be made regarding the themes of the current parable, taking the reversal of fates as one of the themes will make the story ready to stop at verse 26 and the discussion between Father Abraham and the rich man in Luke 16:27–31 will appear meaningless to the parable. In fact, the second part of the parable suggests that the reversal of fates is not the core issue of the story. The rich man in the story realizes that repentance is necessary. However, what is the object of repentance? If it is about the use of wealth, it will become a work-based repentance in that a person will be rewarded with good results after death by being generous to others while living. However, such a good person may not need to have any connection with God for treating others well. It also runs against the teaching of faith-based conviction in turning to God throughout the Bible. Thus, it may be difficult to take the position of repentance from the use of wealth to be a major theme of the parable but such a theme may possibly construct a part of a bigger theme. In fact, the direct object is not provided after the verb μετανοήσουσιν (will repent) in Luke 16:30. The answer from Father Abraham in Luke 16:31 also shows that even repentance from the teaching of OT or repentance owing to someone rising from dead may not help. That is, the theme of the parable is not just about obeying the teaching of OT. What one needs to repent from, perhaps, is the general attitude toward God. By returning to God, it is no longer a work-based life to follow some rules in the Scriptures, to treat others well for the purpose of getting future reward, or to avoid ultimate judgment. A person who is genuinely repentant to God in the heart will obey the Scriptures willingly and will employ personal resources properly. Therefore, the themes (image receivers) of the current parable are probably: returning to God truly from the heart while one is living, so that one may live out the word of God willingly and make a good use of resources accordingly.

The various perspectives of the same parable indicate the difficulty in interpreting a parable with implicit allegory expressed in a good drama. By putting several themes together in a sentence, it does not mean that there is only one point in this parable. Rather, it shows the complexity of the subject matters or the points build in a story by the author. Some commentators may touch on some points of the author but no one gets the complete picture. This is particularly the case when the subject matters are broad in a parable expressed through an implicit allegory. That is, whether the meaning of the Rich Man and Lazarus is about wealth, social justice, and repentance, they all hit somewhere on the big target regarding the author's intended subject matters. The difference among these positions from various commentators perhaps is a matter of which explanations are closer to the author's intended meaning.

Wicked Tenants (Luke 20:9-19; Matt 21:33-46; Mark 12:1-12)

The Wicked Tenants is attested among the synoptic gospels. Before delivering the parable, Jesus entered into the temple teaching the gospel (Luke 20:1; Mark 11:27; Matt 21:23). However, the chief priests, scribes, and elders came challenging his authority for doing these things (Luke 20:2). In return, Jesus asked them whether the baptism of John was from heaven or earth, but they refused to answer (Luke 20:3-8). So Jesus also declined to answer their question.

The plot of the Wicked Tenants contains two major parts. The first section is found in Luke 20:9-16. It began with a certain owner who planted a vineyard. Then, he rented it out to vine growers and he went on a journey (Luke 20:9). He sent a servant to the vine growers to collect the produce during harvest time, but his servant returned empty handed (Luke 20:10). The owner sent the second servant, but the vine growers beat and insulted him (Luke 20:11). The owner sent the third one, but the vine growers wounded and then cast him out (Luke 20:12). So the owner talked to himself, "What shall I do?" He decided to send his beloved son to the vineyard thinking that his son would be respected (Luke 20:13). However, when the vine growers saw the owner's son, they decided to murder him so that they might take away his inheritance (Luke 20:14). So they cast the son out of the vineyard and they killed him (Luke 20:15). At that point, Jesus, the narrator, asked, "What then will the vineyard's owner do to them?" He continued, "He will come and destroy the vine growers and give the vineyard to others" (Luke 20:15–16). The audience responded at that point, "May it never be." The drama then shifted to the second part (Luke 20:17–19). Jesus asked them about the meaning of Psalm 118:22 that the stone being rejected by the builders became the chief corner stone (Luke 20:17). He went on to elaborate upon it. Whoever fell on that stone would be broken to pieces, but on whom it fell, it would crush him (Luke 20:18). The scribes and chief priests wanted to lay hands on Jesus but they feared the people. They knew the parable was spoken against them (Luke 20:19).

What are the interpretative hints concerning the allegorical transference in the parable? While Mark and Luke place the Wicked Tenants right after the conflict between the religious leaders and Jesus concerning his authority to teach, Matthew includes the parable of Two Sons in between (Matt 21:28–32). The Two Sons was about a father asking two sons to go to work in his vineyard. The first son refused initially but then he regretted his refusal and worked for his father (Matt 21:29). The second son agreed to go but then he did not go (Matt 21:30). Jesus asked them which son did the will of the father. They all said the first one (Matt 21:31). So Jesus explained the Two Sons immediately. He pointed out that because the tax collectors and prostitutes believed John the Baptist, they were entering the kingdom of God before the religious leaders (Matt 21:31–32). In other words, the first son indirectly referred to the tax collectors and the prostitutes since they responded to God through the ministry of John the Baptist. In contrast, the second son who said yes but then did not go to work in his father's vineyard indirectly pointed to the religious leaders. That is, their rejection of John the Baptist was indeed an indication of not doing God's will, which was contrary to what they claimed initially before God. The preceding context of the Wicked Tenants already sets the stage against the religious leaders.

The reactions of the religious leaders shows that they knew the Wicked Tenants was spoken against them (Luke 20:19). When the audience including the religious leaders heard that the vine growers would be destroyed by their lord and their vineyard would be given to others, they responded, "May it never be" (Luke 20:16). The religious leaders and those who rejected Jesus understood exactly that the vine growers (image givers) in the parable referred to them (image receivers). In fact, the vineyard in the parable is explained indirectly in Matt 21:43 as the kingdom of God. Thus, the Wicked Tenants is not speaking generally to everyone, but specifically to whoever rejects Jesus at the scene especially the religious leaders. As the vine growers are identified and the authority of Jesus to teach was challenged before delivering the Wicked Tenants, the owner's son in the story referred implicitly to Jesus.

An allusion from Isa 5:2 is found at the beginning of the parable (Luke 20:9; Matt 21:33; Mark 12:1). Isa 5:1–7 is a song about a vineyard (Isa 5:1). John D. W. Watts regards Isa 5:1–7 as a poem with YHWH as the singer (Isa 5:1–2), the owner of the vineyard (Isa 5:3–4), and the one who proclaims judgment (Isa 5:5–7) in the rest of the passage (Isa 5:8–30).[30] Thus, the vineyard belongs to YHWH (Isa 5:7) and he is also the beloved (Isa 5:1). The vineyard referred to the house of Israel with the plant as the men of Judah (Isa 5:7). YHWH planted the vineyard carefully and expected its good production (Isa 5:2). However, the result was unsatisfactory (Isa 5:3–4). Because of the unfruitfulness of the house of Israel and the house of Judah, YHWH announced its destruction including the removal of protection that he put around the vineyard. The vineyard would be a wasteland with no more maintenance work being done and no rain from the clouds (Isa 5:5–6). The reason for the destruction of Israel and Judah is that they refuse to do justice and righteousness (Isa 5:7).

In spite of the similarity in using vineyard as the background, there are remarkable differences between Isa 5:2 (LXX) and the parable in the synoptic gospels. Matt 21:33 and Mark 12:1 are more similar in content to Isa 5:2 than Luke 20:9. However, ἀγαπητός (beloved) in Isa 5:1 becomes ἄνθρωπος (a man) in Mark 12:1 and ἄνθρωπος ἦν οἰκοδεσπότης (there was a land owner) in Matt 21:33. The owner in Isa 5:2 dug around, removed stone, and planted the choicest vine in the vineyard, while the owner in Matt 21:33 and Mark 12:1 set a wall around the vineyard. Luke 20:9 does not contain the part about the owner setting up protection around the vineyard. Apart from that, both the owner in Isa 5:4 and the one in synoptic paused to ask what he should do (Isa 5:4; Luke 20:13; Matt 21:40, Mark 12:9). However, the objects of the questions of these owners refer to different things. The object that the owner referred to in the Synoptic Gospels is the vine growers, namely those who rejected Jesus particularly the religious leaders (Matt 21:45; Mark 12:12; Luke 20:19). On the other hand, the object in Isa 5:4–7 is the vineyard and everything in it namely Israel and Judah. Indeed the Isaiah passage does not include vine growers. So the Wicked Tenant takes a different direction in the development of the story than the story in Isa 5:1–7. The Isaiah passage is a pre-warning of the exile and destruction of Israel and Judah (Isa 5:13), while the Wicked Tenants

---

30. Watts, *Isaiah 1–33*, 51.

speaks specifically against whoever rejects Jesus regarding the consequence of removal and destruction (Luke 20:16). This may be why the audience responded with "May it never be!"

A quotation from Psalm 118:22–23 is found in the Wicked Tenants (Matt 21:42, Mark 12:10 and Luke 20:17). However, Luke does not include Psalm 118:23. The parable in *Gos. Thom.* 65—66 is also very similar to the current parable in the synoptic even though it is very brief. The allusion to Psalm 118:22 in *Gos. Thom.* 66 is indeed similar to Luke in that they are equally shortened. Although some suggest that the passage from Psalm 118 in the current parable is allegorization from the early church, or it is an addition from the evangelists, the attestations of the synoptic gospels as well as *Gos. Thom.* 65—66 bring a strong refutation to this kind of skepticism.[31] Snodgrass points out that the suspicion about the later addition of the Psalm passage is related to what they see as disconnection between Psalm 118:22 and the first part of the parable.[32] However, he finds that the Psalm passage in the parable is linked through the word play of בֵּן (son), אֶבֶן (stone), and הַבּוֹנִים (builders, the root form is בָּנָה).[33] He suggests that "builders" also traditionally referred to religious leaders.[34] In other words, there are two connections between the Psalm 118:22 and the Wicked Tenants. One of them is the association of the son with the stone as related to Jesus, while another connection is found between the builders and the religious leaders.

Psalm 118 is a royal song of praise concerning military victory. The psalmist remembers the goodness of YHWH in the past and looks forward

---

31. Dodd, *The Parables of the Kingdom*, 99. Dodd suggests that the Psalm 118 passage in the Wicked Tenants is added by the evangelists. Crossan, "The Parable of the Wicked Husbandmen," 464–65. Crossan prefers a shorter version with no quotation as the original form of this parable. So he considers that the original form of the parable is like *Gos. Thom.* 65 without including *Gos. Thom.* 66. Jeremias, *Die Gleichnisse Jesu*, 55–76. Jeremias regards Psalm 118:22 as allegorical application by the early church to prove the resurrection and rejection of Christ. In fact, when Jeremias comes across *Gos. Thom.* concerning this parable with the ending phrase "whoever has ears let him hear," he says that such a conclusion makes it hard to treat the parable as an allegory. If allegory to Jeremias means church addition for testifying the work of Christ, a later text having similar content with the synoptic with the inclusion of the Psalm passage like *Gos. Thom.* helps to point this verse back to an earlier time. This can shake the belief about church allegorization. Lanier, "The Rejected Stone," 741. Lanier also suggests that if *Gos. Thom.* 66 contains Psalm 118:22, it should belong to "part of the earlier form."

32. Snodgrass, *The Parable of the Wicked Tenants*, 63.

33. Ibid., 64–65. Snodgrass, "Recent Research on the Parable of the Wicked Tenants," 204–5. He finds similar word play between "son" and "stone" in Matt 3:9 and Luke 3:8.

34. Snodgrass, "Recent Research on the Parable of the Wicked Tenants," 204.

in hope for the future.³⁵ The psalm began with a call for praise (Ps 118:1–4). Even when enemies were all around, the psalmist could depend on the Lord to get rid of them and to provide deliverance (Ps 118:5–18). The psalmist gave thanks to the Lord in great joy because what was rejected by humans became very useful to God (Ps 118:19–29). The "stone" verse is located in the end of the section giving thanks to YHWH. According to Leslie C. Allen, verse 22 is a citation of a proverb to praise the Lord for uplifting a person from low to high. He suggests that אֶבֶן (stone) in verse 22 is "a generally discarded stone," which will be "the foundation stone stabilizing two adjacent walls."³⁶ Instead of just a cornerstone being laid at inauguration, Joseph A. Fitzmyer emphasizes that it is indeed a key stone for holding up the walls of the whole building, which means "essential and crucial."³⁷ Psalm 118:23 goes on to praise what the Lord has done. In general, what the psalmist praises the Lord for is that even a readily discarded stone by builders will be the most useful and important stone in the hand of God. It implies that God can work even though the situation sounds impossible or unappealing to humanity. If the conflict between the religious leaders and Jesus is all about who has the authority to teach or to be the leader (Luke 20:2), Psalm 118:22 is quoted to remind the religious leaders of the difference between the choice of human and of God. What is considered as useless, impossible, and ready to be rejected by humans, can be very useful to God.

Jesus did not stop with the quotation of Psalm 118:22. He questioned them concerning the meaning of this verse (Luke 20:17). He explained immediately in Luke 20:18. The useless stone to the builders can cause everyone who falls on it to be broken into pieces. On whom that stone falls, it causes such one to be crushed. As religious leaders (image receivers) are referred to the vine growers (image givers) in the first part of the parable and the context is a head on collision between the religious leaders and Jesus concerning "who has the authority," the owner's son (image giver) is implicitly referred to Jesus himself (image receiver). If Jesus is using word play between "son" and "stone" to make transition between the first and second part of the parable, the stone (image giver) in the second part of the drama continues to refer to Jesus himself implicitly. Another possible connection of the two parts of the parable drama centers the idea on rejection.³⁸ Darrell Bock sees

---

35. Allen, *Psalms 101–50*, 165–68. It is the closing song of Hallel psalms.
36. Allen, *Psalms 101–50*, 167.
37. Fitzmyer, *The Gospel according to Luke X—XXIV*, 1282.
38. Lanier, "The Rejected Stone," 745–46. Lanier sees a rejection motif through the

the shift not on "the image of the cornerstone" but "the stone's significance."[39] He suggests that not only is the stone "rejected yet exalted," but also it will have "the authority to judge those who reject it."[40] The pattern of rejection of the religious leaders toward the authority of God was already pointed out by Jesus when he questioned them on whether the baptism of John was from heaven or earth (Luke 20:4). Then, the Two Sons stated explicitly that the religious leaders refused to believe the one whom God sent (Matt 21:32). In the first part of the Wicked Tenants, the vine growers were repeating the pattern of rejection of the owner's servants and each rejection was more intense than the one before (Luke 20:10–12). When the owner finally sent his son to them, the rejection of the vine growers to the owner's authority rose to the climax that they decided to kill his son and to take over his inheritance (Luke 20:14–15). The quotation of Psalm 118:22 matches with the flow of rejecting the authority of God. What humans treat as rejected, unimportant, and ready to be discarded, becomes uplifted by God to be the most important and powerful one, which can cause the religious leaders and those who reject the choice of God to be crushed.

A parallel story with the Wicked Tenants is found in Wis 2:10–20. Certain evil people want to test a righteous man to see if his word is true (Wis 2:17). Indeed, the righteous man called himself the child of the Lord (Wis 2:13) and God his father (Wis 2:16). The test of these evil people was to put the righteous man to death and to see if the righteous man is under the protection of the Lord (Wis 2:17, 20). Their assumption is that if he is the son of God, God will come to help and will deliver him from adversaries (Wis 2:18). So they insulted, tortured, and condemned him to a shameful death (Wis 2:19–20). There is some similarity between Wis 2:10–20 and the Wicked Tenants concerning the son being ill-treated and killed. However, the righteous man in Wis 2:10–20 explicitly calls himself "the child of God" and God "his father" (Wis 2:13, 16). On the other hand, the son in the parable is simply regarded as the son of the vineyard owner. Apart from that, the evil people in Wis 2:10–20 want to test the claim of being the son of God by killing him, whereas the idea of testing is not present in the Wicked Tenants. The vine-growers in the synoptic indeed killed the owner's son to seize his inheritance.

---

ministry of Jesus.

39. Bock, *Luke:9:51—24:53*, 1604.

40. Ibid.

Application of Allegorical Spectrum

Thus, what is the dominant image giver in the Wicked Tenants? Is it the vine growers, the owner, the owner's son, the rejected stone, or the whole story? The drama indeed has two sections. As the first part of the drama centers on the vine growers (image givers), which refer to those who reject Jesus (image receivers) in the context, the image receiver (theme) is: those who persistently reject the authority of God will turn out to be their own rejection from the kingdom of God (Luke 20:16; Matt 21:43). The drama shifts gear to the rejected stone (image giver), which implicitly refers to Jesus himself (image receiver). Thus, the second part of the story (image giver) is: the one being rejected becomes the most powerful leader from God causing those who disown him to be destroyed (image receiver).

Snodgrass affirms the allegorical feature in this parable.[41] He suggests that the focus of the story is about God and his people namely the owner and the tenants instead of the son.[42] The tenants are those who stand in the way of "God's purpose for his people."[43] Although the "son" does not need to be a messianic term, it is significantly an "indirect self-reference to Jesus" concerning his "relationship with God."[44] The twist of the story is found in the quotation of the stone passage concerning the motif of "rejection-vindication."[45] The themes (image receivers) of the parable are found in two areas of condemnation aimed at the religious leaders. One of them is about their unfaithfulness in presenting fruit to God while the other is their rejection of the messenger of God.[46] He points out that through the parable, Jesus shows his authority in the temple although he has not answered the question of the religious leader.[47] The kingdom is taken away from them and given to others because of their opposition to the work of God.[48] Snodgrass sees the themes (image receivers) building around the religious leaders in the parable though Jesus shifted the story into an indirect self-reference to the son.

Blomberg also finds the parable complicated and allegorical. He sees at least three referents related to allegorical transference.[49] The owner (im-

---

41. Snodgrass, *Stories with Intent*, 292.
42. Ibid., 293–94.
43. Ibid., 293.
44. Ibid., 294.
45. Ibid., 294–95.
46. Ibid., 295.
47. Ibid.
48. Ibid.
49. Blomberg, *Interpreting the Parables*, 248.

age giver) is God. The original tenants (image giver) refer to the religious leaders. The second group of tenants (image givers) is related to those who take the place of the first group. In relation to the image givers, he has three themes (image receivers). The first theme is "God's patient and long suffering" in waiting for his people to produce fruit even though they are rebellious.[50] The second theme focuses on the destruction of those who continue to reject God until his patience finally ends. The third theme is related to God's usage of new leaders to replace the former leaders so that they can continue to produce fruit. He also finds an implicit self-reference by Jesus regarding the son.[51] Similar to Snodgrass, Blomberg does not consider the son as a major theme (image receiver).

Donald A. Hagner sees the linkage between the scene at the vineyard and the stone passage as the rejection of the son.[52] From the murder of the son to the rejected stone in the parable, not only did the original group lose their "favored position" by having the kingdom transferred to others, but also they would be judged.[53] Obviously, Hagner ties the theme (image receiver) to the son and the stone instead of the tenants.

To summarize, there are several themes (image receivers) found in the Wicked Tenants. At least three themes (image receivers) are related to the religious leaders. One of them is about their rejection of the messenger of God. Another theme is about their unfaithfulness in producing fruit for the kingdom. The third theme is the destruction and rejection from the kingdom of God concerning those who persistently refuse him. A theme is related to the character of God in showing patience to those who rebel him. A debatable theme is using rejection of "the son" as pivotal to the whole story. The "rejected son" is certainly a theme related to this drama. However, the parable story mainly shows what the religious leaders do and the condemnation against them.

Which themes (image receivers) may be closer to the intended meaning of the author? As the development of the plot divides into two parts, there are at least two themes in this story. The response of the audience particularly religious leaders after hearing the parable suggests that one of the major themes is related to them. Although the backdrop of the parable is related to the vineyard and the vine growers, the parable gives very little

---

50. Ibid., 249.
51. Ibid., 251.
52. Hagner, *Matthew* 14–28, 622.
53. Ibid., 624.

Application of Allegorical Spectrum

attention to their production. Matt 21:43 does mention that the kingdom of God will be taken from the religious leaders and given to people who produce fruit of it. However, Matt 21:43 does not say the reverse is true in that the religious leaders are rejected from the kingdom of God because they do not produce fruit unless the entry requirement of the kingdom of God counts work. Thus, the theme is less likely about the productiveness of the religious leaders regarding kingdom's work. Rather, the focus of the parable is more about the pattern of rejection of the vine growers to the servants and the owner's son leading to their own destruction and rejection from the vineyard. Thus, themes concerning the rejection of religious leader to the authority of God and their rejection from the kingdom of God because of their refusal of his leadership are right on the target. Indeed, these two themes are better put together: owing to the rejection of the authority of God, whoever rejects God is rejected from the kingdom of God.

Whether the patience of God is a theme is unclear from the parable. Rather, as the second part of the parable is mainly about the effect of the rejected stone on those who discard it, it should be a theme or better, a sub-theme. The reason is that the stone passage exists to elaborate the first part of the parable but the reverse is not the case. Thus, making the rejected son as a linkage and theme without associating with the main characters, the vine growers, will make the theme incomplete. Although the two parts of the parable can be linked by word play, it demands that the audience understand Hebrew to see the connection.

The linkage of the two parts of the parables better uses something obvious. The idea of rejection indeed links up the whole context starting from the rejection of the religious leaders to the authority of Jesus in the temple, to the authority of the baptism of John, to the servants of the vine owner as well as his son, and finally, to the stone. If the stone passage is used to elaborate upon the story of the vine growers, the theme in the second part should be something related. Although the stone passage does indirectly point to Jesus so as the owner's son in the story, his identity as the Son of God and Messiah are not obviously revealed. By answering his own question, Jesus takes the quotation from Ps 118:22 in a different direction (Luke 20:17–18), namely the effect of the rejected stone on those who throw it away. Therefore, the sub-theme of the parable is: what these people reject will be the most powerful and important one causing them to fall and be destroyed. The significance is that there is a severe consequence of rejecting the authority of God. It is also the major reason that the religious leaders and those who reject Jesus are cast out from the kingdom of God. The themes of this parable can be combined: whoever rejects the authority of God through the one that he entrusts will be rejected from the kingdom of God and be destroyed by what one rejects.

It is interesting to see the different opinions from various scholars about the themes of these two parables, the Rich Man and Lazarus and the Wicked Tenants. The very nature of these two parables is unexplained or implicit. When the subject matters are unclear, it is not surprised at all that each interpreter may touch on a part of the themes. As mentioned earlier, a possibility is that behind these implicit parables, the themes are so general and vague that many points can be covered under each story. As a result, whoever follows the text to expound the meaning will get something though no one can give a full certainty about all the subject matters intended by the author in an implicitly allegorical parable. Citing from McNeile, Black explains why the allegorical nature of a parable can have multiple points, "When more than one truth is illustrated (in a parable) the picture approaches an allegory."[54] In other words, an allegorical parable is expected to contain a complexity of points. Obviously, it is harder to grasp all the points crafted carefully by a storyteller in a parable that is implicitly allegorical than one that is explicitly expressed.

To conclude, this is an application chapter of the model, Allegorical Spectrum of the Parables of Jesus, from chapter 3. Hermeneutic guidelines that are developed from previous chapter for handling parables with allegorical features are applied on two allegorically implicit parables. The Rich Man and Lazarus gets a score of eight and is placed under the category of implicit-drama major on the Allegorical Spectrum of the Parables of Jesus. In comparison with the Rich Man and Lazarus, the Wicked Tenants contains more indirect hints for interpretation. This is why it gets a score of seven and it is located under the category of implicit-complex drama in the allegorical spectrum. Although the two parables reflect different levels of implicitness in allegory, they both demonstrate the difficulties in completely understanding the themes (image receivers) that the parable stories (image givers) are transferring, particularly when they contain more than one point in the subject matters.

---

54. Black, "The Parables as Allegory," 287. McNeile, *The Gospel according to St. Matthew*, 186.

Conclusion

JESUS USED MANY PARABLES in his speech. While some of them contain allegorical features, his parables are not equally allegorical. The need for exploring the allegorical features in his parables becomes necessary. However, the hindrance in understanding the rhetorical use of allegory in parables comes from the misunderstanding to the point of total rejection of allegory in Adolf Jülicher's theory of parable categorization. Although Jülicher identifies four parables as example stories with no referential feature in them, many disagree regarding the existence of such a parable group. By exploring the allegorical nature in example stories and other parables, not only is the regrouping of the parables of Jesus necessary, but it also shakes the theory of parable categorization of Jülicher. The current work evaluates the following thesis statement:

> The existence of allegorical elements in the parables of Jesus exposes the inadequacies of the definition of example stories so that a new categorization for the parables of Jesus is named for a better expression of their allegorical features.

Chapter 1 sets the stage for investigating allegory in the parables of Jesus. The nature of parables is not just about parallel comparison of two things. Terms like מָשָׁל or παραβολή carry a wide range of meaning. As the term "parable" is not used in some passages, the parables of Jesus cannot be identified by means of term, but by how they are used. His parables are better considered as special rhetorical speeches for handling conflict, persuading, and moving audience into decision for action. Unfortunately, allegorical features in parables have been notoriously mixed up with the bad practice of allegorical interpretation. Allegorical interpretation is never the

PART II: ON EXAMPLE STORIES

position of the current work. Instead, the purpose is the proper handling of allegory as the rhetorical feature in parables so that good interpretation guidelines can be developed for exploring the author's intended use of allegory in parables. Thus, a working definition of allegory for use in rhetoric is necessary. Allegory is defined as referring one thing through words to the meaning of another thing or contrary thing, which involves the transference either between things or between contexts.

Allegorical transference can happen between an image giver such as a thing, an image, or any visible material of the world and an image receiver such as theme, subject matter, idea, or immaterial. In a good allegory, an image giver and its image receiver are tightly fused connecting with the details throughout the story. Thus, good allegory is usually implicit and the link between image giver and image receiver is not clearly shown in the context. Bad allegory however shows the allegorical referents so explicitly that the story appears to be fragmented by teaching points. That is, the link between image giver and image receiver can be easily found in the context in the latter type of allegory.

Chapter 2 and chapter 3 focus on the exploration of allegory in the parables of Jesus particularly the implicit relationship between image giver and image receiver. In fact, allegory in parables is better understood through a spectrum. An earlier form can be found in the description of Quintilian about various types of allegory. Though he does not call it as a gradient, he presents types of allegory ranging from explicit to implicit in expression. Thus, I name the gradient as Quintilian's Gradient. Northrop Frye is the first to explain allegories with a sliding scale. Graham Hough modifies the model of Frye by placing the relation of image and theme on an allegorical circle. The more implicit an allegory, the better an allegory. From the gradation of allegories in various models, factors that contribute to the making of a good allegory can be seen. These factors become the basis for developing an allegorical model. One of them is the fusion between theme (image receiver) and image (image giver). It looks for whether or not explanation is provided. Another factor concerns the fluency of an allegory in a drama, which observes the difficulty in detaching the metaphorical details from a story. The third one deals with the dominant image giver that connects with the details throughout the whole drama. The last factor is the length of the story. These factors are modified into four sets of questions as assessment criteria for the allegorical level of the parables of Jesus. The result helps to spread out the parables on a new allegorical spectrum ranging

CONCLUSION

from the least allegorical (zero points) to the most allegorical (eight points). The new categorization is named as Allegorical Spectrum of the Parables of Jesus. The categories on the new spectrum include explanatory-brief (zero points), explanatory-point (one point), explanatory-illustrative story (two points), implicit-short analogy (three points), implicit-explicit mixed (four points), implicit medium (five points), implicit-simple drama (six points), implicit-complex drama (seven points), and implicit drama major (eight points).

The four example stories are not found in the same category on the Allegorical Spectrum of the Parables of Jesus. Instead, they are scattered among three categories toward the implicit end of it. It indicates not only that example stories contain allegorical features, but also they are not located in one category but several categories together with other parables. This supports the first part of the thesis statement in that example stories carry allegorical features and they do not form a homogenous group. These reflect problems in the categorization of Jülicher that demands a critique of his parable model.

Chapter 4, chapter 5, and chapter 6 explore and evaluate critically the term "example stories" and the categorization of Jülicher as a whole. Three major areas of problems are found in the theory of categorization of Jülicher which resulted in the rejection of his whole parable categorization. The first area is his concept of "sameness" between a story and its proposition found in his definition for example stories. Behind his idea of the "same," he unrealistically searches for a particular kind of comparison between heavenly and earthly realms, or between higher and lower areas in the parables of Jesus. As a result, even though example stories do make comparison implicitly between the stories and their propositions, they are considered by Jülicher as examples only with no comparison. His reason is that their comparison occurs in the "same" area, the higher area. However, whenever a story makes a referent to a proposition, whether they are both from the higher area or both from the lower area, it is in fact comparison, or better transference. In fact, coming from the same area does not equal to identical. Neither is making comparison within the same area a reason to call a parable story as an example. Indeed, anything can be an example when it is used for illustration, such as parables in *Parabeln*. So the real issue is less about if example stories are examples or not. Rather, it is more about a different style of comparison in these parables that Jülicher has missed and mistaken as examples.

Part II: On Example Stories

The second area of problem in Jülicher's theory of parable categorization is related to what he does and does not consider as comparison. While he limits explicit comparison between earthly and heavenly things to be the only style of comparison in parables, the referential framework of some narrative parables including example stories is indeed implicit instead of explicit. The real issue is not whether a parable contains an explicit comparison between heavenly and earthly realms. Rather, it is all about how a parable expresses the transference between the story and the subject matter, either explicitly or implicitly. Reading explicit comparison into an implicit parable that expresses its proposition partially, indirectly, or even completely missing can only result in misidentifying it as an example without referent. However, the kind of comparison that Jülicher embraces concerning example stories is entirely different. Although Jülicher initially finds no comparison in example stories and he does not consider them as parables, he amends these later in the revised edition by considering them now as parables. What he sees as comparison in example stories is not from the author. Instead, it is a comparison which a reader makes between oneself and the characters in the story. Although embracing reader's approach comparison puts example stories back to be parables, Jülicher has never found the author's intended comparison in these parables.

The third area of problem in Jülicher's parable theory is found in his system of categorization. The term "example stories" is indeed misleading. As example stories point implicitly toward some themes or subject matters, they are more than just examples. The term "example stories" is not a good description for distinguishing this group from the other two categories of Jülicher. The reason is that he relates *Gleichnisse* and *Parabeln* to παραβολή (comparison) and fables of Aristotle, which fall under the category of invented παράδειγμα (example) for inductive proof. It means that all three parable categories of Jülicher can be considered as examples. Apart from that, his grouping of the categories is not homogeneous. Some parables that use implicit transference are grouped under *Parabeln* owing to their heavenly-earthly realms of expression, while other parables such as those in "example stories" are not all equally implicit. Implicitness in expressing the subject matters in parable stories significantly upsets the homogeneousness of the categories of Jülicher. To put it in another way, using explicit comparison between heaven and earth as a framework for categorization cannot bring a good coverage to all parables of Jesus particularly those that are allegorically implicit. If implicit transference is the

Conclusion

real concern that causes difficulty in categorization, continuing with the categorization of Jülicher that runs in a framework of explicit comparison and renames "example stories" as something else will just lead to the same problem again.

It seems better to regroup all parables of Jesus into new categories with a new system. In fact, it is all along a problem finding a place for example stories in Aristotle's system of inductive examples. After all, the focus of the inductive examples of Aristotle is mainly logical persuasion instead of distinguishing various types of narratives or comparisons in the parables of Jesus. Thus, it is better to replace the inductive system of Aristotle with something that can distinguish rhetorical features in the parables of Jesus for categorization. The parable teaching of Jesus is probably a unique style among the various types of rhetorical speeches of his time. In fact, rhetoric needs to be delivered by a person with virtue and the good use of ornament in the speech. Not only is Jesus a virtuous teacher, but also he demonstrates a good use of allegorical transference in his parables. From explicitness to implicitness in allegorical expression, the parable speech of Jesus shows a stylish ornament, which lures the audience into the parables and convicts them with a punch at the scene. Thus, it is better to categorize the parables of Jesus according to his style of speech instead of trying to fit them into the system of anyone.

In view of the problematic definition for example stories of Jülicher and his questionable concept of comparison in the parables of Jesus, together with a system of categorization that does not fit the style of speech of Jesus, the whole theory of Jülicher for categorizing the parables of Jesus needs to be rejected. Consequently, the need for the second part of the thesis statement is established.

Chapter 7 and chapter 8 provide an application of the new categorization developed in chapter 3, Allegorical Spectrum of the Parables of Jesus. Some essential guidelines for interpreting parables with allegorical features are developed. Among them, the most important rule for interpreting a parable is the context. It is preferable to read a parable as a whole with a good balance of attention on the details. Interpretative hints from within the context of the story and its surrounding narrative are very important in understanding a parable. In good allegory, the relationship of image giver and image receiver is so fused forming a tight unit with the whole parable drama and making allegorical transference cannot be immediately identified. Therefore, three more factors help to find additional hints for understanding the allegorical transference between image givers and image receivers in a parable. In the case of good fusion, it is necessary to explore the relationship between image giver and image receiver, whether it is explicit or implicit. When an allegory runs fluently in a parable, observation concerning how the image givers connect with a parable drama is important to search for hints regarding their image receivers (themes). Apart from that, more than one image can always be found in a parable. Thus, searching for the dominant image giver that leads through the entire story for its image receiver (theme) is necessary. If a parable occurs in the synoptic, making a good comparison among the gospel stories can help to provide further hints for interpretation particularly in their differences. Background materials such as OT and extra-biblical literature offer further understanding for some ancient contexts. However, in order to avoid confusion of contexts, it is necessary to beware of the differences between the contexts of background materials and the unique context of a parable. The purpose of interpreting a parable is always about getting closer to what the author meant instead of what others say in their situations.

The value of this study brings attention to the proper understanding of allegory as a rhetorical feature in the parable speech of Jesus. Allegory no longer needs to be rejected by neglecting its existence, or being abused by interpreters who see it wherever they want in a parable. With proper hermeneutic in handling of allegory as rhetorical feature in biblical parables, it brings audience closer to the author's intention. This is particularly helpful when parables are not explicitly explained. Apart from that, not only does the Allegorical Spectrum of the Parables of Jesus help to reflect the various levels of allegory in parables, but also does the new categorization provide better groupings of the parables of Jesus. This allegorical spectrum helps us to see and appreciate the creativity that our great teacher, Jesus, uses to draw the attention of his audience into learning.

Bibliography

Allen, Leslie C. *Psalms* 101–50. Rev. ed. Word Biblical Commentary 21. Dallas, TX: Word, 2002.
Aristotle. *The "Art" of Rhetoric.* Translated by John Henry Freese. Loeb Classical Library 193. Cambridge. MA: Harvard University Press, 1926. Reprint, 1991.
Aristotle, Longinus, and Demetrius. *Aristotle: Poetics; Longinus: On the Sublime; Demetrius: On Style.* Translated by Stephen Halliwell, W. H. Fyfe, and Doreen C. Innes. Loeb Classical Library 199. Cambridge, MA: Harvard University Press, 1995. Reprint, 2005.
Bauckham, Richard. *The Fate of the Dead: Studies of the Jewish and Christian Apocalypses.* Supplements to Novum Testamentum 93, edited by A. J. Malherbe and D. P. Moessner. Leiden: Brill, 1998.
Black, Matthew. "The Parables as Allegory." *Bulletin of the John Rylands University Library of Manchester* 42 (1960): 273–287.
Blomberg, Craig L. *Interpreting the Parables.* Downers Grove, IL: InterVarsity, 1990.
Bloom, Edward A. "The Allegorical Principle." *A Journal of English Literary History* 18 (1951): 163–190.
Bock, Darrell L. "The Words of Jesus in the Gospels: Live, Jive or Memorex?" In *Jesus under Fire: Modern Scholarship Reinvents the Historical Jesus*, edited by Michael J. Wilkins and J. P. Moreland. Grand Rapids: Zondervan, 1995.
———. *Luke:9:51—24:53.* Vol 2. Baker Exegetical Commentary on the New Testament 3B. Grand Rapids: Baker, 1996.
Boucher, Madeleine. *The Mysterious Parable: A Literary Study.* Catholic Biblical Quarterly Monograph Series 6. Washington, DC: Catholic Biblical Association of America, 1977.
Brouwer, Anneus Marinus. *De Gelijkenissen.* Leiden: A.W. Sijthoff, 1946.
Brown, E. Raymond. "Parable and Allegory Reconsidered." *Novum Testamentum* 5 (1962): 36–45.
Bullinger, E. W. *Figures of Speech Used in the Bible: Explained and Illustrated.* London: Eyre and Spottiswoode, 1898. Reprint, Grand Rapids: Baker, 1968.
Cicero. *Cicero Letters to Atticus in Three Volumes II.* Translated by E. O. Winstedt. Loeb Classical Library 8. London: William Heinemann, 1913. Reprint, 1966.

———. *Cicero in Twenty Eight Volumes IX: Pro Lege Manilia, pro Caecina, pro Cluentio, pro Rabirio, Perduellionis*. Translated by H. Grose Hodge. Loeb Classical Library 198. London: William Heinemann, 1927. Reprint, 1979.

———. *Cicero in Twenty Eight Volumes XIV: Pro Milone, in Pisonem, pro Scauro, pro Fonteio, pro Rabirio Postumo, pro Marcello, pro Ligario, pro Rege Deiotaro*. Translated by N. H. Watts. Loeb Classical Library 252. London: William Heinemann, 1931. Reprint, 1979.

———. *Cicero in Twenty Eight Volumes X: In Catilinam I–IV, pro Murena, pro Sulla, pro Flacco*. Translated by C. Macdonald. Rev. ed. Loeb Classical Library 324. London: William Heinemann, 1937. Reprint, 1977.

———. *Cicero in Twenty-Eight Volumes II: De Inventione; de Optimo Genere Oratorum; Topica*. Translated by H. M. Hubbell. Loeb Classical Library 386. London: William Heinemann, 1949. Reprint, 1976.

———. *Cicero in Twenty Eight Volumes I: [Cicero] Ad C. Herennium de Ratione Dicendi (Rhetorica Ad Herennium)*. Translated by Harry Caplan. Loeb Classical Library 403. London: William Heinemann, 1954. Reprint, 1981.

Crossan, John Dominic. "The Parable of the Wicked Husbandmen." *Journal of Biblical Literature* 90 (1971): 451–465.

———. *In Parables: The Challenge of the Historical Jesus*. New York: Harper & Row, 1973. Reprint, Sonoma, CA: Polebridge, 1992.

Dodd, C. H. *The Parables of the Kingdom*. Rev. ed. New York: Charles Scribner's Sons, 1961.

Eggen, Renate Banschbach. *Gleichnis, Allegorie, Metapher: Zur Theorie und Praxis der Gleichnisauslegung*. Texte und Arbeiten zum neutestamentlichen Zeitalter, edited by Klaus Berger. Tübingen: Francke, 2007.

Evans, Craig A. *Ancient Texts for New Testament Studies: A Guide to the Background Literature*. Peabody, MA: Hendrickson, 2005.

Fiebig, Paul. *Altjüdische Gleichnisse und die Gleichnisse Jesu*. Tübingen: J. C. B. Mohr, 1904.

Fish, Stanley Eugene. *Is There a Text in This Class? The Authority of Interpretive Communities*. Cambridge, MA: Harvard University Press, 1980.

Fitzmyer, Joseph A. *The Gospel according to Luke X–XXIV*. Anchor Bible 28A. Garden City, New York: Doubleday, 1985.

Frye, Northrop. *Anatomy of Criticism: Four Essays*. Princeton, NJ: Princeton University Press, 1957. Reprint, 1990.

Funk, Robert W. *Language, Hermeneutic, and Word of God: The Problem of Language in the New Testament and Contemporary Theology*. New York: Harper & Row, 1966.

Gerhardsson, Birger. "The Narrative Meshalim in the Synoptic Gospels: A Comparison with the Narrative Meshalim in the Old Testament." *New Testament Studies* 34 (1988): 339–63.

Goebel, Siegfried. *Die Parabeln Jesu: Methodisch Ausgelegt*. Vol. 1. 2 vols., combined ed. Gotha: Friedrich Andreas Perthes, 1879.

———. *Die Parabeln Jesu: Methodisch Ausgelegt*. Vol. 2. 2 vols., combined ed. Gotta: Friedrich Andreas Perthes, 1880.

"Gospel of Thomas." In *The Complete Gospels: Annotated Scholars Version*, edited by Robert J. Miller. Santa Rosa, CA: Polebridge, 1992.

Grensted, L. W. "The Use of Enoch in St. Luke 16:19–31." *Expository Times* 26 (1914–15): 333–34.

Bibliography

Gressman, Hugo, and Georg Möller. *Vom reichen Mann und armen Lazarus: Eine literargeschichtliche Studie*. Philosophisch-Historische Klasse 7. Berlin: Königl Akademie der Wissenschaften, 1918.

Hagner, Donald A. *Matthew 14–28*. Word Biblical Commentary 33B. Dallas, TX: Word, 1995.

———. "Matthew's Parables of the Kingdom: Matthew 13:1–52." In *The Challenge of Jesus' Parables*, edited by Richard N. Longenecker. Grand Rapids: Eerdmans, 2000.

Harnisch, Wolfgang. *Die Gleichnis-Erzählungen Jesu: Eine hermeneutische Einführung*. Göttingen: Vandenhoeck & Ruprecht, 1985.

———. "Language of the Possible: The Parables of Jesus in the Conflict between Rhetoric and Poetry." *Studia theologica* 46 (1992): 41–54.

Hoskyns, Edwyn, and Noel Davey. *The Riddle of the New Testament*. 3rd ed. London: Faber and Faber, 1952.

Hough, Graham. "The Allegorical Circle." *Critical Quarterly* 3 (1961): 199–209.

IJsseling, Samuel. *Rhetoric and Philosophy in Conflict: A Historical Survey*. Translated by Paul Dunphy. The Hague: Martinus Nijhoff, 1976.

Jeremias, Joachim. *Die Gleichnisse Jesu*. Zürich: Zwingli, 1947. Reprint, Göttingen: Vandenheock & Ruprecht, 1958.

Jülicher, Adolf. *Die Gleichnisreden Jesu*. 1st ed. Freiburg: J. C. B. Mohr, 1888.

———. *Die Gleichnisreden Jesu: Die Gleichnisreden Jesu im Allegemeinen*. Rev. ed. Freiburg: J. C. B. Mohr, 1899.

———. "Parables." In *Encyclopaedia Biblica: A Critical Dictionary of the Literary Political and Religious History the Archaeology Geography and Natural History of the Bible*, vol 3. New York: Macmillan Company, 1902.

———. *Die Gleichnisreden Jesu*. 2 vols. Rev. and combined ed. Tübingen: J. C. B. Mohr, 1910. Reprint, Darmstadt: Wissenschaftliche Buchgesellschaft, 1963.

Kierkegaard, Søren. *Søren Kierkegaard's Journals and Papers*. Edited and trans. by Howard V. Hong and Edna H. Hong, vol. 1. Bloomington, IN: Indiana University Press, 1967.

Kissinger, Warren S. *The Parables of Jesus: A History of Interpretation and Bibliography*. American Theological Library Association Bibliography Series 4. Metuchen, NJ: Scarecrow, 1979.

Klauck, Hans-Josef. *Allegorie und Allegorese in synoptischen Gleichnistexten*. Neutestamentliche Abhandlungen, edited by Joachim Gnilka. Münster: Aschendorff, 1978.

Kubczak, Hartmut. *Die Metapher: Beiträge zur Interpretation und semantischen Struktur der Metapher auf der Basis einer referentialen Bedeutungsdefinition*. Heidelberg: Carl Winter, 1978.

Kurz, Gerhard. *Metapher, Allegorie, Symbol*. 6th ed. Göttingen: Vandenhoeck & Ruprecht, 2009.

Lancaster, Steven P., and James M. Monson. *Regional Study Guide: Introductory Map Studies in the Land of the Bible*. 6th ed. Rockford, IL: Biblical Backgrounds, 1999. Reprint, 2014.

Lanier, Gregory R. "The Rejected Stone in the Parable of the Wicked Tenants Defending the Authenticity of Jesus' Quotation of Ps 118:22." *Journal of the Evangelical Theological Society* 56 (2013): 733–51.

Lausberg, Heinrich. *Handbook of Literary Rhetoric: A Foundation for Literary Study*, edited by David E. Orton and R. Dean Anderson. Leiden: Brill, 1998.

Bibliography

Lehtipuu, Outi. *The Afterlife Imagery in Luke's Story of the Rich Man and Lazarus*. Supplements to Novum Testamentum 123. Leiden: Brill, 2007.

Lewis, C. S. *The Allegory of Love: A Study in Medieval Tradition*. London: Oxford University Press, 1936. Reprint, 1976.

McNeile, Alan Hugh. *The Gospel according to St. Matthew: The Greek Text with Introduction, Notes, and Indices*. London: Macmillan, 1915.

Milton, John. *Paradise Lost: A Poem, in Twelve Books*. Snow-Hill, London: T. Spilsbury and Son, 1794.

Nickelsburg, George W. E., and James C. VanderKam. *1 Enoch 2: A Commentary on the Book of 1 Enoch Chapters 37–82*. Minneapolis: Fortress, 2012.

The Old Testament Pseudepigrapha: Apocalyptic Literature and Testaments. Anchor Bible Reference Library, edited by James H. Charlesworth, 2 vols. New York: Doubleday, 1983.

Osborne, Grant. *The Hermeneutical Spiral: A Comprehensive Introduction to Biblical Interpretation*. Downers Grove, IL: InterVarsity, 1991.

Plato. *Plato I: Euthyphro; Apology; Crito; Phaedo; Phaedrus*. Translated by Harold North Fowler. Loeb Classical Library 36. Cambridge, MA: Harvard University Press, 1914. Reprint, 1947.

———. *Plato V: Lysis; Symposium; Gorgias*. Translated by W. R. M. Lamb. Loeb Classical Library 166. London: William Heinemann 1925. Reprint, 1946.

Quintilian. *Quintilian: The Orator's Education Books 1–2*. Translated by Donald A. Russell. 5 vols. Loeb Classical Library 124. Cambridge, MA: Harvard University Press, 2001.

———. *Quintilian: The Orator's Education Books 3–5*. Translated by Donald A. Russell. 5 vols. Loeb Classical Library 125. Cambridge, MA: Harvard University Press, 2001.

———. *Quintilian: The Orator's Education Books 6–8*. Translated by Donald A. Russell. 5 vols. Loeb Classical Library 126. Cambridge, MA: Harvard University Press, 2001.

———. *Quintilian: The Orator's Education Books 9–10*. Translated by Donald A. Russell. 5 vols. Loeb Classical Library 127. Cambridge, MA: Harvard University Press, 2001.

Ryken, Leland. *How to Read the Bible as Literature*. Grand Rapids: Zondervan, 1984.

———. *Words of Life: A Literary Introduction to the New Testament*. Grand Rapids: Baker, 1987.

Sellin, Gerhard. "Allegorie und Gleichnis: Zur Formenlehre der synoptischen Gleichnisse." In *die neutestamentliche Gleichnisforschung im Horizont von Hermeneutik und Literaturwissenschaft*, edited by Wolfgang Harnisch. Darmstadt: Wissenschaftliche Buchgesellschaft, 1982.

Sider, John W. *Interpreting the Parables: A Hermeneutical Guide to Their Meaning*. Grand Rapids: Zondervan, 1995.

Smith, B. T. D. *The Parables of the Synoptic Gospels: A Critical Study*. London: Cambridge University Press, 1937.

Snodgrass, Klyne. *The Parable of the Wicked Tenants: An Inquiry into Parable Interpretation*. Wissenschaftliche Untersuchungen zum Neuen Testament 27. Tübingen: J. C. B. Mohr, 1983.

———. "Recent Research on the Parable of the Wicked Tenants: An Assessment." *Bulletin for Biblical Research* 8 (1998): 187–216.

———. *Stories with Intent: A Comprehensive Guide to the Parables of Jesus*. Grand Rapids: Eerdmans, 2008.

Spenser, Edmund. *The Faerie Queene: Book One*. Riverside Literature Series, edited by Martha Hale Shackford. Boston: Houghton Mifflin, 1905.

Bibliography

Stockmeyer, Immanuel. *Exegetische und praktische Erklärung Ausgewählter Gleichnisse Jesu*. Basel, Switzerland: R. Reich, 1897.

Strack, H. L., and Günter Stemberger. *Introduction to the Talmud and Midrash*. Edited & translated by Markus Bockmuehl. Minneapolis: Fortress, 1991. Reprint, 1996.

The Apostolic Fathers, Justin Martyr, Irenaeus. Rev. ed. Ante-Nicene Fathers. Vol. 1. Translated by Alexander Roberts, James Donaldson, and A. Cleveland Coxe. Edinburgh: T. & T. Clark, 1871. Reprint, Buffalo, NY: Christian Literature, 1885.

Theon. *The Progymnasmata of Theon: A New Text with Translation and Commentary*. Translated by James R. Butts. Claremont: Claremont Graduate School, 1986.

Thiselton, Anthony C. *New Horizons in Hermeneutics: The Theory and Practice of Transforming Biblical Reading*. Grand Rapids: Zondervan, 1992.

Tinsley, E. J. "Parable, Allegory and Mysticism." In *Vindications: Essays on the Historical Basis of Christianity*, edited by Anthony Hanson. New York: Morehouse-Barlow, 1966.

———. "Parable and Allegory: Some Literary Criteria for the Interpretation of the Parables of Christ." *Church Quarterly* 3 (1970): 32–39.

Tucker, Jeffrey T. *Example Stories: Perspectives on Four Parables in the Gospel of Luke*. Journal for the Study of the New Testament: Supplement Series 162. Sheffield: Sheffield Academic, 1998.

Van Koetsveld, Cornelis Elisa. *De Gelijkenissen van den Zaligmaker*. Vol. 1. rev. ed. Schoonhoven: S. E. Van Nooten & Zoon, 1869.

———. *De Gelijkenissen van den Zaligmaker*. Vol. 2. rev. ed. Schoonhoven: S. E. Van Nooten & Zoon, 1869.

Virgil. *Virgil in Two Volumes: I Eclogues, Georgics, Aeneid I–VI*. Translated by H. Ruston Fairclough. Rev. ed. Loeb Classical Library 63. London: William Heinemann, 1916. Reprint, 1978.

Watts, John D. W. *Isaiah 1–33*. Word Biblical Commentary 24. Dallas, TX: Word, 1985.

Weinrich, Harald. *Sprache in Texten*. Stuttgart: Klett, 1976.

Weiss, Bernhard. "Ueber das Bildliche Im Neuen Testament." *Deutsche Zeitschrift für christliche Wissenschaft und christliches Leben* 4 (1861): 309–31.

———. *Das Leben Jesu*. 2 vols. Berlin: W. Hertz, 1882.

Wilder, Amos N. "Semeia, an Experimental Journal for Biblical Criticism: An Introduction." *Semeia* 1 (1974): 1–16.

Zimmermann, Ruben. "Parabeln—Sonst Nichts! Gattungsbestimmung jenseits der Klassifikation in ‚Bildwort', ‚Gleichnis', ‚Parabel', und ‚Beispielerzählung'." In *Hermeneutik der Gleichnisse Jesu: Methodische Neuansätze zum Verstehen urchristlicher Parabeltexte*, Wissenschaftliche Untersuchungen zum Neuen Testament 231. Tübingen: Mohr Siebeck, 2008.

Scripture and Ancient Document Index

Old Testament

Leviticus

19:18   131

Numbers

23:7–10, 18–24   126

Deuteronomy

6:5   131

1 Samuel

24:13   5, 126

2 Samuel

12:1–14   126
14:4–13   5, 6

Psalms

23   15
49:4   126
80:8–15   15
118   152
118:1–29   153
118:22   136, 150, 152, 153, 154, 157
118:23   152, 153

Proverbs

1:6   126
26:20   5

Isaiah

5   81
5:1–7   5, 6, 151
5:1–30   151
5:2   151
61:1–2   132

Jeremiah

24:9   126

Scripture and Ancient Document Index

Ezekiel

12:22	126
17	126
24:1–14	126
31:2–6	5, 6

Daniel

7	126

Malachi

3:7	140, 141

OT Apocrypha and Pseudepigrapha

Sirach

1:25	126
13:26	126

Tobit

3:4	126

Wisdom of Solomon

5:4	126
2:10–20	154

1 Enoch

9	126n105
22	143
22.2	143
22.5–6	143
22.9–11	143
37.1–4	126n104
37–71	126
38	126n104
46–47	126n105
68.1	126n104
83–90	126n104

4 Ezra

7.36, 80–99	143

New Testament

Matthew

3:9	152n33
5:13	52, 66
5:14–15	66
5:25–26	52, 66, 86
6:22	66
6:24	66
7:9–11	66, 96
7:16–20	66
7:24–27	52, 70, 114
9:12	66
9:14	22, 52, 66, 115
9:15	22, 52
9:16	52, 66
9:17	52
10:24	66
10:26	66
11:16–19	52, 66
12:22–30	66
12:29	52
13:1–9	52
13:18–23	30, 35, 52, 70, 89n64

13:24–30	38, 53, 69, 70, 87, 89n64
13:31–32	52, 70, 89n64
13:33	52, 89n64
13:36–43	38, 53, 134
13:44	53, 87, 89n64
13:44–46	53, 70, 81n7
13:45–46	53, 87, 88, 89n64
13:47–50	38, 53, 70, 87, 89n64
13:52	53, 66, 87
15:10–20	53, 66
15:14	52, 66
15:26	66
18:10–14	70
18:21–35	53, 70, 77, 81n7, 87, 89n64
20:1–16	53, 70, 81n7, 87, 89n64
21:23–27	139, 149
21:28–32	53, 70, 77, 81n7, 139, 150
21:32	154
21:33–46	8, 53, 70, 81n7, 89n64
21:33	151
21:40	151
21:42	152
21:43	150, 155, 157
21:45	8, 151
22:1–14	xiii, 21, 53, 56, 70, 81, 87, 89n64, 135, 139, 140
22:14	56, 135
24:14	85
24:28	66
24:32–35	53, 66
24:43–51	52, 66, 139
25:1–13	53, 70, 87, 89n64
25:14–28	53, 70, 81n7, 89n64
25:29	30
25:31–46	53

Mark

2:17	66
2:18–20	52, 66, 115
2:21	52, 66
2:22	52, 66
3:22–27	52, 66
4:1–9, 13–20	xiii, 52
4:11	5
4:21	66
4:22	66
4:26–29	53, 70, 89n64
4:30–32	5, 52, 70
7:5	134
7:14–23	53, 66
7:15	5, 134
7:27	66
9:49	66
9:50	52
11:27–33	139, 149
12:1–12	5, 8, 53, 70, 151
12:9	151
12:10	152
12:12	8, 151
13:28–31	53, 65, 66
13:33–37	66, 89n64

Luke

3:8	152n33
4:16–20	132
4:21	132
4:22	133
4:23	5, 40, 52, 66, 98, 132
4:23–24	133
4:24–30	40, 133
5:31	66
5:33–35	52, 66, 115
5:33–39	55
5:36	5, 52, 66
5:37–39	52, 66
6:39	66
6:40	66
6:43–46	66
6:46–49	52
7:29	70
7:31–35	52, 66
7:36–50	70

Luke (*continued*)

7:40–43	52
8:4–8	xiii, 39, 40, 52, 70, 138
8:11	xiii, 39, 51, 132
8:11–15	xiii, 39, 40, 52, 55, 70, 136, 138
8:16	66
8:17	66
10:25–37	5, 6, 52, 81n7, 89, 131
10:29	38, 106, 110, 114, 131, 135, 138
10:30–35	85
10:36	83, 131
10:36–37	35, 38, 114, 132, 135, 138
10:37	83, 106, 110, 131
11:5–8	52, 70, 81n7
11:11–13	66
11:14–26	66
11:21–22	52
11:34–36	66
12:13–21	52, 114
12:13	125, 135
12:14	125, 135
12:15	135
12:15–20	114
12:16	98, 118
12:16–21	81n7, 85, 89, 135
12:20	125
12:21	135
12:33–34	52
12:35–38	52, 66
12:39	66
12:39–48	52, 139
12:41–48	66
12:57–59	52, 66
13:6–9	52, 70, 81n7, 89n64, 136
13:18–21	52, 70
13:20–21	52, 89n64. 134, 137
13:23–30	52, 70
13:28–29	88
14	140
14:1	139
14:7	5
14:7–11	52, 66
14:11	55
14:12–24	52, 70, 89n64, 98, 136, 139
14:15	87
14:21	140
14:25–33	52, 66
14:34	66
15	96
15:1–10	70
15:3–7	53
15:7	113, 135
15:8–10	53, 89n64, 137
15:10	113, 135, 137
15:11–24	57
15:11–32	4, 38, 53, 70, 81n7, 85, 89n64
15:18	23
15:18–19	113
15:20	141
15:21	113
15:24	57, 113, 119, 135
15:31–32	135
15:32	57, 113, 119, 135
16:1–12	53, 70
16:13	66
16:13–18	142
16:19–22	83, 110, 111, 142, 144
16:19–26	146
16:19–31	53, 81n7, 85, 89, 136
16:22–23	142
16:23–26	110, 143
16:27–28	143, 145
16:27–31	83, 110, 111, 144, 146, 148
16:29	143
16:30	143, 145, 148
16:31	110, 143, 145, 148
17:5–6	53
17:7–10	53, 56, 66
17:37	66
18:1	107, 113, 119, 135
18:1–8	53, 70, 85, 89n64, 107

18:4–5	107
18:9	57, 98, 118, 132
18:9–14	53, 81n7, 85, 89, 114
18:10–11	132
18:13	132
18:14	57, 114, 132
19:11–27	53, 70, 89n64
20:1	149
20:1–8	136, 139
20:2	149, 153
20:3–8	149
20:4	154
20:9	149, 151
20:9–19	8, 53, 70, 149
20:10–15	137, 154
20:10	149
20:11	149
20:12	149
20:13	149, 151
20:14	149
20:15	149, 150
20:16	136, 150, 152, 155
20:17–18	136, 137, 150, 152, 153, 157
20:19	8, 136, 150, 151
21:29–33	53
22:19–20	24, 44

John

1:4	18
3:16	22
8:12	44
10:1–6	88
10:7	44

Romans

11:16–24	29
11:17	29–30
11:18, 23–24	30

1 Corinthians

10:6	90

Galatians

4:21–31	22
4:22–24	22

1 Timothy

4:12	90

Hebrews

9:9	5

Revelation

3:12	45

Rabbinic Writings

Pesiqta Rabbati

44.9	140

y. Sanhedrin

6.6	144

Greco-Roman Writings

Atticus

9.9.1n1	12

Cluentio

91nb	13

De Inventione

1.7.9	123
1.14.19	123
1.19.27	123

Eclogues

3.104–5n1.	12
9.7–10.	10

Elocutione

8–9	12
99–101	12
102	12
241	12

Gorgias

452e	121
453a	121
453d	121
454a	121
454b–c	121, 122
454e–455a	122
460c, 508c	122

Institutio Oratoria

2.15.1	122
2.15.3	122
2.15.5–6	122
2.15.10	121, 122
2.15.12–13	122
2.15.12–18	122
2.15.19–22	122
2.15.33	122
2.15.34	122, 123
3.1.8	121
3.3.1–3	124
3.4.1–3	123
3.4.11, 15–16	123
8.3.1	124
8.3.2	124
8.3.5	124
8.3.7	124
8.3.11	124
8.3.15	125
8.3.72	20
8.3.73	20
8.5.1	125
8.6.1–3	4, 20, 125, 130
8.6.9	20, 21, 134
8.6.14	21
8.6.19–20	23
8.6.22	20
8.6.23	22
8.6.44	10, 49, 130
8.6.46	10, 29
8.6.47	10, 11, 18
8.6.48	11
8.6.49	11, 15, 18, 21
8.6.52	11, 12
8.6.53	12
8.6.54	10, 12, 49
8.6.55	10, 12
8.6.56	12, 13
8.6.57	13
8.6.58	13
8.6.59	13
9.1.1	125
9.1.4	20, 125, 130

Scripture and Ancient Document Index

9.1.5	125	1.2.9	116
9.1.7	20, 125	1.3.3	116, 123
9.1.8	20	1.4.1–2	116
9.1.9–11	20	1.9.1, 40	116
9.1.16	125	1.10.1	117
		2.20.1	112, 115
		2.20.2	117
		2.20.2–3	101, 117

Milone

		2.20.3	75, 115, 120
5	11	2.20.4	4, 64, 75, 77, 78
		2.20.5	67, 75, 76
		2.20.6	76

Murena

		3.16.1, 6	117
		3.16.11	116, 117
35	11	3.17.5	116

Rhetorica ad Herennium

		lvi–lviii	19

Phaedrus

		1.2.3	123, 124
260c	122	4.7.10	123
		4.12.18	20, 123
		4.31.42	124

Rhetoric

		4.32.43	22
xxxvi	74, 79	4.34.46	10, 124
xlii	74		
1.2.1	116		
1.2.2	116		

Theon

1.2.6–7	116		
1.2.8	116	1.21	5

Early Christian Writings

Gospel of Thomas

65–66	152

Author Index

Allen, Leslie C., 153

Bauckham, Richard, 144, 146
Black, Matthew, 158
Blomberg, Craig L., xv, 8, 9, 28, 40, 130, 132, 136–37, 147, 155, 156
Bloom, Edward A., 14, 15, 33, 36
Bock, Darrell L., 24, 153
Boucher, Madeleine, 4, 5, 6, 9
Brouwer, Anneus Marinus, 9
Brown, E. Raymond, 8
Bullinger, E. W., 14–15, 21

Crossan, John Dominic, 9, 28, 152n31

Dodd, C. H., 152n31

Eggen, Renate Banschbach, 18, 21, 36

Fiebig, Paul, 6, 8
Fitzmyer, Joseph A., 153
Frye, Northrop, xiv, 9, 16, 23, 26, 27, 28, 29, 30, 31, 32, 35, 41, 42, 46–47, 49
Funk, Robert W., 4

Gerhardsson, Birger, 5
Goebel, Siegfried, 88, 89, 90, 92, 93, 95, 101
Grensted, L. W., 143
Gressman, Hugo, 144n4

Hagner, Donald A., 156
Harnisch, Wolfgang, xiv, 6, 7, 73, 74, 79, 112
Hoskyns, Edwyn, 24
Hough, Graham, 16, 17, 23, 26, 28, 29, 30, 31, 32, 35, 41, 42, 43, 44, 45, 46–47, 130, 133

IJsseling, Samuel, 121n59

Jeremias, Joachim, xiii, 5, 6, 152n31
Jülicher, Adolf, xiv, xv, 4, 7, 64, 65, 67, 68, 69, 71, 72, 73, 76, 77, 78, 80, 84, 92, 93, 94, 95, 99, 100, 101, 102, 105, 107, 108, 109, 111, 112, 114, 115, 116, 118, 119, 120, 163

Kierkegaard, Søren, xv
Kissinger, Warren S., xiii, 14n74
Klauck, Hans-Josef, xiv, 8, 9, 28
Kubczak, Hartmut, 18, 21, 110, 134
Kurz, Gerhard, 18, 133

Lancaster, Steven P., 131
Lanier, Gregory R., 152n31, 153
Lausberg, Heinrich, 10, 11, 12, 20
Lehtipuu, Outi, 145–46
Lewis, C. S., 15, 21, 23, 31, 44, 130

McNeile, Alan Hugh, 158
Milton, John, 32
Monson, James M., 131

Author Index

Nickelsburg, George W. E., 126

Ryken, Leland, xiv, 9, 26, 28, 30, 31, 35, 37, 39, 43, 45, 47, 49, 130n3, 131, 137n24, 140

Sellin, Gerhard, 18
Sider, John W., 4
Smith, B. T. D., 9
Snodgrass, Klyne, xiv, xv, 5, 6, 21, 129, 130, 132, 137, 139, 140, 143–44, 147, 152, 155
Spenser, Edmund, 31
Stockmeyer, Immanuel, 71, 80, 95, 96, 97, 99, 100, 118

Thiselton, Anthony C., 109n13
Tinsley, E. J., 17, 23, 24, 28, 29, 33, 34, 35, 36, 37, 38, 39, 40, 41, 43, 44, 49, 133
Tucker, Jeffrey T., xiv, 71, 72, 73, 78, 80, 82, 84, 85, 86, 87, 88, 89, 90, 99

Van Koetsveld, Cornelis Elisa, 85, 86, 87, 113

Watts, John D. W., 151
Weinrich, Harald, 18, 130
Weiss, Bernhard, 80, 81, 82, 83, 84, 92, 93, 101, 111, 113, 135, 145
Wilder, Amos N., 4

Zimmermann, Ruben, xv

Subject Index

Aesop, 76, 77
Allegory, 9, 16, 19, 21, 23, 24, 25, 130, 160
Allegorical circle, 16, 26, 28, 32, 35, 41, 42, 43, 45, 46, 47, 48, 49, 59, 133, 160
Allegorical interpretation or allegorizing, 3, 8, 9, 14, 24, 31, 147, 159
Allegorical model, 16–17, 41, 46, 50, 54, 160
Allegorical proper, 16, 30
Allegorical spectrum, 25, 26, 27, 31, 37, 39, 50, 51, 59, 60, 158, 160, 164
Allegorical Spectrum of the Parables of Jesus, 54, 58, 59, 60, 63, 128, 129, 142, 158, 161, 163, 164
Allegorical transference, 128, 129, 133, 134, 138, 139, 141, 142, 150, 155, 160, 161, 163, 164
Allegorische Schilderung, 96, 97, 99, 100, 101
Allegorization, 7, 126n104, 152
Analogy, 4, 55, 81
Analogical formula, 4
Anti-allegorical, 16, 27, 41, 47, 49
Aristotle, 64, 74–76, 79, 102, 116–20, 128, 163
Author's intended or author's intention, 9, 95, 99, 108, 127, 130, 133, 149, 160, 162, 164

Bad allegory, 29, 30, 160
Beispielerzählungen, 64, 70, 71, 72, 78, 79, 82, 83, 84, 93, 99, 100, 101, 105
Bild, 64, 65, 67, 76

Categorization, 25, 26, 58, 60, 63, 74, 78, 79, 86, 88, 99, 100, 101, 102, 103, 104, 111, 113, 115, 118, 119, 120, 121, 125, 127, 128, 129, 159. 161, 162, 163, 164
Cicero, 10, 19, 22, 122, 123, 124
Combined allegory, 11, 14, 15, 18, 21, 27, 59
Comparison, 4, 5, 7, 8, 10, 13, 19, 20, 47, 64–65, 69, 71, 72, 73, 74, 75, 76, 77, 90, 91, 92, 95, 97, 98, 99, 100, 102, 103, 105, 106, 108, 109, 112, 114, 115, 117, 119, 120, 124, 127, 139, 161, 162
Context, 12, 19, 20, 21, 25, 38, 125, 127, 130, 132, 133, 134, 135, 136, 140, 141, 160, 163, 164
Continued hypocatastasis, 15
Continued metaphor, 15
Continuous allegory, 16, 30, 31, 39, 46, 48, 49
Corax, 121

Dominant image, 39, 40, 41, 138, 141, 160, 164
Double reference, 18, 36

Subject Index

Drama, 34, 36, 37, 38, 39, 40, 41, 46, 57, 58, 60, 131, 136, 138, 141, 149, 160, 163
Dramatic coherence, 29, 30, 34, 136

Empedocles, 121
Enigma and enigma allegory, 12, 14, 21, 27, 34, 42, 48, 59
Evangelists, 7, 152
Example, 5, 7, 11, 17, 71, 74, 75, 76, 79, 82, 83, 87, 90, 91, 93, 95, 97, 98, 103, 107, 108, 111, 112, 116, 120, 127, 161, 162
Example stories, 36, 59, 60, 70–71, 72, 73, 78, 79, 83, 84, 93, 94, 95, 99, 103, 106, 107, 108, 109, 110, 111, 112, 113, 114, 115, 116, 118, 120, 127, 161, 162, 163
Explanatory-brief, 54, 55, 58, 59, 161
Explanatory-point, 55, 58, 59, 161
Explanatory-illustrative story, 55, 58, 59, 161
Explicit allegory, 19, 22, 24, 35, 36, 37, 41, 42, 133, 134, 141
Explicit comparison, 8, 77, 87, 94, 104, 105, 107, 109, 110, 111, 112, 119, 120, 123, 127, 162, 163
Explicit metaphor, 18, 19, 21, 22, 39, 40, 51

Fable, 5, 7, 64, 67–68, 69, 74, 75–76, 77, 84
Figures of diction, 19, 20, 123, 124
Figure of speech, 6, 67
Figures of thought, 19, 20, 123
Free style allegory, 16, 17, 27
Fusion, 16, 32, 35, 36, 37, 38, 40, 41, 50, 60, 133, 141, 160, 164

Gleichnisse, xiv, 4, 64, 65, 66, 67, 68, 76, 77, 79, 80, 99, 100, 103, 105, 112, 115, 162
Gleichniserzählungen, 69, 80
Good allegory, 33, 34, 36, 37, 38, 39, 40, 41, 60, 131, 133, 136, 137, 138, 141, 160, 163
Gorgias, 121, 122

Hermeneutic guidelines, 129
Historical example, 64, 74, 75, 78, 101, 102, 117
Hypotypose, 95, 97, 99, 100, 101, 102, 103, 118

Image, 10, 11, 16, 17, 24, 26, 28, 29, 30, 31, 32, 33, 34, 35, 36, 37, 38, 39, 40, 41, 42, 43, 44, 45, 46, 54, 55, 56, 57, 58, 60, 133, 135, 141, 160
Image giver, 18, 19, 21, 24, 30, 33, 34, 36, 38, 50, 130, 160
Image receiver, 18, 19, 21, 24–25, 30, 33, 34, 36, 50, 130, 160
Implicit allegory, 19, 24, 25, 41, 135, 141
Implicit-short analogy, 55, 58, 59, 161
Implicit comparison, 92, 110, 111, 113, 119, 120, 121, 127
Implicit-simple drama, 57, 58, 59, 60, 161
Implicit-complex drama, 57, 58, 59, 60, 158, 161
Implicit drama major, 58, 59, 158, 161
Implicit medium, 56, 58, 161
Implicit metaphor, 18, 19, 21, 24, 40, 51, 87, 110
Implicit-explicit mixed, 56, 58, 59, 161
Incarnation, 16, 17, 32–41, 44, 46, 59
Incarnational allegory, 16, 17, 32, 33, 34, 35
Inductive example, 102, 117, 118, 119, 120
Interpretative hints, 81, 138, 140, 141, 163
Irony, 12–13, 20, 27, 34, 42, 48, 59
Isocrates, 122

κοιναὶ πίστεις, 64, 68, 72

Lexical referent, 18, 36
Logical proof, 64, 68, 74, 75, 76, 77, 78–79

Mashal, 5, 6, 24, 72, 73, 108, 159
Maxim-in-example allegory, 12, 14, 27, 34

Subject Index

Metaphor, 4, 5, 7, 8, 10, 18, 19, 20, 21, 24, 34. 36, 38, 40
Metaphorical referent, 18, 36, 129, 136
Metonymy, 22, 23, 124n87
Mixed allegory, 11, 14, 27
Motif, 23, 146, 153n38, 155

Naive allegory, 16, 17, 28–30, 41, 42, 45, 46
Narrative, 33, 38, 58, 67, 77, 78, 84, 88, 91, 92, 100, 101, 110, 116–19, 123, 133, 138
Narrative parables, 77, 80
No metaphor allegory, 10, 14, 27, 48

Parabeln, 67–69, 77, 80, 84, 88, 89, 91, 92, 94, 101–2, 109, 112
Parables, 4, 5–6, 7
Persuasion, 6–7, 24, 74, 116, 119, 120, 121, 122, 123
Plato, 122
Predicate, 18, 19, 24
Proposition, 64–65, 67–68, 71, 72, 73, 78, 105, 106, 109, 110, 112, 114, 161
Proverb, 5, 7, 12, 40, 98, 126, 153
Pure allegory, 11, 14, 18, 27

Quintilian, 10–13, 14, 18, 19, 20, 21, 22, 124–25
Quintilian's Gradient, 11, 12, 14, 27, 48, 59

Reader's approach, 108–9, 127, 162
Realism, 17, 41, 42–43, 46
Realms, 4, 36, 98, 99, 100, 102, 104, 105, 106, 107, 127, 161, 162
Referent, 15, 18, 29, 34, 36, 37, 57, 84, 87, 94, 98, 104, 105, 106, 109, 110, 127, 129, 136, 160, 161
Rejection, 153, 154, 155, 156, 157
Repentance, 57, 82, 96, 113, 135, 145, 146, 147, 148, 149
Rhetoric, 6, 12, 74, 116, 121, 122, 123, 124, 125, 126, 128, 160, 163

Rhetorical allegory, 14, 17, 24, 25, 26, 60
Riddle, 5, 7, 12, 98

Sache, 64, 65, 67, 68, 76
Simile, 5, 7, 8, 11, 15, 19, 20–21, 24, 54, 77, 98, 134
Similitude, 5, 7, 10, 13, 21, 24, 55, 56, 98, 134
Sliding scale, 16, 27, 28, 32, 35, 41, 42, 46, 47
Socrates, 4, 75, 121, 122
Speech, 5, 6, 7, 10, 24, 67, 74, 79, 116, 117, 118, 121, 122, 123, 124, 125, 128, 159, 163
Spectrum, 16, 26, 37, 38, 51, 54, 59, 114, 127, 158, 160-61, 164
Stesichorus, 67, 75, 76, 77
Subject, 18, 19, 25, 64, 65, 68, 110, 112, 127, 130, 158, 160, 162
Symbol, 5, 7, 23–24, 42, 45, 46, 98
Symbolic *parabeln*, 89, 91, 92, 94
Symbolism, 17, 23, 24, 41, 42, 43–45, 46, 47, 49
Synecdoche, 20, 22, 23
Synoptic comparison, 139–40

Tertium comparationis, 64, 67
Theme, 16, 17, 25, 26, 28, 29, 30, 31, 32, 33, 34, 35, 36, 37, 38, 40, 41, 42, 43, 44, 45, 46, 50, 54, 55, 56, 57, 58, 60, 112, 130, 133, 135, 136, 137, 138, 141, 144, 149, 156, 158, 160, 162
Tisias, 121
Transference, 20, 24, 25, 125, 127, 128, 130, 133, 138, 160, 161, 162, 163, 164
Trope, 4, 19, 20, 125, 130
Typical *parabeln*, 89, 90, 91, 92, 93, 94, 95, 102

Undetachability, 38

Virtue, 122, 123, 124, 125, 126, 163

www.ingramcontent.com/pod-product-compliance
Lightning Source LLC
Chambersburg PA
CBHW062042220426
43662CB00010B/1607